Visions of Development

For my parents

Visions of Development

A Study of Human Values

David Alexander Clark

Von Hügel Institute, Saint Edmund's College, University of Cambridge

Edward Elgar
Cheltenham, UK • Northampton, MA, USA

Published by
Edward Elgar Publishing Limited
Glensanda House
Montpellier Parade
Cheltenham
Glos GL50 1UA
UK

Edward Elgar Publishing, Inc.
136 West Street
Suite 202
Northampton
Massachusetts 01060
USA

A catalogue record for this book
is available from the British Library

Library of Congress Cataloguing in Publication Data
Clark, David, 1972–
    Visions of development : a study of human values / David Alexander Clark.
        p. cm.
    Includes index.
    1. Economics—Moral and ethical aspects. 2. Economic development—Moral and ethical aspects. 3. Economics—Methodology. I. Title.

    HB72 .C54 2002
    303.44—dc21

2002072162

ISBN 1 84064 982 8

Printed and bound in Great Britain by MPG Books Ltd, Bodmin, Cornwall

Contents

Boxes

Figures

Tables

Acronyms

APU	Asia Pacific Update
ATG	Augmented Theory of the Good
CSS	(South African) Central Statistics Service
EA	Enumerator Area
GNP	Gross National Product
GNU	(South African) Government of National Unity
HDI	Human Development Index
OED	Oxford English Dictionary
RDP	Reconstruction and Development Programme
SOAS	School of Oriental and African Studies
SALDRU	Southern African Labour and Development Research Unit
SSA	Statistics South Africa (formerly the CSS)
TFP	Total Factor Productivity
TVTG	Thick Vague Theory of the Good
UNDP	United Nations Development Programme
WIDER	World Institute for Development Economics Research

Foreword

Peter H. Nolan

When David first came to me to discuss his proposed PhD topic I was sceptical about the possibility of such a topic producing a worthwhile thesis, let alone a book. Moreover, I was concerned that this would remain an abstract piece of research of little real-world relevance. However, his infectious interest in this issue made it easy to be won over. Throughout the PhD and its revision into book form, David has consistently wished to integrate rigorous philosophical investigation with real-world relevance. This has made it highly rewarding to follow his research closely over the years. I am delighted that this research has borne fruit in the form of this book. I am honoured to be asked to write the foreword.

The question 'What is development?' typically occupies the first chapter of textbooks on 'development'. For many years, this usually offered a relatively standardised account of the debate. The chapter typically discussed the issue of structural change and 'development' along the lines developed by Simon Kuznets in his pioneering work on measurement of national product. It typically examined different conventional national output-based measures of 'development', evaluating the relative advantages of converting national product to a common dollar value using the official exchange rate or using 'purchasing power parity dollars'. In later editions of the textbook, the chapter began to consider the use of a 'Human Development Index' in its various forms, which built on the 'basic needs' approach towards 'development'. Still more recently, the account might devote some space to the discussion of 'environment'-adjusted measures of national product. It then typically compared the different results of using these different measures of 'development', and drew conclusions about the relationship between attaining these different measures of 'development'.

In more recent years, thinking about the meaning of 'development' has begun to change substantially, largely under the influence of A. K. Sen's pioneering work on 'capabilities' and 'entitlements'. These have involved a significant group of philosophers, such as Martha Nussbaum, who have rigorously explored different aspects of human well-being, using a tradition in philosophy that stretches back to the Ancient Greeks. These debates have heavily influenced practical issues, such as the way in which the UNDP's 'Human Development Index' has been constructed.

David Clark's approach has been to build on these conceptual advances in order to investigate the meaning of 'development' in a way that is susceptible to concrete investigation among poor people in real-life situations. Like Sen, Nussbaum and others, he has gone back to the philosophical foundations of the meaning of the 'good life'. He has developed a rigorous taxonomy of the precise ways in which people can be considered to have become 'better-off' or 'worse-off'. He has taken scrupulous care to tease out operationally useful concepts from the abstract philosophical ideas of a wide range of writers. The key to the usefulness of this approach is the case study and fieldwork aspect of David's research. He is almost alone in having undertaken such research, which directly links the philosophy of 'development' with real-world fieldwork. David struggled to ensure that all the concepts he used could be expressed in the form of simple questions in a questionnaire among ordinary people.

David has not tested a particular thesis about development. Rather, he has tried to develop empirically testable versions of all of the main strands of philosophical thinking about the meaning of 'development'. The confrontation of these concepts with the lives of ordinary people in South Africa enables David's research to shed deep light on the meaning of development for poor people. This gives his research a unique place in the development literature. It also made this an extremely exciting piece of research to be involved with, if only at a distance. I am confident that this book will be widely referred to for a long while to come, not only because people will debate the significance of its concrete results, but also for its pioneering methodology, which integrates rigorous philosophical analysis with fieldwork in developing countries.

Preface

David A. Clark

This book is the product of five years of full time research, most of which have been spent thinking about the concept and meaning of human development. It started life as a doctoral research project at the University of Cambridge and some of the core ideas were later developed in a series of working papers and other publications (Clark, 1998; 2000a, b, c; 2001). The following pages represent the definitive record of this research.

In stark contrast to many Western philosophers and some social scientists, I have been fortunate enough to visit many poor and vulnerable communities during the course of my work. Much of what I have to say has, therefore, inevitably been influenced by what I have seen and heard in remote rural villages and urban townships. My experiences in these places have, without doubt, fundamentally transformed my understanding of development and underline the old dictum *experience is the best teacher*. I have gained a new appreciation and respect for those at the bottom of society, which not all of my associates in academic or policy circles always share. This new appreciation has been accompanied by the realisation that we have just as much to learn from the poor and vulnerable as they have to learn from us. A range of participatory studies have now been conducted in the context of development (for an extensive list see Narayan et al., 2000). We must be careful not to misinterpret or misrepresent the results of these studies. Nor should we dismiss the studies out of hand (perhaps on the grounds that the views expressed must be ill-informed) if the results are sometimes unpalatable or fail to slot naturally into whatever framework or paradigm we happened to be utilising. To do so not only defeats the object and purpose of participatory research but reeks of hypocrisy.

This particular inquiry draws on the results of fieldwork in an impoverished rural village called Murraysburg and a new urban township known as Wallacedene (both situated in Province of the Western Cape, South Africa). I am heavily indebted to local people in both these communities for making this study possible. I have been deeply touched by the kindness and generosity of these individuals, who not only made me feel welcome but also willingly gave their time in order to participate in what turned out to be long and tedious interviews.

I am also grateful to my former supervisor, Peter H. Nolan, not just for his guidance and advice over the last five years, but for his friendship, encouragement and moral support. I owe similar debts of gratitude to Ron Ayres, Dudley Horner, Gay Meeks and Mozaffar Qizilbash. I have also benefited from useful discussions with many other individuals. In particular I would like to thank Sabina Alkire, Floya Anthias, Frank Carey, Isaac Dokter, Dorit Engster, Faldie Esau, Ben Fine, John Friend, Des Gasper, Jaqui Goldin, Geoff Harcourt, Stephan Klasen, Tony Lawson, Valerie Moller, Steve Pressman, Robert Rowthorn, Jochen Runde, John Sender, Dorothy Thompson and Francis Wilson for helpful comments and suggestions. I regret that it has not been possible to address all of the points these people have raised. Any errors or omissions are, of course, entirely my own. Christine Clark, David M. Clark, Bill Ireson, Stephen Morris, Michael Pridham, Allison Stevens, Sylvia Trevis, Matthew Welch and Lynn Woolfrey have rendered technical and administrative support. I am grateful to the Southern Africa Labour and Development Research Unit for supporting my fieldwork activities and the School of Social Sciences and Law at the University of Greenwich for making their facilities available.

Finally, I would like to thank my parents (who funded my doctoral research and the bulk of this study) for their encouragement and support over the years. Without them, this book would not have been written. I would also like to thank my aunt, Mrs Linda A. Morris, for many kind words of encouragement and support. Funding from The Cambridge Political Economy Society, The Smuts Memorial Foundation, The Thomas Carpenter Trust and Linda A. Morris is gratefully acknowledged.

Introduction

1. CONCEPTUAL FOUNDATIONS

The concept of human development is as old as philosophy itself. Discussions of what makes a good life date back at least to Aristotle's *Nicomachean Ethics* and the Ancient Greek tradition. In fact, much of ancient philosophy concerns itself with the question of *eudaimonia*, i.e. 'the state of having an objectively desirable human life' (Honderich, 1995, p.252). The objective character of *eudaimonia* distinguishes it from the ancient philosophies of the Epicureans and Stoics, who saw the good in terms of mental tranquillity; and from modern concepts of utility, which are concerned with the achievement of a subjectively satisfactory life.

But Ancient Greek philosophy (and subsequent moral theories[1]) had little influence upon the development of modern political economy and social science – the disciplines that eventually gave rise to the birth of development studies as an independent field of inquiry in the 1950s. Social scientists expressed little interest in ancient concepts of *eudaimonia* and *human flourishing*.[2] Outside the domain of Classics and Philosophy these concepts were largely forgotten. Economists in particular were uncomfortable with ethical questions and sought to avoid subjective value judgements by divorcing their 'science' from the realms of politics and moral philosophy.[3]

Most development economists turned to more practical issues, such as the determinants of economic growth and the merits of competition and trade. Modern conceptions of development concerned themselves with growth, capital accumulation, technological change, structural transformation of the economy, and the modernisation of the social, cultural and political institutions necessary to facilitate economic development (see Chapter 1). In the early days of the development studies discipline comparatively little attention was devoted to the development of human beings as ends in themselves.

In fact economists and other social scientists have said little of substance about the meaning of 'development'. No books appear to be devoted to an exclusive or systematic treatment of the concept of 'development'.[4] Instead, discussions have been restricted to a small number of academic papers and introductory chapters in elementary textbooks. Some meaningful contributions have been made (e.g. Hicks and Streeten, 1979; Seers, 1972; Sen, 1983), but most of the available literature takes the form of criticising existing concepts rather than developing new ideas or building upon old ones. In most cases little direct interest is expressed in the concept of development.[5] Most treatments seem to be motivated by other objectives, such as the desire to reassess existing development strategies or construct basic social and economic indicators to guide public policy (e.g. Adelman, 1975; Bastar, 1972).

There are several practical reasons for studying the concept of development. In particular a more thorough and comprehensive exposition of the meaning of development could help to improve policy and form a foundation for building new and better theories. In the words of one of the pioneers of development studies:

> . . . we have to dispel the fog around the word *development* and decide more precisely what we mean by it. Only then will we be able to devise meaningful targets and indicators, and thus help to improve policy, national or international. (Seers, 1972, p.22)

By the 1990s however, the 'fog' surrounding the concept of development had not cleared. The notion of development still seemed to require clarification before it could be used to inform public policy, as another prominent scholar of development observed:

> . . . the main question – What does development mean? – is important. The failure to have an objective that is widely understood, and accepted and has relevance for policy, is an important reason for the many difficulties that nations encounter in designing consistent and effective policies. (Bruton, 1990, p.870)

Yet despite the widespread interest in designing development strategy and the calls to clarify and agree the goals of development, few economists or social scientists made a serious effort to work in the field of development ethics.

An early exception was Denis Goulet whose book, *The Cruel Choice*, aimed to introduce – in the words of the sub title – 'a new concept in the theory of development'. Goulet however, devotes only seven pages (of a 362 page book) to the actual formulation of a development ethic (Goulet, 1971, pp.87–94).[6] Moreover, Goulet's notion of development (life sustenance, self-esteem, and freedom from servitude) is remarkably thin in comparison to Aristotle's original account of human flourishing, and contains little that is genuinely new. Subsequent attempts to conceptualise development in the 1970s and early 1980s were typically confined to the enumeration of basic needs or the construction of a small selection of socio-economic indicators.

Few social scientists concerned themselves with the big picture. Instead, attention centred on a narrowly defined set of human needs.

One distinguished economist-philosopher however, has adopted a different approach. In a series of journal papers and books dating from the late 1970s, Amartya Sen began to construct a more comprehensive framework for conceptualising human well-being and development. According to Sen development is about the expansion of human capabilities. One argument in favour of the capability approach is the need to (re)focus on people, who are the ultimate beneficiaries of real development. Following the eighteenth century philosopher Immanuel Kant, Sen argues for the necessity of viewing people as ends in themselves and never as only means to other ends:

> Human beings are the agents, beneficiaries and adjudicators of progress, but they also happen to be – directly or indirectly – the primary means of all production. The dual role of human beings provides a rich ground for confusion of ends and means in planning and policy making. Indeed, it can – and frequently does – take the form of focusing on production and prosperity as the essence of progress, treating people as the means through which the productive process is brought about (rather than seeing the lives of people as the ultimate concerns and treating production and prosperity merely as means to those lives). (Sen, 1990, p.41)

Meanwhile some modern philosophers had already given some thought to the ultimate ends of a good human life. Perhaps the most notable is James Griffin (1986) whose book *Well-Being* proposed a list of Prudential Values.[7] But in stark contrast to most other philosophers, Sen's approach is firmly rooted in social science.[8] His philosophy has profoundly influenced the way in which economists and policy makers think about the real world. By focusing on ends rather than means, Sen has revolutionised the way in which social science understands the concept of 'development'.[9]

Sen is also responsible for inspiring other social scientists to take an active interest in development ethics. By the 1990s the capability approach had emerged as the leading alternative to traditional concepts of welfare.[10] Sen's conceptual framework (and friendship with the late Mahbub ul Haq) encouraged the UNDP to compile a *Human Development Report,* which has been published annually since 1990 (e.g. UNDP, 1990; see also Haq, 1995). Meanwhile WIDER published the proceedings of two major conferences attended by leading economists and philosophers from around the world, both of which were concerned with the foundations and application of Sen's capability approach (see Nussbaum and Glover, 1995; Nussbaum and Sen, 1993).[11] New terminology began to enter the social science and development literature. Phrases like 'development ethic', 'human good', 'good living' and 'well-being' were finally used alongside more familiar terms such as 'living standards', 'quality of life' and 'human development' (e.g. Crocker, 1991; Gasper, 1996a; Qizilbash, 1996).

But most of the debates that transpired were conducted by philosophers or economists with a keen interest in philosophy from elite universities in the UK and North America. (Consider the list of contributors to the WIDER conferences in the two volumes cited above.) These philosophers operated strictly at the level of theory. While most economists were uncomfortable with ethical questions, social philosophers expressed little interest in solid empirical work. The possibility of testing their grand designs in the public domain or constructing an account of human well-being that rests squarely on the values and attitudes of ordinary people were not seriously considered.[12] Some philosophers regarded such endeavours as superfluous and perhaps even misguided. Most felt that such tasks fell outside the domain of philosophy and should be left to social scientists or anthropologists who are better equipped to handle these kinds of investigations.

While Sen's capability approach has revolutionised our understanding of human development, further research is required to make his framework operational (see Clark, 2000b; Saith, 2001). Before human development can be assessed a list of relevant ends is required. Although countless lists have appeared in the literature, no systematic attempt has been made to develop an account of capability or need through scientific investigation. There are no apparent examples of what might be called an 'empirical philosophy' in development ethics, where theoretical accounts of human well-being and development are informed by empirical studies of human values.[13] It is therefore prudent to reflect on the usefulness and relevance of some of the abstract concepts of human development and hypothetical accounts of well-being advocated by philosophers and social theorists. An authentic development ethic should not be divorced from the hopes, expectations and aspirations of ordinary people.[14] This point has been underlined in the South Report, which was compiled by an independent team of scholars from developing countries:

> True development has to be people centred. It has to be directed at the fulfilment of human potential and the improvement of social and economic well-being of the people. And it has to be designed to secure what the people themselves perceive to be their social and economic interests. (South Commission, 1990, p.11)

Taking account of the views of ordinary people from poor countries may also provide philosophers and social theorists with some useful and potentially unique insights into human development.

In fact one solitary social scientist (who wrote long before Sen inspired a small group of economists and social theorists to take an active interest in development ethics) has called for a more direct approach for understanding poverty and human development. In a passage which has been overshadowed by more recent contributions to development ethics, Goulet observes:

> Underdevelopment is shocking: the squalor, disease, unnecessary deaths, and hopelessness of it all! No man understands if underdevelopment remains for him a mere statistic reflecting low income, poor housing, premature mortality or underemployment. The most emphatic observer can speak objectively about underdevelopment only after undergoing, personally or vicariously, the 'shock of underdevelopment.' This unique culture shock comes to one as he is initiated to the emotions that prevail in the 'culture of poverty' . . . Chronic poverty is a cruel kind of hell, and one cannot understand how cruel that hell is merely by gazing upon poverty as an object. Unless the observer gains entry into the inner sanctum of these emotions and feels them himself, he will not understand the condition he seeks to abolish. (Goulet, 1971, pp.23–4)

While Goulet may overstate the necessity of encountering the phenomena we seek to understand, there can be no substitute for experience itself.[15] Yet since this passage was written, many of those who have made key contributions to development ethics have managed to avoid encountering 'development' or 'undergoing personally or vicariously, the shock of underdevelopment'.

The preceding remarks suggest that efforts to conceptualise human well-being and development would benefit from the closer integration of the philosophy and social science disciplines. This book represents an ambitious attempt to bridge the gap between social science and philosophy in the field of development ethics. The aim is to introduce a new kind of 'empirical philosophy' that is informed by scientific inquiry and firmly rooted in social reality. In order to achieve this goal our inquiry attempts to: (1) identify and clarify some of the academic concepts of development commonly found in the social science and philosophy literature; (2) consider how poor people themselves perceive development (a 'good' form of life); and (3) confront abstract concepts of development with the views of ordinary poor people living in two distinct locations.

The results of this study help to throw light on two fundamental questions. The first asks if there are any common human values upon which we can build a theory of the good. In contrast to traditional wisdom, the evidence presented below suggests that it is possible to achieve a broad consensus regarding the central features of a good human life. The second question relates to the nature and character of human values themselves. What are the objects of a good human life? One interesting aspect of this question concerns the distinction between a 'morally good life' and the kind of life in which 'comfort' and 'enjoyment' play a large part (see Walsh, 1995). The evidence presented in this study implies that most people value a life of comfort and satisfaction, but also believe that such a life should be combined with ethical behaviour that includes at least some altruistic acts.

Terms such as 'the good life', 'human good' and 'development ethic' are used interchangeably throughout this study. While these terms (like other concepts in social science) are clearly 'value loaded' and carry 'emotive connotations' (see Myrdal, 1962), an effort has been made to employ them in a neutral and scientific way (insofar as this is possible). By using these terms one does not necessarily 'beg the question'. Ultimately our respondents have the final say on what constitutes a good form of life. This inquiry is concerned with the dimensions of human development rather than the process of economic development. It is not my intention to underplay or deflect attention from the significance of economic growth for long-term improvements in living standards and social well-being. But the success of economic development does ultimately have to be judged in terms of its consequences for human beings.

A final point remains. The word 'concept' is used to refer to the idea of development. The term 'definition' is resisted in this context. A 'definition' consists of a rigid statement or description of the precise nature and meaning of an object or word and therefore implies a high degree of precision and objectivity that the notion of development seems to lack. In contrast, a 'concept' is composed of a set of ideas, beliefs and values about a particular object, and thus more adequately portrays the subjective character of development.

2. ANALYTICAL STRUCTURE

Chapter 1 reviews some of the abstract concepts of development employed in economics and social science. A *prima facie* case is made for conceptualising development in terms of human capability. It is also suggested that a new approach, which draws on perceptions of development among the poor, is required to provide potentially sterile debates about the nature of human well-being and development with new impetus. Chapter 2 considers the case for viewing development as capability expansion. The capability approach is also compared and contrasted with more traditional ways of conceptualising development, which typically focus on income, commodity command and utility. Chapter 3 paves the way for making the capability approach operational. A methodology is developed for forging an international development ethic; and a list of potentially valuable ends is identified by drawing on the work of philosophers and social theorists. Chapter 4 provides a detailed analysis of our surveys, which investigated how ordinary poor people from a rural village and urban township view a good life. The results are used to evaluate the usefulness and relevance of some of the theoretical accounts of human well-being and development advanced in the academic literature, and provide the foundation for developing a more realistic and robust theory of the good.

NOTES

1. For an overview of early Christian ethics and other moral theories in the period between Aristotle and the rise of modernity see the relevant entries in Honderich's (1995) dictionary of philosophy. It is not practical to review early contributions to ethics here. The following pages only try to get to grips with the literature that is familiar to modern social scientists.
2. The concept of 'welfare' in economics in not unrelated to human flourishing but is usually reduced to some notion of income or commodity command. The Pareto criterion, for example, tells us that there is a welfare gain if at least one person is made better off (in terms of money) without making anybody else worse off. Of course income and wealth are not in themselves the ends we are seeking (as Aristotle himself recognised). Nor may they be reliable proxies for human flourishing. These arguments are considered in Chapter 2.
3. Heilbroner (1973), Myrdal (1962), Sen (1980a) and Streeten (1981) have all argued that value judgements of one kind or another invariably manage to creep into economics and social science.
4. In an effort to locate material I have searched the catalogues of Cambridge University's copyright library, made use of two electronic databases (BIDS and EconLit) and consulted several scholars of development. The only volume I have managed to locate which devotes substantial space to the concept of 'development' restricts itself to charting the history of the idea and to the clarification of different streams of work (see Arndt, 1987). See also the history of thought material described in Chapter 1, n.4.
5. Two notable exceptions include Dower (1988) and Sen (1988).
6. A further chapter places this 'ethic' in the context of forging a strategy for development (Goulet, 1971, ch. 6).
7. Griffin's concern with these questions is not new. His work stems from a vast utilitarian tradition. The academic literature on well-being is endless, but it should be noted that other philosophers have also advanced comprehensive accounts of the human good. For the appropriate references see Chapter 3. See also Alkire (2002), Clark (2001), Gasper (1996) and Saith (2001).
8. The publication of Partha Dasgupta's *An Inquiry into Well-Being and Destitution* (1993) more than a decade after Sen first proposed viewing development in terms of capability expansion represents another landmark in social science.
9. The need to recognise that human beings are both a means and the end of economic development has been popularised by Haq (1995). Some of the architects of the basic needs approach have emphasised the overlap between their original framework and the capability perspective. For example, in the Foreword to Haq's book, Paul Streeten remarks: 'The concept of basic needs as we understood it, was not (as is sometimes thought) centred on the possession of commodities. Instead, it was concerned with providing all human beings, but particularly the poor and deprived, with the opportunities for a full life' (ibid., p.ix).
10. In recognition of his contribution to welfare economics (which includes the development of the capability approach) Sen was awarded the 1998 Nobel Prize in Economics.
11. More recently, the *Journal of International Development* has published two special issues on development ethics (Vol.9, No.2, 1997; and Vol.12, No.7, 2000) and the UNDP has launched the first *Journal of Human Development* (dating from January 2000), which publishes work that analyses the concept, measurement and practice of human development at global, national and local levels.
12. Nussbaum's theory of the good does not draw directly on human values and experience (as the discussion of her methodology sometimes implies) but is in fact based on the myths,

legends and stories of ancient history. This is discussed at length in Chapter 3.

13. It is perhaps worth recalling that Aristotle's philosophy was, in fact, based on practical experience and common sense. Nonetheless, his theory of flourishing is not derived from modern scientific principles or meant to apply to those at the bottom of the heap such as farm labourers or manual workers (who, like women, did not even qualify for citizenship).

14. Of course, human values and aspirations are socially constructed. So an authentic development ethic should only include rational and informed value judgements. We should not allow ourselves the luxury of assuming that such considered judgements necessarily exclude certain goods, e.g. 'de-merits' or 'bads'.

15. We need not restrict ourselves to experiencing the 'emotions' of poverty and development, as the quotation from Goulet suggests. Human well-being or development is not just a state of mind; there is also a strong physical dimension. The distinction between physical and mental aspects of human development is explored in Chapter 2 (see also Clark, 2000a, b). Much of the development and basic needs literature concerns itself with the person's physical condition.

1.   Abstract Concepts of Development

1. INTRODUCTION

This chapter reviews some of the abstract concepts of development employed in economics and social science over the last forty or fifty years. These concepts constitute the foundations of the development studies discipline, but are rarely discussed. It is argued that some deeper notion of human development (call this $development_X$) is behind all of these concepts. The idea of human development is perhaps best expressed in terms of the expansion of people's capabilities (see Section 7). This approach is explored and developed in Chapters 2 to 4.

2. THE CONCEPT OF DEVELOPMENT

Before proceeding, it is worth taking a closer look at the word *development* itself, and comparing and contrasting the term with the allied notions of *social change* and *economic evolution*. In general usage, it is possible to distinguish between a dynamic and a static concept of development.[1] The former implies a 'gradual unfolding' and 'fuller working out' of a principle or activity. To develop is to unroll, disclose and bring to a more advanced or highly organised state (call this $development_1$). In contrast, the static concept of development ($development_2$) describes a 'well grown state' or 'stage of advancement' of some principle or activity (i.e. a mature stage of $development_1$).

In the social context a fairly broad concept of development ($development_3$) implies a process of social and economic change, of transformation and evolution. But while all societies are constantly going through changes of one description or another, not all countries or regions can be said to be *developing* in the sense often given to this word. Development ($development_4$) involves positive social change. The word is 'almost a synonym for improvement' (Seers, 1972, p.22). Presumably then, development precludes negative social and economic transformation.[2,3]

Attempts to specify the nature of different aspects of $development_4$ are scattered throughout the social science literature. In the following pages an effort is made to identify, clarify and evaluate some of the abstract concepts of development$_4$ typically found in the post-war development studies literature.[4] These concepts of 'development' are summarised in Box 1.1.

3. ECONOMIC DEVELOPMENT

3.1 Economic Growth and Technological Change

In strictly economic terms development is traditionally defined in terms of the capacity of the economy to generate growth, i.e. an annual increase in Gross National Product (GNP) (development$_5$). A more popular and alternative indicator of economic growth is GNP per capita (development$_6$). This statistic 'take[s] into account the ability of a nation to expand its output at a rate faster than the growth rate of its population' (Todaro, 1994, p.14). The growth of GNP per capita 'is widely accepted as the best single indicator of [economic] development, both historically and for international comparisons . . .' (Hicks and Streeten, 1979, p.567). This approach can be found in most standard textbooks, such as Paul Samuelson and William Nordhaus's *Economics* (1992) and Charles Kindleberger's handbook of *Economic Development* (1958). Most economists tend to fall back on these two statistics, which provide simple, convenient and quantifiable measures of development, despite their limitations.[5]

'The process of economic growth can be formally described as the result of the expansion in productive resources and the increase in the efficiency of their use' (Syrquin, 1988, p.224). As economic development proceeds, the growth of inputs (labour and capital) and total factor productivity (TFP) accelerates. Early estimates led to the conclusion – surprising at the time – that by far the most important source of historical growth in advanced countries was the increase in TFP (development$_7$).[6] This increase in productive efficiency was soon explained in terms of technological progress.

3.2 Capital Accumulation

Economic development also depends, to a large extent, on the rate of capital accumulation (development$_8$). Accumulation refers to the use of resources to increase the productive capacity of the economy and takes the form of investment in physical capital, infrastructure and R&D, together with investment in resource use (education and health).

A great deal of weight has been attached to the importance of capital accumulation in the literature. In the 1940s capital appeared as a critical variable in the Harrod-Domar model. Later Rostow (1956) argued that a necessary condition for a country to 'take off' into automatic self-sustained growth is the mobilisation of enough domestic savings to generate a sharp increase (doubling) in the rate of productive investment.

In another well-known essay, 'Economic Development with Unlimited Supplies of Labour', Lewis (1954) points to a similar rise in the rate of investment as a defining feature of the transition to economic growth:

> The central problem in the theory of economic development is to understand the process by which a community which was previously saving and investing 4 or 5 per cent of its national income or less, converts itself into an economy where voluntary saving is running at about 12 to 15 per cent of national income or more. (Lewis, 1954, p.416)

In Lewis's model the shift of resources from the subsistence to the modern sector increased the profit share of capitalists and thus raised the rate of saving. 'The central fact of economic development is that the distribution of incomes is altered in favour of the saving class' (ibid., p.417).

The main message of these studies and later work is that a sustained increase in the rate of accumulation is a necessary requirement for long run growth and transformation.[7] Capital accumulation also plays an important role in economic development by facilitating technological progress, and may also be required to sustain aggregate demand and prevent excess capacity from arising.

3.3 Structural Transformation

Economic development has also typically been seen in terms of the structural transformation of an economy. Structural development refers to the set of interrelated changes in the economic structure of a country that both contribute to and are affected by economic growth (Chenery and Srinivasan, 1988, p.199). The modern analysis of structural transformation and sectoral change can be found in the writings of Colin Clark, Simon Kuznets and Hollis Chenery, Moshe Syrquin and their associates. Their studies, both time series and cross sectional, of countries at different levels of per capita income, led to the identification of several characteristic features (the stylised facts) of development.[8]

The most notable characteristic of economic transformation is the rise of industry and corresponding decline of agriculture.[9] The key features of successful industrial development (development$_9$) are changes in the structure of production and employment so that agriculture's share of both decline and that of secondary and manufacturing industry in particular increase.[10] The essence of this process is described in the Lewis model in terms of migration from a traditional, overpopulated, rural subsistence sector characterised by low productivity to a high productivity modern urban industrial sector (Lewis, 1954). The transfer of workers to sectors characterised by higher productivity accelerates growth.

The structure of the manufacturing sector also changes considerably during the process of industrialisation. As incomes rise, the composition shifts from light to heavy industry (development$_{10}$). The transformation of manufacturing and the rise of heavy industry has important implications for economic development. On the whole, heavy industry tends to be more capital and skill intensive, enjoy faster productivity growth, and is more prone to exhibit economies of scale.

Attempts to model industrial development have traced the rise of industry to changes in domestic demand, growing intermediate use of industrial products, and to shifts in international trade, as well as to socio-economic factors such as urbanisation and changes in the growth and distribution of population. Since the 1960s economists have also increasingly emphasised the importance of agricultural modernisation for economic growth and structural change.

3.3.1 Domestic demand
Two phenomena typically dominate the shift in the overall pattern of domestic demand as incomes rise. The first is a substantial decline in the share of food in private consumption, which reflects an increase in demand for other non-food products (development$_{11}$). At the same time private consumption of all goods as a *proportion* of GNP declines, permitting the share of investment to rise (like development$_8$ above). Together, the increase in the share of non-food consumption and investment imply a shift in domestic demand away from agricultural to industrial products.

3.3.2 Intermediate demand
The use of intermediate goods (inputs) as a proportion of total output tends to increase (development$_{12}$) with growth and industrialisation. This phenomena stems from technological progress within the economy which leads to greater use of inputs, and also from the shift in production towards manufacturing and other sectors that typically use more inputs. In addition to the overall rise in intermediate use, the relative use of primary products as intermediates tends to decline while the use of intermediates from manufacturing increases (development$_{13}$). These two trends produce rapid growth in the intermediate demand for manufactured goods, thereby reinforcing industrialisation and growth.

3.3.3 International trade
A third major source of industrialisation is the transformation of international trade. Trade generally expands as development takes place (development$_{14}$).[11] There is also a marked change in the structure of international trade. Through import substitution and the expansion of manufactured exports, economies tend to shift away from specialisation in agricultural and other primary products and towards specialisation in industrial goods (development$_{15}$) as they develop. Underlying the transformation of trade are changes in supply conditions including the accumulation of skills and physical capital, greater availability of intermediate inputs, and the expansion of economies of scale based on a growing domestic market for manufactured goods.

3.3.4 The demographic transition and urbanisation
Structural development also includes demographic factors. Population changes underlie the activities of the rest of the economy. Economic growth is thought to be associated with a set of factors that produce first a widespread decline in the mortality rate and then, after a discrete lag, a decline in the birth rate (see Dasgupta, 1993, ch. 12).[12] The result is a rise and then a decline in the rate of population growth (development$_{16}$), as the gap between mortality and birth rates change over the course of economic development$_5$.[13] At the same time the proportion of people living in towns and cities increases rapidly (development$_{17}$). Urbanisation reflects not only the increase in population growth, but also the shift away from agricultural production. The existence of economies of scale in the manufacture of industrial products generally results in the growth of industrial organisations. In addition, there is an incentive for industrial enterprises to locate in the same place in order to take advantage of common support facilities like power stations and transport as well as links to suppliers and markets. Consequently, industrialisation and urbanisation reinforce one another.

3.3.5 The agricultural transformation
Often economists focus on industrialisation at the expense of agricultural and rural development. One reason for the neglect of agriculture is related to the misconception that this sector is unimportant because its relative share of the economy declines naturally as growth and development proceeds. Since the 1960s, however, economists have increasingly recognised that agricultural development, in the form of a substantial increase in labour productivity (development$_{18}$), is nothing less than a prerequisite for growth and industrialisation. The modernisation of agriculture increases the supply of food for domestic consumption, releases labour to the industrial sector and generates savings and foreign exchange (see Timmer, 1988).

The main criticism levelled against structural models of development is that the process of growth and transformation is not uniform (e.g. Hirschman, 1981, p.11). Although many theories of structural development recognise that the pattern of growth typically varies (for example Chenery and Syrquin, 1986 in contrast to Rostow, 1956), it is still conceivable that there may be other viable routes to economic prosperity. For example, some islands and small states have been able to develop through tourism (Ayres and Briguglio, forthcoming).

In recent years institutional economics has started to consider the factors that account for variation in historical growth. One of the most prominent institutional economists to put forward a theory of growth is Nobel Prize winner Douglas North. By drawing on the history of development in the Western world, North argues that high transaction costs prevent some economies from realising their potential. According to North, economic growth depends on the development (development$_{19}$) of a range of 'well-specified and well-enforced property rights' that ensure markets function with low transaction costs (North, 1989). The kind of institutions that promote growth include formal contracts and elaborate monitoring and enforcement mechanisms, which help sustain the legal basis of a competitive market economy. A key stumbling block with North's approach is that an efficient system of property rights may be viewed as a *consequence* as well as a *cause* of economic development.[14]

4. SOCIO-CULTURAL ASPECTS OF ECONOMIC DEVELOPMENT

In the 1950s and early 1960s some sociologists turned their attention to the social and cultural modernisation of traditional society. Most of the theories put forward were derived from the writings of Emile Durkheim, Max Weber and to a lesser extent Karl Marx. In essence these theories argued that development depends upon displacing traditional 'values, attitudes and norms' with modern ones (Webster, 1993). In particular, commentators like Bert Hoselitz, Talcott Parsons and David McClelland identified the weakening of traditional ties and power structures (especially the kinship system) (development$_{20}$), and the growth of individual motivation and rise of an entrepreneurial class (development$_{21}$) as key features of the social and cultural modernisation required for economic growth and structural change. These theories have been heavily criticised for equating modernisation with Westernisation (Ingham, 1995, pp.40–42; Wiarda, 1983). In particular, several empirical studies have shown that traditional structures can survive and even contribute to the process of economic development (see Webster, 1993, pp.114–9).

5. SOCIAL DEVELOPMENT

The experience of the 1950s and 1960s, when many poor countries recorded impressive growth rates but did not manage to make much progress in terms of improving the standard of living signalled that something was wrong with narrow economic concepts of development like GNP per capita. The assumption that 'all good things go together' no longer seemed to be valid (Hirschman, 1981, pp.19–24). An increasing number of economists called for the dethronement of GNP and the elevation of attacks on the social problems of development$_X$.[15] Initially, the emphasis shifted from growth to the creation of employment and then to the redistribution of benefits to the poor, before the more recent emphasis on basic human needs (see Streeten, 1979; 1995).

In two classic papers Dudley Seers (1969; 1972) argues the case for measuring development$_X$ more directly and suggests criteria for doing just that. For Seers, development$_X$ means 'creating the conditions for the realisation of human personality' and implies a reduction in (absolute) poverty, unemployment and income inequality (development$_{22}$) (Seers, 1972, p.21). Increases in GNP per capita are not sufficient for development$_X$ unless they are accompanied by reductions in these three crucial variables.

While the concept of development$_{22}$ proposed by Seers is more sensitive to changes in aggregate social welfare than GNP per capita, it can be criticised on several different grounds. In some ways his criteria for development$_X$ goes too far. In other respects it does not go far enough.

For example, Gary Fields (1980) has shown that a reduction in absolute poverty is compatible with, and in many cases has accompanied, an increase in relative income inequality. In terms of the Seers criteria this does not constitute development$_X$. Development$_X$ requires nothing less than the *simultaneous* reduction of poverty and inequality (not to mention unemployment).[16] On balance this *all or nothing* requirement for human development$_X$ seems a little too strict. It can be argued that an improvement in the average incomes and living conditions of the poorest must constitute a valuable form of development$_X$, even if the poorest lose out in relative terms because inequality becomes more pronounced.[17]

Furthermore, there may be a conflict between the objective of greater equality on the one hand, and the goals of growth, poverty alleviation and employment on the other (see Bauer, 1981; Little, 1982, pp.209–14). Several economists have concluded that a redistribution of income in favour of the rich who typically save a relatively high proportion of their income will lead to greater investment and growth. Adding the premise that growth makes it possible to reduce poverty and boost employment implies Seers's concept of $development_{22}$ is internally inconsistent. In fairness to Seers however, the logic behind the contention that inequality contributes to growth rests on a number of potential flaws (Herrick and Kindleberger, 1983, ch. 2), and it can be argued that the reverse may be true in $underdeveloped_1$ societies (Myrdal, 1970, ch. 3).

Alternatively, it could be argued that the greatest weight should be given to changes in income inequality because growing income differentials make people *feel* worse off.[18] For example, it is conceivable that the envy of the rich by the poor might more than offset the gain in utility from those who were fortunate enough to become richer.[19] Some commentators have also pointed out that social justice may be a public good. People may find it enjoyable to live in a society with a comparatively egalitarian distribution of income (Morawetz et al., 1977; Thurow, 1971). These arguments imply that $development_X$ requires greater equality.

In other respects Seers's criteria for assessing $development_X$ does not go far enough. Measuring poverty, unemployment and inequality provides an inadequate foundation for assessing well-being.[20] Providing villagers with an adequate income does not guarantee access to basic necessities such as education and medical treatment if there are no school or hospitals nearby (Sen, 1983, p.756). Nor will money or jobs guarantee access to food in a famine resulting from a per-capita food shortage (see Nolan, 1993). A rise in real income only adds to a person's purchasing power over the goods and services currently *available* in the market. Moreover, even if the basic necessities of life are affordable and available, there is in fact no guarantee that a person or family will purchase a sufficient quantity of these goods.[21] It follows that $development_X$ should not just be judged in terms of the ability to command goods and services or what Sen refers to as people's *entitlements* (call this $development_{23}$). We also need to look at the things (doings and beings) individuals manage to achieve (see Section 7 below).

A related approach is to evaluate $development_X$ ($development_{24}$) in terms of a variety of different social indicators, many of which capture some of the consequences of $development_X$ (see Bastar, 1972; Herrick and Kindleberger, 1983; Hicks and Streeten, 1979). Social indicators are concerned with ends as well as means or at least intermediate ends. Even social indicators that measure inputs (like the number of doctors or hospital beds per thousand of the population or enrolment rates in schools) rather than the outputs or results (such as life expectancy and literacy rates), are closer to the actual objectives of $development_X$ than indicators of absolute and relative income.

In the literature however, there is a regrettable tendency to concentrate on measuring inputs into the $development_X$ process, rather than on analysing the concrete results of development$_X$.[22] Moreover, social indicators are *partial* in that each one provides a useful but incomplete insight into development$_X$. Problems typically arise in absorbing the content and meaning of a large number of overlapping and sometimes conflicting indicators and there is no obvious way of combining them.

6. POLITICAL DEVELOPMENT

From the late 1960s there was growing concern about a series of 'political disasters' (civil wars, revolutions and the rise of authoritarian regimes) that had swept through a number of developing countries (Hirschman, 1981, p.20). Many liberals called for greater political freedom and the democratisation of repressive regimes (development$_{25}$). Some studies even tried to show that greater political freedom promotes economic growth and social welfare (e.g. Dasgupta, 1993, ch. 5). However, there is no straightforward relationship between democracy and development in terms of growth or social welfare. Some anthropologists have even suggested that some cultures and societies may not value freedom highly.

Some social scientists incorporated the concept of grass roots participation into rural development strategies (see Chambers, 1994; Ingham, 1995). It was hoped that participation (development$_{26}$) would integrate people into the decision-making process, empower the weak and improve responsiveness to local needs. In practice however, those at the bottom of the heap have not always benefited from efforts to decentralise development initiatives. At its worst, encouraging participation can simply mean transferring power from regional to local elites.

Since the publication of Esther Boserup's (1970) pioneering book *Women's Role in Economic Development*, a range of empirical studies have shown that women (and their dependants) are among the most vulnerable, disadvantaged and deprived members of society. Women typically have less education and training, face discrimination in the labour market and have lower earning potential. They are often barred from higher paying occupations, lack property rights and access to credit, and undertake work that is unremunerated. Studies of resource allocation in the household have also found evidence of sex-bias against women in the areas of nutrition, health care, education and inheritance (e.g. Sen, 1984). Hence the demand for social and political reform to fully integrate women into the development$_X$ process. This entails promoting equality for women, especially in the areas of education, formal employment, legal rights and access to government resources such as social security and agricultural extension programmes (development$_{27}$).

7. HUMAN DEVELOPMENT

By the early 1980s a new conceptual framework for evaluating human well-being and development$_X$ began to emerge. In contrast to income, resource and basic need approaches, this framework concerned itself exclusively with the development of people rather than the development of things. This approach owes much to the pioneering work of Amartya Sen and views development$_X$ as the expansion of human capabilities (development$_{28}$). The foundations of the capability approach are explored in the following chapter. For now it is sufficient to note that this approach seems to offer the most robust and comprehensive framework for conceptualising human well-being and development.

Research at the United Nations has drawn on the capability approach to compile a *Human Development Report*, which provides a 'Human Development Index' (HDI) based on GNP per capita, literacy and life expectancy (development$_{29}$). According to the first of these reports:

> Human development, is a process of enlarging people's choices. The most crucial ones are to lead a long and healthy life, to be educated and to enjoy a decent standard of living. (UNDP, 1990, p.10)

If these three key choices are not available, then many other options are not likely to be accessible as well.

Two sides to human development are identified: (1) the formation of human capabilities (such as improved health and knowledge); and (2) the use people make of their capabilities for work and leisure. This approach then, brings together the production and distribution of commodities and the expansion and use of human capabilities (ibid., pp.10–11). The emphasis on longevity and knowledge relate to the formation of human capabilities and income serves as a proxy measure for the choices people have in putting their capabilities to use (ibid., p.14).

While the HDI has been modified and improved since 1990, and provides a much wider, richer and deeper conception of development$_X$ than any single indicator, it remains conceptually weak (see Kelley, 1991; Srinivasan, 1994; Streeten, 1995, pp.19–26). The weights attached to the three core indicators are necessarily arbitrary, and the index only provides a relative estimate of how well a certain country is doing in relation to the performance of other countries. Moreover, like GNP per capita, the HDI is an average and therefore says nothing about inequality between the rich and poor, men and women or urban and rural people.

8. SUSTAINABLE DEVELOPMENT

Over the last twenty years the sustainability of development$_x$ has become a big issue. Several different concepts of sustainable development have been advanced by geographers, ecologists, environmentalists and physical scientists as well as economists (see Ingham, 1995, pp.55–8). It is not practical to review all of these concepts here. For our purposes it is sufficient to note that sustainability basically refers to 'meeting the needs of the present generation without compromising the needs of future generations' (World Bank, 1992, p.34). Implicit in this statement is the idea that future growth and human well-being depend on the quality of the environment. Steps must be taken to ensure the protection and renewal of natural resources. Water pollution and water scarcity, soil degradation, loss of forests, the decline of biodiversity and harmful atmospheric changes (such as ozone depletion) all need to be tackled (ibid., p.4). The goal of sustaining natural resources (development$_{30}$) however, can conflict with economic growth and may not be practical in developing countries where people live in extreme poverty and do not have the luxury of respecting the environment.

9. FIFTY YEARS OF CONCEPTUALSING DEVELOPMENT

Since the 1950s there has been a shift in emphasis from economic growth to some of the social and political aspects of development$_x$. The last two decades have seen the advent of the capability approach and increasing concern with issues of sustainability. Yet the primary concern for economists and policy makers always was and still remains the elimination of poverty and promotion of human development (see Srinivasan, 1994, pp.238–9; Streeten, 1979).

Early discussions of economic development were heavily influenced by Arthur W. Lewis and others who expressed concern with the development of people. In his monograph *The Theory of Economic Growth* published in the mid 1950s, Lewis remarks that:

> The advantage of economic growth is not that wealth increases happiness but, that it increases the range of human choice . . . The case for economic growth is that it gives man greater control over his environment, and thereby increases his freedom . . . Economic growth also gives us freedom to choose greater leisure. (Lewis, 1955, pp.420–421)

Lewis was emphatic that economic growth would overcome poverty and facilitate freedom from servitude:

... Woman gains freedom from drudgery, is emancipated from the seclusion of the household, and gains at last the chance to be a full human being, exercising her mind and her talents in the same way as men. It is open to men to debate whether economic progress is good for men or not, but for women to debate the desirability of economic growth is to debate whether women should have the chance to cease to be beasts of burden, and to join the human race. (ibid., p.422)

These remarks imply that development is really about the expansion of human capabilities or positive freedom of choice.

Even the strongest advocates of economic growth have adopted a broader perspective. In their classic textbook *Economics*, Paul Samuelson and William Nordhaus (1992) effectively equate 'growth' with 'development' and employ the concepts interchangeably. But they recognise that:

... economic growth is not just an abstract concept. It is vital for the citizens of a country because economic growth, in terms of growth of output per capita, means growing real wages and rising living standards. (ibid., p.547)

Even the World Bank pays homage to a broader conception of development:

The challenge of development . . . is to improve the quality of life. Especially in the World's poor countries, a better quality of life generally calls for higher incomes – but it involves much more. It encompasses, as ends in themselves, better education, higher standards of health and nutrition, less poverty, a cleaner environment, more equality of opportunity, greater individual freedom, and a richer cultural life. (World Bank, 1991, p.4)

Some of the most ardent critics of economic growth have also appealed to some deeper notion of human development. In his critique of the affluent society, Galbraith (1958) remarks that

The family which takes its mauve and cerise, airconditioned, powerbraked car out for a tour passes through cities that are badly paved, made hideous by litter, blighted buildings, billboards, and posts for wires that should long since have been put underground. They pass on into a countryside that has been rendered largely invisible by commercial art . . . They picnic on exquisitely packaged food from a portable icebox by a polluted stream and go on to spend the night at a park which is a menace to public health and morals. Just before dozing off on an air-mattress, beneath a nylon tent, amid the stench of decaying refuge, they may reflect vaguely on the curious unevenness of their blessings. (Galbraith, 1958, pp.196–7)

Two decades later Hirsch (1977) tried to expose the social limits to growth. His basic argument is that there is a social dimension to private consumption. As average consumption rises the satisfaction each person derives from a given bundle of goods declines 'as the conditions of [their] use deteriorate' (ibid., p.3). This means that individuals increasingly have to compete against one another for economic opportunities in order to maintain their position and outperform one another to advance their position. In the end not everyone can enjoy the benefits of economic growth (ibid., pp.5, 12).

10. A FINAL WORD

The commitment to a broad notion of human development is widespread. Although the emphasis and rhetoric have changed over the last four or five decades, the basic underlying concepts themselves remain the same. Since the 1950s many of the basic principles taught to students of economic development have not fundamentally changed. In the first edition of Kindleberger's classic handbook *Economic Development* (1958), students are told that 'development is accompanied by a more equal distribution of income' and incorporates social and political stability. The significance of declining mortality rates, avoiding violence, increasing employment, and rising living standards are also mentioned (ibid., pp.178, 205–8, 236–7). The main change in the latest edition of the handbook is to devote more space to the discussion of these concepts (see Herrick and Kindleberger, 1983).[23] This chapter has tried to show that a deeper notion of human development is behind these concepts.

In the following chapters an effort is made to investigate the concept of development$_X$. In particular the capability approach is developed by appealing to the values and aspirations of poor people themselves. It is hoped that this approach will breathe new life into potentially sterile debates about the nature of human well-being and development. We begin with the case for viewing development$_X$ in terms of human capabilities.

Box 1.1 A Clarification of Some of the Abstract Concepts of Development Employed in Economics and Social Science

---

General Concepts:

Development$_X$ is a good human life (whatever that may be).

Development$_1$ implies a 'gradual unfolding' and 'fuller working out' of a principle or activity; to develop is to unroll, disclose and bring to a more advanced or highly organised state.

Development$_2$ describes a 'well grown state' or 'stage of advancement' of a given principle or activity, i.e. mature development$_1$.

Development$_3$ is a process of social and economic change, of transformation and evolution.

Development$_4$ is a process of *positive* social and economic change.

Development$_{4a}$ is a process of overall (or net) positive social and economic change.

Economic Development:

Development$_5$ is an increase in GNP, i.e. the total national output or income of a country.

Development$_6$ is an increase in GNP per capita, i.e. the total GNP of a country divided by total population.

Development$_7$ is an increase in TFP, i.e. the average productivity of all factors employed in the economy. (TFP measures changes in output per unit of all inputs combined.) An increase in TFP represents technological progress, i.e. new and improved ways of accomplishing traditional tasks.

Development$_8$ is an increase in the rate of capital accumulation. (Key indicators of accumulation are saving and investment rates.)

Development$_9$ is industrialisation, which is characterised by an increase in the industrial sector's share of output and employment.

Development$_{10}$ is the transformation of the manufacturing sector, which is characterised by a shift from light to heavy industry.

Development$_{11}$ is a shift in the composition of domestic demand away from food and agricultural products in favour of consumer durables.

Continued/....

Box 1.1 (cont.)

Development$_{12}$ is an increase in the demand for and use of intermediate products as a proportion of GNP.

Development$_{13}$ is a change in the composition of intermediate demand involving the substitution of manufactured for primary inputs.

Development$_{14}$ is an increase in international trade.

Development$_{15}$ is a shift in the composition of exports away from agricultural products and towards manufactured goods.

Development$_{16}$ is a rise and then a decline in the rate of population growth as the gap between mortality and birth rates first widens and then narrows over the course of economic development$_5$. (Known as the Demographic Transition.)

Development$_{17}$ is an increase in the proportion of people located in towns and cities. (Urbanisation.)

Development$_{18}$ is an increase in agricultural labour productivity.

Development$_{19}$ is the efficient functioning of the market economy (or relatively low transaction costs), which depends on clearly defined and well enforced property rights.

Socio-Cultural Development:

Development$_{20}$ is the weakening of traditional ties and power structures.

Development$_{21}$ is the growth of individual motivation and the expansion of enterprise.

Social Development:

Development$_{22}$ implies a reduction in absolute poverty, unemployment and income inequality. (Dudley Seers's criteria.)

Development$_{23}$ is the expansion of people's entitlements or command over goods and services.

Development$_{24}$ is an improvement in social indicators. The most notable include rates of life expectancy, adult literacy and infant mortality.

Continued/....

Box 1.1 (cont.)

Political Development:

Development$_{25}$ is the growth of political freedom and democratisation.

Development$_{26}$ is the growth of participation in the development process. It is characterised by an increase in decision-making and the control over resources and institutions by those at the bottom of society.

Development$_{27}$ involves promoting equality for women, especially in the areas of education, employment and formal and informal rights.

Human Development:

Development$_{28}$ is the expansion of human capabilities.

Development$_{29}$ is a process of enlarging people's freedom of choice which is measured by an index of human development based on GNP per capita, literacy and life expectancy.

Sustainable Development:

Development$_{30}$ is a pattern of resource allocation that permits future generations to live at least as well as current generations.

Concepts of Underdevelopment:

Underdevelopment$_1$ is an early stage of social and economic development$_4$.

Underdevelopment$_2$ is a qualitative process of negative social and economic change (i.e. the opposite of development$_4$).

NOTES

1. The following remarks draw on the definitions of 'development' presented in various dictionaries. The sources consulted were Fowler and Fowler (1975), OED (1933) and Schwartz (1993).
2. In practice social and economic development is not a purely positive process. Development (development$_{4a}$) is a process whose net effect is positive. Development$_{4a}$ does not preclude any negative elements but it does preclude a negative overall balance.
3. This process of negative change is sometimes referred to as underdevelopment. The Classical view of underdevelopment (underdevelopment$_1$) identified the concept with backwardness or an early stage of development$_4$. Today the concept is more usually associated with a country's incorporation into the world capitalist system in a subordinate position. In the original (strong) version of dependency theory, underdevelopment (underdevelopment$_2$) and development$_4$ are viewed as 'opposite faces of the same coin' (Frank, 1967, p.33). On other concepts of 'dependency' see Brewer (1990), Cardoso and Faletto (1979) and Rao (1994).
4. In a longer book it would have been useful to consider earlier attempts to conceptualise

development, which can be traced back to Adam Smith (1776) and Karl Marx (1848; 1853; 1877; 1959) if not to Aristotle himself. Some useful surveys of this material include Dorfman (1991), Harcourt (1996), Hodgson et al. (1994), Kerr (1993), Lange (1963, chs 1-3), Larrain (1989), Lewis (1988), Meier and Baldwin (1962, chs 1-6), Palma (1978), Samuelson (1977) and Spengler (1949). There seems to be considerable overlap between the concepts of development endorsed in the eighteenth, nineteenth and early twentieth century and more recent approaches.

5. The drawbacks associated with the GNP and GNP per capita statistics as measures of development have been well documented. There are well-known difficulties relating to data collection and to inter-country comparisons of GNP, not to mention the indicator's inadequacy as a measure of welfare. See Bastar (1972), Hicks and Streeten (1979) and Streeten (1981; 1995). See also Ekins and Max-Neef (1992), Herrick and Kindleberger (1983, ch. 6), Sen (1984; 1987; 1988), UNDP (1990; 1996) and World Bank (1991, ch. 2).

6. Calculations indicate that increases in TFP accounts for anywhere from half to three-quarters of historical growth in developed countries. See Chenery, Robinson and Syrquin (1986, ch. 2) and Ingham (1995, pp.143–4).

7. For a critique of the view that investment spending is a primary determinant of economic development see Bauer (1981, ch. 14).

8. Structural development is by no means uniform across countries. It is affected by national factors such as resource use, and the initial structure of the economy as well as by the choice of development policies. For these reasons most comparative studies of structural change have concentrated on analysing average patterns of development over time. The following remarks draw heavily but not exclusively on Chenery and Syrquin (1986), Kuznets (1973) and Syrquin (1988) who provide useful summaries of the stylised facts of development.

9. There is a vast literature on industrialisation. See for example, Ayres and Clark (1998), Bagchi (1989), Chenery, Robinson and Syrquin (1986), Hirschman (1968), Lewis (1954; 1955; 1980), Little (1982), Rosenstein-Rodan (1943), Warren (1973; 1980) and World Bank (1987).

10. The main indicator of this shift is the relative importance of the contribution of manufacturing to growth. Over the course of the transition there is a significant shift in value added from primary production to manufacturing.

11. Exports typically expand as countries become more competitive and imports generally rise in response to rising demand for (foreign) consumer durable goods and industrial inputs. Several studies have pointed to a weak but positive correlation between the extent of a country's international trade and growth (e.g. Clark, 1995, p.38; World Bank, 1987, p.85).

12. See also Birdsall (1977) and Lewis (1955, pp.304–19).

13. This is known as the demographic transition. In contrast to the Western experience, not all developing countries have been able to complete the demographic transition, despite a prolonged period of sustained growth in the post-war years that lasted at least until the 1980s. (The most notable exceptions include China and Sri-Lanka.)

14. It is beyond the scope of this chapter to consider other economic concepts of development, such as the capacity of the economy to combine growth with low inflation or Rosenstein-Rodan's (1969) criteria for 'development potential'.

15. More recently the links between growth and human development have been explored by the UNDP (1996). See also the literature on the limitations of the UNDP's Human, Gender and Poverty Indices (some of which is cited below) along with recent econometric work by Pritchett, Ravallion and others on the relationship between the growth of GNP per capita and health or other 'human development' variables.

16. Seers (1972, p.24) writes 'if one or two of these central problems [poverty, unemployment and inequality] have been growing worse, especially if all three have, it would be strange to call the result development, even if per capita income had soared'.

17. Of course, one can still rank reductions in poverty accompanied by a move towards a more egalitarian distribution of income above a similar reduction in poverty associated with rising income inequality.

18. See Gary Fields (1980, esp. ch. 3) on the subjective value judgements and welfare

implications associated with concepts of poverty and inequality.

19. Hirschman (1981, essay 3) points out that an increase in income inequality generated by economic growth adds to everyone's social welfare, providing the 'tunnel effect' is strong. The tunnel effect refers to the utility or gratification the people who failed to benefit from a rise in income derive from the expectation that there own economic position will improve in line with their more fortunate associates in the not too distant future. In this eventuality an increase in income inequality actually contributes to development$_x$. However, Hirschman notes the tunnel effect is unlikely to be strong in all social, political and psychological settings and will quickly decay if expectations of a higher income are not realised.

20. Seers (1972, p.24) acknowledges that 'the true fulfilment of human potential requires much that cannot be specified in these terms' including adequate education levels, participation in government and belonging to a truly independent nation. He also makes it clear that development$_x$ is about change in social, economic and political structures and 'with relations between countries as well as relations within countries'.

21. Research suggests that many more poor families possess the income to purchase a nutritionally adequate diet than in fact do so, and the intra-family distribution of consumption is often far from equitable.

22. If development$_x$ is about what people achieve, then the latter set of indicators must be the most relevant.

23. In particular, some new material on social indicators is included and entire chapters are set aside for discussions of Structural Change and Socio-Cultural approaches to economic development.

2. Capability and Human Development

1. INTRODUCTION

The aim of this chapter is to provide a detailed assessment of the capability approach – particularly in relation to more traditional concepts of development, which typically focus on utility or commodity command. It also paves the way for making the capability approach operational by considering some of the capabilities thought to facilitate a good form of life. The discussion is illustrated by drawing on some examples from fieldwork in South Africa, which investigated how poor people living in a rural village and urban township perceive human development.

The following discussion is meant to be constructive and is intended to strengthen the capability approach. To avoid possible misunderstandings, it is worth pausing to spell out the full implications of the proceeding discussion for the capability approach. My basic position is that while there are difficulties with Sen's approach, it still has clear advantages over more traditional notions of well-being. In particular, the results of our surveys indicate that Sen's critiques of utility (happiness, desire-fulfilment) and resource (income, commodity command) based approaches should be endorsed. Neither of these frameworks have an informational base that is broad enough to capture all aspects of human development. In fact, these frameworks can provide fairly misleading guides to well-being (as Sen himself has argued). In contrast, the capability approach is broad enough to avoid these pitfalls (see Sections 2–4).

However, if Sen's framework is going to be used to evaluate human well-being a far more extensive list of capabilities than Sen cares to provide is required. Perhaps the only reasonable way of arriving at such a list is to consult the poor themselves. Any other method risks imposing our own ethnocentric views on those we propose to develop. I do not particularly want to quarrel with Sen's examples of 'intrinsically valuable capabilities' (which are summarized in Section 4 and Table 3.1 below). The examples Sen provides, however, do seem to be somewhat selective. This is partly because Sen's goal is to distinguish the capability approach from rival frameworks. He is concerned with proposing and defending a conceptual space for evaluating development rather than articulating an account of good living.

Yet his discussion of different frameworks and, perhaps more noticeably, his examples of valuable capabilities both seem to imply a fairly specific vision of development (even though this vision is *never* explicitly endorsed). It is worth keeping this in mind as Sen writes extremely persuasively on such matters, and it is not difficult for the reader to come away with the impression that certain fundamental capabilities *ought* to be included in any rational view of a good life. Sen tends to emphasise the value of basic capabilities that relate to a person's *physical condition*. He also acknowledges the value of a small and fairly select number of social capabilities. But these are not the only ends that matter. A diverse combination of physical, social and psychological achievements contribute to a good life style (as our fieldwork results clearly show). In particular, more emphasis should be given to the role of utility (valuable mental states broadly construed) and hedonistic ends. Psychological achievements such as happiness, confidence and peace of mind not only have intrinsic value but immense instrumental significance. Chronic depression or madness can seriously undermine the capability to function well. The capability approach also directs attention away from income and commodities. While many material things may not have intrinsic value, they certainly are endowed with considerable instrumental power. In short, they are necessary (if not by themselves sufficient) for human development (a fact that even the most ardent humanist should not overlook). Reflecting on these issues leads to the more general conclusion that there is greater overlap between the categories of *commodities*, *functioning* and *utility* than the current literature on the capability approach suggests. It is not always clear how certain things should be classified using these distinctions; and many things (irrespective of how they are classified) seem to be endowed with both intrinsic and instrumental value, to greater or lesser degrees (see Sections 5–6).

The chief advantage of the capability approach then, is that it is broad enough to capture all aspects of human development. In contrast, utility and resource-based approaches only capture part of the picture. The former is preoccupied with mental states while the latter is only concerned with the material requirements for good living. Sen helps to fill the gap between these perspectives by voicing the value of certain basic physical capabilities together with some more complex social achievements. But in doing so he only provides a partial account of the good, which fails to cover all relevant spheres of life. This is only problematic insofar as it misdirects deliberation about the nature and character of human well-being. What is far more problematic and misleading is the kind of approach that not only tries to develop a full account of the human good, but also discriminates either in favour of, or against, potentially controversial ends. Examples of such approaches include Baran and Sweezy's theory of 'genuine human need', and

Vance Packard's critique of capitalist production and consumption. The final part of this chapter considers the problem of paternalism in relation to the general approach of capabilities. It is argued that Sen's framework (in marked contrast to some other theories of human need) is flexible and can escape the charge of paternalism, provided that it is not abused.

2. THE COMMODITY APPROACH

There is a long tradition of viewing the process of economic development in terms of economic growth and the expansion of goods and services. Since Adam Smith (1776) wrote about the 'progress of opulence' economists have been preoccupied with characterising and measuring living conditions in terms of income and commodity command.[1]

There is certain logic behind this approach. Economic growth and material prosperity are necessary (if not sufficient) for human development. People cannot live, let alone live well, without goods and services. This point is often lost or obscured in radical critiques of development. A credible critique of the commodity approach however, does not entail overlooking (or challenging) the material basis of well-being. In a well-known paper in the *Economic Journal* Sen (1983) comes close to adopting this position. He acknowledges the link between growth and living standards and praises traditional development economics for identifying the factors that promote growth in poor countries. But he also offers a critique of the commodity approach and proposes an alternative that is concerned with what people can do and be. In recent years Martha Nussbaum has tried to reinforce this critique. I shall consider the merits of their arguments against the commodity approach.

First, Sen and Nussbaum advise us that commodities are not valuable in themselves but only by virtue of what they can do *for* people:

A person's well-being is not really a matter of how rich he or she is . . . Commodity command is a *means* to the end of well-being, but can scarcely be the end itself. . . (Sen, 1985, p.28)

. . . commodities are no more than means to other ends. Ultimately the focus has to be on what life we lead and what we can or cannot do, can or cannot be. (Sen, 1987, p.16)

. . . wealth, income and possessions simply are not good in themselves. However much people may actually be obsessed with heaping them up . . . what they have really, when they have them, is just a heap of stuff. A useful heap, but a heap nonetheless, a heap that is nothing at all unless it is put to use in the doings and beings of human life. (Nussbaum, 1990, p.210)

These statements may be compelling. But to make the argument stick Sen and Nussbaum need to demonstrate that ordinary people only value material things on instrumental grounds. It is doubtful that this can be done (see Chapter 4). Appealing to our intuition, considered judgement or Aristotelian values is not a sufficient foundation for a scientific argument.

A second avenue of attack turns on showing that the commodity requirements of individuals can vary quite widely (e.g. Nussbaum, 1990, p.211; Sen, 1984; 1985; 1999, pp.70–71). People typically *differ* in their capacity to convert a given bundle of goods into valuable achievements. A cripple, for example, or a person with a parasitic disease and relatively high metabolic rate, may have extra-ordinary needs (for wheelchairs, ramps or food, etc.) that ought to be catered for. This argument does not depend on appealing to a few special cases. Iliffe's (1987) history of African poverty suggests that the ranks of the 'very poor' are typically made up of a substantial number of lepers, cripples and blind people[2] (among others). Nor should we overlook other very real and widespread differences between people (Sen, 1982, p.366). A manual labourer, for example, given his activity level, needs more food than most other people to function well. Pregnant or lactating women have different nutritional requirements. The protein needs of a growing child are different from those of adults, and so on (see Section 4). We need to consider how well a particular person can *function* with the goods and services at his or her command.

Third, there may also be variations in commodity requirements between cultures and societies (Sen, 1984, essay 14). More clothing, heating and food is required for basic living in colder climates. Sen is particularly keen to emphasise the importance of cultural and social factors. He often refers to Adam Smith's example of the eighteenth century labourer who requires a linen shirt to appear in public without shame (see Chapter 4). It is unlikely that a modern-day manual worker would possess a linen shirt, let alone feel obliged to wear one in public. The advantage of the capability approach is that it can view well-being (and poverty) as *absolute* in the space of capabilities and relative in the space of commodities. We can say that things like avoiding shame, self-respect and taking part in the life of the community are central parts of life, while recognising that the resources required to achieve these ends will vary with social and cultural conventions (Sen, 1984, pp.333, 335–7; 1987, p.18; 1992, ch. 7.5).

I do not want to quarrel with these three criticisms – although the first may well be difficult to sustain. The fourth and final criticism is more problematic. Following Aristotle, Nussbaum (1990, p.211) has reiterated the idea that 'more is not, in fact, always better, where wealth and income are concerned'. Too many goods can encourage 'excessive competitiveness' and make people insolent, arrogant and have 'a mercenary attitude towards other things' (ibid., pp.211, 245, n.20). The pursuit of material things can also distract 'people from social interaction, from the arts, [and] from learning and reflecting' (ibid., p.211). It is possible to imagine scenarios in which more resources may indeed have bad results. But these are few and far between in the field of development. In poor countries the real issue is 'not enough' goods and services rather than 'too much'. The assumptions (values) behind Nussbaum's brand of Aristotelian wisdom can also be challenged. Do ordinary people really think competition, the desire to succeed and the pursuit of material things have bad results? Or do they regard these things as valuable parts of a good life? The survey findings considered below provide little support for Nussbaum's position (see Table 2.1 below and Chapter 4).

The most credible arguments against the commodity approach turn on showing that material prosperity is an inaccurate and incomplete guide to personal well-being rather than a potential obstacle to human development. These arguments imply that we cannot evaluate the quality of life or make inter-personal comparisons of well-being in terms of income or commodity command. None of this detracts from the importance of having material things and benefiting from economic growth. In most poor countries, living standards could be substantially improved by greater access to (and the better use of) appropriate resources.

3. THE WELFARE (UTILITY) APPROACH

An alternative approach is to judge well-being and development in terms of utility, which is what traditional welfare economics tends to do. In contrast to the commodity approach, this perspective has the advantage of viewing well-being as a feature of persons themselves (Sen, 1985, pp.23–4). But like the commodity approach, the three most common interpretations of utility (in terms of happiness, desire-fulfilment and choice) all provide unsatisfactory accounts of development. Sen dismisses the choice based approach as a 'non-starter' on the grounds that people do not always choose in accordance with their own personal interests, but often wish to take account of wider concerns (Sen, 1985, pp.18–20). The bulk of his critique is directed against the happiness and desire-fulfilment views, which he regards as more serious contenders.[3]

Sen (1982, pp.362–3; 1984, p.308) begins by endorsing the criticism that Utilitarianism is unable to distinguish between different types of pleasures and pains or different kinds of desires.[4] In particular, the utilitarian account of the human good does not discriminate against 'offensive tastes' (Cohen, 1993, pp.11–2).

> In calculating the greatest balance of satisfaction it does not matter, except indirectly, what the desires are for. We are to arrange institutions so as to obtain the greatest sum of satisfactions; we ask no questions about their source or quality but only how their satisfaction would affect the total of well-being . . . Thus if men take a certain pleasure in discriminating against one another, in subjecting others to a lesser liberty as a means of enhancing their own self respect, then the satisfaction of these desires must be weighed in our deliberations according to their intensity or whatever, along with other desires. (Rawls, 1971, pp.30–31)

Notice that this argument applies to Welfarism in general (and not just the special case of Utilitarianism) as the adequacy of relying upon utility information for judging the well-being of individuals is questioned (Sen, 1980, p.363).[5] However, accepting that the 'offensive tastes' argument defeats Welfarism does not necessitate abandoning the utility approach (Cohen, 1993, p.12). A natural response is to regard some kinds of utility (such as the satisfaction derived from subjecting another person to a lesser liberty) as 'wrong', and to strike these pleasures and desires from utility functions before evaluating well-being (e.g. Rawls, 1971, p.31). Alternatively, offensive pleasures and desires could be regarded as less valuable than those arising from more virtuous sources.[6]

Sen also points out that there is more to life than achieving utility:

> Happiness or desire fulfilment represents only one aspect of human existence. (Sen, 1984, p.512; see also Sen, 1987, p.8; 1992, p.54; 1999, p.62)

> The Welfare approach, of which utilitarianism is a prime example, overemphasises people's mental states and neglects other aspects of their well-being . . . It goes astray . . . by paying exclusive attention to but one aspect of human well-being, namely, utility. (Crocker, 1992, pp.599–600)

Many types of non-utility information appear to have intrinsic importance for the assessment of well-being and development (Sen, 1982, p.363 and part IV). For example, we could reject the Welfare approach and its single-minded concern with utility by appealing to other principles, such as the irreducible value of negative liberty (e.g. Rawls, 1971).[7] Sen is particularly concerned about Welfarism's apparent lack of interest in positive freedoms.

> Hunger, starvation and famines are awful social phenomena not just because they cause disutility. An elementary failure of freedom is involved in this, and we do not judge the seriousness of the situation by the precise extent of the unhappiness or dissatisfaction. (Sen, 1984, p.512)

For Sen the relevance of non-utility information 'is the central issue involved in disputing Welfarism' (Sen, 1982, p.363). This position gains support from the evidence considered below, which suggests that a credible conception of the human good should take explicit account of the person's physical condition as well as his or her state of mind.

Finally, Sen advances arguments to suggest that 'utility does not adequately represent well-being' (quoted in Crocker, 1992, p.601; see also Sen, 1999, p.62). The first of these arguments recognises that a severely deprived person can be quite cheerful if s/he has learned to take pleasure in small mercies and entertain realistic desires.

> A thoroughly deprived person, leading a very reduced life, might not appear to be badly off in terms of the mental metric of utility, if the hardship is accepted with non-grumbling resignation. In situations of long standing deprivation, the victims do not go on weeping all the time, and very often make great efforts to take pleasure in small mercies and cut down personal desires to modest – 'realistic' – proportions. The person's deprivation, then, may not at all show up in the metrics of pleasure, desire fulfilment etc., even though he or she may be quite unable to be adequately nourished, decently clothed, minimally educated and so on. (Sen, 1990, p.45)

Expectations and aspirations typically adapt to allow the poor and deprived to cope with the harsh realities of life.[8] Some empirical support can be found for the thesis of false consciousness. For example, Sen (1984, p.309; 1985, pp.82–3) cites evidence from a post famine health survey in India that indicates significant disparities between the externally observed health of widows and their own impressions of their physical state.

Sen is also concerned that social, cultural and religious ideas may condition the poor and deprived to accept and even find justification for their fate (Sen, 1982, p.367; 1985a, p.188; Sen and Williams, 1982, p.6). Social influences, for example, may distort *perceptions* of the relative needs of different family members, and can give rise to significant differences in the quality of life between different groups of people. Sen's estimates of sex and age bias in poverty underline this point (Sen, 1984, essay 15; 1985, pp.81–104). It is also possible that the poor and disadvantaged may lack the necessary experience and knowledge to harbour grand desires, and are therefore more likely to be content with little.[9]

It follows that achieving happiness and realising desires are not necessarily indicative of high levels of personal well-being. In many ways a grumbling rich man is better off than a content peasant. These arguments may help to explain the 'Easterlin Paradox' – the finding that people in rich countries do not appear happier than those in poor ones (Easterlin, 1974). More recently, a report in the *Scientific American* that draws on a range of studies conducted throughout the world confirms that 'happiness does not appear to depend significantly on external circumstances' (Myers and Diener, 1996, p.54).

Together these considerations indicate that utility constitutes an incomplete concept of well-being that cannot be used as a reliable proxy for human development. What is required is an approach that considers what people can do and be – where achieving happiness and realising desires only count as one valuable aspect of life (Nussbaum, 1990, p.213; Sen, 1980, p.211; 1984, p.318).

4. FUNCTIONING, CAPABILITY AND DEVELOPMENT

We have seen that a person's well-being cannot be judged exclusively in terms of utility (happiness, desire-fulfilment) or commodity command. These approaches exclude relevant information and typically provide inaccurate guides to well-being. Instead, we need to look at how well a person manages to function with the resources at his or her disposal. Sen (1985) models this in terms of an index of function(ing)s. A *functioning* is 'an achievement of a person: what she or he manages to do or to be' (ibid., p.12). Sen's substantive claim is that the evaluation of a person's well-being must take the form of an assessment of the functionings achieved by that person (e.g. Sen, 1985, p.25; 1988, p.15; 1992, p.39). This implies that development entails – *inter alia* – the expansion of valuable functionings, i.e. the 'achievement of a better life' (Sen, 1988, p.15).

Sen emphasises the importance of distinguishing between *commodities* (and their *characteristics*), *functionings* and *utility* (Sen, 1980; 1982; 1984; 1984a; 1985; 1985a; 1988). The hypothetical examples Sen uses to illustrate these distinctions are summarised in Figure 2.1. Following Gorman (1956) and Lancaster (1966), Sen recognises that a characteristic is a 'feature' or attribute of a good. While the ownership of goods and the corresponding characteristics (attributes and qualities) of goods is usually a personal matter, he observes that the 'quantification of characteristics does not vary with the personal features of the individual possessing the goods' (Sen, 1985, p.10). A bicycle, for example, is treated as having the characteristic of transportation regardless of whether or not the owner is able-bodied or crippled. A functioning, on the other hand, relates to the *use* a person can make of the commodities and characteristics at his or her command. In the case of the cripple, for example, the notion of functioning acknowledges that s/he may be unable to do many of the things (e.g. moving around) an able-bodied person can achieve with the same commodities (e.g. a bicycle).

	Intervention of personal and social factors ↘		
Commodity → e.g. bicycle	**Characteristic** → e.g. transportation	**Functioning** → e.g. cycling around	**Utility** Happiness or Desire-fulfilment
e.g. bread (or rice)	e.g. provides nutrition e.g. facilitates social occassions	e.g. living without calorie deficiency e.g. entertaining others	" " " " " " " "

Source: adapted from Sen (1982, p.31). The examples are taken from Sen (1984, pp.315–7, 333–4; 1984a, pp.84–7; 1985, pp.9–10, 25–6).

Figure 2.1 From Resources to Functioning – Sen's Concept of Human Well-Being

On closer inspection it becomes clear that the conversion of commodities (and their characteristics) into personal achievements of functionings are subject to a range of personal and social factors (see Sen, 1985, pp.25–6; 1999, pp.70–71). Take a commodity like bread which exhibits the attributes of: (1) yielding nutrition; and (2) facilitating social occasions (among other characteristics). According to Sen, the nutritional achievements derived from consuming bread (or food more generally) typically depend on factors such as '(1) metabolic rates, (2) body size, (3) age, (4) sex (and, if a woman, whether pregnant or lactating), (5) activity levels, (6) health (including the presence or absence of parasites), (7) access to medical services and the ability to use them, (8) nutritional knowledge and education, and (9) climatic conditions' (Sen, 1985, p.25).[10] In the case of functionings relating to social behaviour and entertaining friends and family, Sen notes that what a person is able to achieve will be determined by such influences as '(1) the nature of social conventions in force in the society in which the person lives, (2) the position of the person in the family and in the society, (3) the presence or absence of festivities such as marriages, seasonal festivals and other occasions such as funerals, (4) the physical distance from the homes of friends and relatives, and so on' (ibid.). In comparing the functionings of different people, not enough information is provided by looking only at the commodities each can successfully command.

On the other hand, Sen has remarkably little to say about the role of utility (and its bearing on well-being) in his discussions of the examples in Figure 2.1. He simply notes that a *functioning*, such as bicycling, 'has to be distinguished from' and 'must not be identified with' the happiness generated by that act (ibid., p.10). I will have more to say about this presently.

Sen is not in favour of restricting his account of well-being to human functioning. He also wants to assess development in terms of the *capability* to function (Sen, 1984; 1988; 1990). This 'represents the various combinations of functionings (beings and doings) that the person can achieve' (Sen, 1992, p.40). It reflects the person's real opportunities or *positive* freedom of choice between possible life styles (see Sen, 1985; 1992; 1999). Sen (1993, p.39) argues that this freedom must have intrinsic value if objects such as 'acting freely' and 'being able to choose' are important features of a good life.

This raises the question of whether development should be seen in terms of (1) functioning; (2) capability; or (3) some combination of these two concepts. No real distinction is drawn between (1) and (2) in Sen's early writings (e.g. Sen, 1980). In later writings Sen appears to favour the second interpretation.[11]

> Ultimately, the process of economic development has to be concerned with what people can or cannot do . . . (Sen, 1983, p.754)

> . . . the process of economic development is best seen as an expansion of people's 'capabilities'. (Sen, 1984, p.509–10)

> Development can be seen . . . as a process of expanding the real freedoms that people enjoy. (Sen, 1999, p.3)

Elsewhere Sen (1988; 1990) has advised us that the quality of life is complex and should be seen in terms of functionings *and* capabilities. He is not always consistent. There are elements in Sen's writings that define well-being in terms of all three of these categories.[12] There are even some inconsistent passages:

> If life is seen as a set of 'doings and beings' [functionings] that are valuable, the exercise of assessing the quality of life takes the form of evaluating these functionings *and the capability to function*. (Sen, 1990, pp.43–4. *My italics*)

One of the strengths of Sen's approach is that it is flexible. His concepts can be employed in different ways and have a wide range of possible applications. To assess poverty, for example, we may want to focus on a small number of basic functionings. Beginning to understand human development, on the other hand, demands a firm grasp of the most central functionings and capabilities in every sphere of life. Sen believes that appropriate conceptual space (functioning, capability, etc.) depends on the purpose of the evaluative exercise in hand – although the ultimate goal is to ensure that each and every individual enjoys the substantive freedoms or capabilities to live the kind of life he or she 'has reason to value' (Sen, 1999, p.74).

Notice that much depends on what is meant by the term 'capability'. If the capability to do X entails that one can definitely choose to do X (without being prevented from realising X in some way), it would probably be sufficient to view development as capability expansion. On this reading, the emphasis on freedom is assured *without* running the risk of jeopardising the actual power of functioning. Viewing freedom in this way also helps to ensure that some of Sen's criticisms of the commodity and utility approaches – specifically the charge that they can provide a misleading guide to human well-being and achievement – cannot be turned against the capability approach. (I have tried to clarify the concept of capability in the Addendum to this chapter.)

Interpreting capability in terms of the *actual ability to function* sits well with the concept of functioning. Indeed, there is nothing to stop us from *refining* the notion of functioning to reflect choice as Sen (1985a) himself suggests. Ultimately, however, we do not need to take a firm position on these matters. Capability and functioning are both defined in terms of the same focal variables (Sen, 1992, p.50). This means that the accounts of human development considered in the following chapters can be viewed in either of these conceptual spaces.

Sen has been reluctant to endorse a unique list of functionings or capabilities as objectively correct for strategic reasons (see Section 7; see also Qizilbash, 2001). He is concerned that such a list may be over specified, and wants to leave space for people to define their own ends. He also wants to avoid compromising the influence and reach of his approach, which can be developed in many other ways some of which are not necessarily consistent with completeness (Sen, 1993, p.47). But while Sen's concept of well-being is intentionally incomplete and open-ended, he does end up endorsing a *partial* theory of good living. For example, in an early paper Sen claims that 'being able to live long, escape avoidable morbidity, be well-nourished, be able to read, write and communicate and take part in literary and scientific pursuits and so forth' are all examples of valuable capabilities (Sen, 1983, p.754). Elsewhere he has argued that more complex social functionings such as achieving self-respect, appearing in public without shame, entertaining family and friends and taking part in the life of the community are relevant for assessing poverty and development (e.g. Sen, 1984; 1985a, p.199; 1992, pp.39, 110). Sen is compelled to appeal to these (and other) examples of intrinsically valuable ends to justify his critique of utility and resource based accounts of well-being and provide the capability approach with normative force. The examples he provides, however, relate largely to the physical and social spheres of life and fail to provide a sufficiently broad overview of well-being. Nor does Sen's work capture the complexity of, or interaction between, different forms of human functioning. The capability approach however, is broad enough to address the former and sophisticated enough to shed light on the latter.

5. USING SEN'S FRAMEWORK

I have tried to show that Sen's approach provides a more comprehensive framework for thinking about human well-being and development than the traditional emphasis on resources or utility (defined in terms of some valuable mental state). His framework moves the emphasis away from the categories of goods and utility (happiness, pleasure, desire-fulfilment) and towards the idea of functioning. However, the distinctions Sen makes between the notions of *commodities, functionings* and *utility* are less robust than his original discussion suggests. A good way of illustrating these complications (and gaining some initial insights into the dimensions of human development) is to consider how certain commodities and activities fit into Sen's conceptual framework. The analysis is illustrated by drawing on some concrete examples from fieldwork in two poor South African communities (see Table 2.1).[13] While some of these examples are deliberately provocative (e.g. Coca-Cola, alcohol, advertising), they do help to illustrate some broader concerns about the presumed nature of well-being.[14] An assessment of the fieldwork together with a full analysis of the results is reserved for Chapter 4 (see also Clark, 2000a).

Before proceeding, notice that the distinctions Sen draws between the categories in Figure 2.1 rest heavily upon two examples (having a bicycle, and having some bread[15]), which refer to only three possible functionings. Sen returns to these two examples again and again, but in order to make the distinctions between the categories stick, it is necessary to consider a much wider and more diverse range of commodities, activities and achievements (see below).

Moreover, both of Sen's examples can be questioned. The first of these examples, which involves the use that an able-bodied person (in contrast to a crippled person) can make of a bicycle, is fairly obscure. While moving around on a bicycle is a potentially valuable achievement (particularly from the perspective of a disabled person),[16] it is not necessarily one of the first things to come to mind when thinking about human well-being and development. Attention is typically directed towards jobs, education, housing, health, income, family, physical security, liberty and happiness – among many other things (see Chapters 3–4).

Furthermore, it is not clear that 'moving around' on a bicycle is the object of (intrinsic) value. For example, it is possible to argue that using the bicycle for exercise, to visit family and friends, to travel to work or go to the cinema or local dance are the kinds of 'beings' and 'doings' people value (see Tables II.13 and II.13.A). Cycling is a means to other ends as well as an end in itself. This point has particular relevance for many poor people, who are not in a position to use other forms of transport. In addition, cycling from A to B may become tedious and cause unhappiness if the function is performed on a regular basis. At the extreme, cycling long distances can be painful, physically exhausting and, in the long term, may even threaten health.[17] In these circumstances moving around on a bicycle turns out to be a *negative* functioning that subtracts from personal well-being. But in Sen's example, achieving the function of moving around on a bicycle is naturally assumed to enhance the cyclist's well-being (and also to yield utility), regardless of the purpose or motive behind the action.

Finally, a bicycle is not the only good that exhibits the characteristic of transportation. There are many other potential modes of transport, and good reasons for believing that a person may be better off travelling one way rather than another. Nearly all the people we spoke to insisted that they would prefer to travel by car instead of by bicycle. Being able to 'travel further' more quickly and efficiently was ranked as the single most important reasons for favouring a car by the majority of people we questioned (Table II.13.B). Many respondents also expressed a strong preference to travel by car to achieve happiness or realise a desire. This is an important part of development for many poor people who are not in a position to think about buying a car. Several respondents also felt that a motor car would enhance their status and help them to gain the respect of peers. According to one teenage male cars are 'faster' and 'look better'.[18] In the light of these remarks, we can conclude that by focusing exclusively on the case of riding a bicycle, Sen inadvertently provides an incomplete view of the functions of transport. (In fairness, this was not Sen's objective.)

Sen's second example is less obscure. In general, a loaf of bread (or a bowl of rice) clearly does facilitate important functionings like 'living without calorie deficiency' and 'entertaining others'.[19] These achievements also tend to facilitate pleasure and satisfy desires. Escaping from persistent hunger by consuming a wholesome and filling loaf of bread can be extremely satisfying (see Table I.7). But Sen has little to say about the contribution of utility (happiness, desire-satisfaction, etc.) when he discusses the example. Moreover, while few people want to dispute the importance of absorbing nutrients (in order to live without calorie deficiency) or disagree that a generally healthy diet is of value (see e.g. Table II.7), many individuals do not actually *choose* to adopt a healthy diet. This implies that consuming food facilitates other functionings, some of which receive priority in most people's assessment of what makes a good life[20] (see Chapter 4, Section 4.2.5.1). Hence the demand for junk food. Considering some additional examples helps to illustrate the point and bring out some of the other difficulties associated with Sen's framework (see Table 2.1).

One product that has been immensely successful (even in some of the world's poorest countries[21]) is Coca-Cola. But Coca-Cola, like most other soft drinks, is not a particularly good source of nutrition. The product is low in protein, fat and fibre – although it does have a high energy content derived from sugar and other carbohydrates. While Coca-Cola does have some nutritional value, it is unlikely that the product's ability to provide nourishment is a decisive factor behind its success.[22] Many products are rich in nutrition but few are as successful as Coca-Cola. Soft drinks such as Coca-Cola (like many other products) can also harm health.[23] Some of the British Co-op's own brands of soft drinks carry the following advice for parents:

> Frequent drinking of sugary drinks and fruit juices may lead to tooth decay and poor nutrition. Try to restrict these drinks to meal times and replace them with sugar free drinks or water. Avoid giving sugary drinks or fruit juices to babies.

In stark contrast to the British Co-op, Coca-Cola product labels provide the consumer with no warning and the bare minimum in terms of nutritional information.[24] A few of the people we interviewed stated that they did not value the opportunity to drink Coca-Cola or consume other soft drinks on the grounds that these products are unhealthy, addictive, too acidic, 'blow you up' and cause wind. The vast majority of survey participants however, were not primarily concerned with the *possible* ill-effects of these beverages.

On the other hand, Coca-Cola products do cater for liquid needs. Many survey participants attached a great deal of value to a 'cool' and 'refreshing' glass of Coca-Cola that 'quenches thirst' (Table I.12). The Coca-Cola company also produces a high-quality product that is clean, hygienic and safe to consume (Nolan, 1995).[25] Many of the people we interviewed valued Coca-Cola on the grounds that it is 'a healthy, clean drink' (Tables I.12 and II.11). Several informants also acknowledged that Coca-Cola promotes health by relieving ailments such as stomach ache, wind and diarrhoea. One person described Coca-Cola as a medicine that can be used to treat migraine attacks.

Another important factor behind Coca-Cola's success was recently captured in a remark made by Curt Ferguson, the Director of Indochina Coca-Cola holdings, when he was interviewed on the subject of the product's expansion in Vietnam:

For just 20 cents a bottle, or 45 cents a can, consumers can enjoy a simple affordable moment of pleasure. (APU, 1996, p.10)

The people we interviewed rated enjoyment well above other motives for consuming Coca-Cola and soft drinks (Tables I.12 and II.11). Several respondents particularly liked the gas in Coca-Cola ('fizz' of the product), as well as the taste.

For many poor people however, the consumption of Coca-Cola is not just about obtaining a simple 'moment of pleasure'. Coca-Cola is widely perceived as a superior first world product.

A Chinese consumer on the streets of downtown Tianjin who buys a Coke for himself and his family from a post-mix machine, and stands to drink it in the street 'transports' his family to the advanced countries for the duration of the consumption of the product. (Nolan, 1995, pp.11–12)

According to Nolan the feeling of being 'transported' depends on the *quality* and the *image* of the product. The family's experience of being 'transported' would be reduced 'if the paper cup were not of high quality and turned to mush in their hands while the product was being consumed' (ibid., p.12). Large scale advertising and marketing also play an important part in facilitating this experience:

The product of local handicraft producers may be sold from dirty wooden boxes covered perhaps with a dirty damp towel containing the remnants of ice. Coca-Cola's products are all sold from packaging and surroundings emblazoned with the Coca-Cola logo, including umbrellas, tables and chairs, awnings covering vending points, cold cabinets, post-mix machines, and bicycles.

They are sold in recognisable distinctive 'Coke' designs, from paper cups, glass, and PET bottles, and cans with the Coke logo, to the 'Coke' crate with its distinctive colour and logo. (Nolan, 1995, p.16)

The visual impact of Coca-Cola in poor communities is enormous (see APU, 1996; Nolan, 1995; 1999). Coca-Cola now plays an important role in the fashion culture of many countries. Reports from Vietnam indicate that growing international awareness and changing life styles have elevated Coca-Cola 'to the modern day symbol of refreshment' since the product re-entered the country after the lifting of the American trade embargo in 1994 (APU, 1996, p.10). Many of the South Africans we spoke to cited popularity or brand loyalty as important reasons for valuing and drinking Coca-Cola. Some respondents simply stated that 'Coke is best', 'Coke is top' or 'Coke is No.1'.[26] One or two respondents even claimed to value Coca-Cola because they 'liked the colour' or 'design on the can' (see Table I.12).[27] These are key features of Coca-Cola's identity and marketing strategy. The 'redness' of the colour and the Spencerian script (curvy contour design denoting the 'Coca-Cola' logo) are both important parts of the product's mystique and pleasure. For many of the world's poor, Coca-Cola represents a cheap, affordable and accessible piece of the good life.

Experiencing pleasure and feelings of 'transportation' however, are not the only valuable achievements Coca-Cola helps to facilitate. In keeping with Sen's approach (and virtue ethics more generally) we can also point, with justification, to the value of using Coca-Cola to achieve other important functionings such as relaxing, facilitating social life and enhancing friendships (see Table I.12). (I shall have more to say about the value of these achievements later.) Moreover, while the nutritional value of soft drinks is questionable, Coca-Cola products do play an important role in terms of fulfilling basic liquid needs.

Similar points can be made about more fundamental goods, such as clothing and housing.[28] The most basic function of clothing is to protect the body from the elements and avoid embarrassment. These achievements slot neatly into Sen's system alongside other basic functionings, such as 'living without calorie deficiency' and 'being in good health'. But in most cultures and societies there is also a strong desire to possess quality clothing in order to achieve a range of very different social, cultural and psychological functions. For example, many of the South Africans we interviewed valued clothing to look smart and presentable in public. Teenagers and young adults in particular, also wanted quality clothes to look 'good' and attract the opposite sex. Younger people were also particularly keen to wear good clothes in order to enhance their image, be fashionable and achieve status. These objectives are not unimportant. Some of the poorest people are extremely fashion conscious and find all sorts of inexpensive ways of establishing and reinforcing a personal identity. Something as simple as adding bobbles, flowers or feathers to hats, sewing attractive buckles and buttons onto garments and coats, and using a small slip of colourful material as a neck scarf can count as examples of major fashion statements.[29] Poor people, particularly women, also tend to supplement their clothing with costume jewellery, headbands and handkerchiefs (among other items). Several respondents reported that clothes bring happiness (Table I.8). Most poor people possess pathetically little clothing and are unable to achieve these functionings satisfactorily. So far Sen has not explicitly discussed these aspects of poverty.[30]

Good housing also makes it possible to achieve basic human functionings such as shelter from the elements and physical security. These items fit naturally into Sen's framework. (In fact, Sen explicitly mentions the capability 'to have adequate shelter'.) Again however, living in a well-constructed house with adequate living space helps promote an important range of social and psychological functionings such as privacy, self-respect and peace of mind. Other important achievements connected with living in a good house include happiness, feeling proud and achieving status (see Tables I.3 and II.3). These observations stand in stark contrast to notions of basic need and physical functioning which typically augment the capability approach. On the other hand, good housing and quality clothing also contribute to physical well-being by improving hygiene, health and the quality of the environment (see Chapter 4).

Moreover, it is not clear how Sen's system should evaluate activities such as taking part in sport, which is particularly important for young people.[31] Achieving physical fitness, acquiring skills and enhancing social life are examples of valuable functionings facilitated by participating in sports (see Tables II.10 and II.10.A). Sen's system would probably regard these achievements as worthwhile ends, but they are not the only (or perhaps the most important) reasons for taking part in sport.[32] Achieving pleasure is also an important objective. Most of the people we spoke to also valued taking part in sports to develop a team spirit[33] and facilitate the love of competition. Winning and scoring goals were particularly important objectives. The majority of informants also confirmed the value of participating in sports to gain status and prestige (Table II.10).

For many people *watching* sport is just as valuable as *playing* sport. In fact, some people prefer to watch sport in order to *avoid* physical exercise.[34] Watching sport (in contrast to taking part in sport) also makes it relatively difficult to acquire skills. There is no substitute for the experience of spin bowling, taking a penalty kick or swinging a golf club. It is the social and psychological impact of watching sport that makes the activity so popular. The South African sports fans we spoke to indicated that it is the excitement, anticipation and enjoyment of these occasions that contribute the most to well-being (Table I.13). This begins to explain why countless thousands of people cram into football stadiums and millions around the globe tune into the World Cup. The presentation of these events, which have increasingly made use of powerful imagery and technology (such as electronic score boards, floodlighting and big television screens for immediate action replays) adds much to the thrill, delight and excitement of watching sport. With the growth of television and satellite communications, many of the world's poor now have the chance to be part of a global audience for high profile sports events (such as the World Cup and Olympic Games), and to participate in these events on an equal footing with sports fans residing in advanced countries. Big sports events also project powerful images of 'development' into the minds of sports fans, who sometimes strive to play for their own team or dream of becoming sport stars (see e.g., Table I.13, items 7, 9, 14 and 29). The people we interviewed also confirmed that watching sport plays an important role in terms of facilitating relaxation and fulfilling the desire for competition and contest. People were keen to support their local team. One man emphasised the value of being able to gamble on the result. These considerations push us in the direction of a Utilitarian rather than an Aristotelian or Marxian ethic (although many of these sentiments can be taken on by non-utilitarians). Watching sport however, also facilitates social gatherings and friendship, provides a valuable topic of conversation and presents useful opportunities to learn the rules, tactics and new techniques of a game (see Table I.13).

Sen's system also needs to cater for activities like watching television and visiting the cinema. These are incredibly important capabilities for poor as well as rich people. The diffusion of televisions, radios and other consumer durable goods in developing countries over the last twenty or thirty years has been remarkable (see PSLSD, 1994, table 8.8; UNDP, 1996, tables 4 and 16; Wells, 1977). Some of the poorest households frequently forgo many of life's necessities in order to acquire a television or radio.[35] During the course of my fieldwork I visited several shacks that contained a colour television or hi-fi system, but had little in the way of quality furniture or other property. A television was a highly prized commodity (see Tables I.11 and II.6). Urban respondents, in particular, were keen to emphasise the importance of watching television to relax or take their mind off worries. Television programmes and cinema trips were also regarded as important sources of pleasure and entertainment. Some respondents also pointed out that television and cinema provide important forms of *escapism*. These activities take you 'away from reality' and help you to 'imagine and daydream'.[36] Watching the television also helps to 'pass time' and avoid boredom and mischief (see Table I.14). Nobody we spoke to mentioned the value of having a television to achieve self-respect or gain status and prestige.[37] These are probably important reasons for desiring a television in many poor societies. On the other hand, a surprisingly large number of people pointed to the educational value of watching television[38] (see Chapter 4). Some people were simply curious about the outside world and wanted to 'see other places'. Several respondents also pointed out that watching television or going to the cinema is an important social activity that can be shared with family and friends (see Table I.14). These objectives are much more consistent with the kinds of *functionings* Sen refers to in his writings.

Nor is it clear how Sen's system would deal with beer or cigarettes. The consumption of these products is widespread among the poor (see Chapter 4). Alcohol and tobacco play a particularly important role in terms of facilitating relaxation, providing pleasurable experiences and satisfying potentially frantic desires. The consumption of alcohol and tobacco also facilitate social interaction and assists with being 'cool' and fashionable. For the poor the consumption of beer, liquor and tobacco also play a crucial role in terms of calming nerves, relieving depression and drowning sorrows. Some people reported that they drink beer and smoke tobacco in order to 'forget problems' and 'feel better' (see Table I.15). These activities, however, also have the potential to generate *negative* functionings that undermine well-being. In particular, the excessive consumption of alcohol and tobacco threatens health. Many of the people we interviewed also pointed out that beer and liquor jeopardise relationships with family and friends, encourage bad, abusive and violent behaviour and lead to crime. Some respondents were also concerned that the consumption of alcohol and tobacco may be addictive or would undermine their status as moral agents by encouraging them to do the wrong things (see Table I.15).

Finally, it is worth considering the role of advertising. Most of the people we spoke to thought advertising served a useful purpose. In particular, respondents valued advertising to 'view products' and gather information about relative prices, product use and the latest fashions (Table I.16). Several people also mentioned the value of finding out about new products and learning how to obtain existing products. This is probably because certain items are not readily available or easy to acquire in poor communities. Many respondents also valued advertising on the grounds that it promotes choice between products. Several informants also pointed out that advertising facilitates economic activity (see Table I.16 items 6, 7, 11–13, 17, 22, and 29). A few respondents valued advertising on the grounds that it is 'likeable', 'entertaining', 'amusing' and facilitates dreams of the future. On the other hand, a small minority of informants refused to endorse advertising on the grounds that it wastes time and money, shows the wrong things and is misleading.[39]

6. SUBSTANTIVE CONCLUSIONS AND FURTHER ANALYSIS

The following conclusions can be drawn from the preceding discussion. In particular, the findings reviewed above imply that the distinctions between the categories in Figure 2.1 are fuzzier than Sen's own analysis suggests. Sen's conceptual framework may also have to deal with some antagonistic aspects of human development.

6.1 Utility and Functioning

There is a great deal of overlap between the concepts of utility and functioning. Experiencing happiness is an important aspect of well-being that features prominently in most activities (see Table 2.1 and Chapter 4 below). Notice that utility consists of much more than feeling happy and avoiding pain in the examples discussed above. The concept can be extended to include a wide range of mental states including pleasure, excitement and the fulfilment of desires. In fact, the concept of utility could even be stretched to cover psychological functionings as diverse as feeling relaxed, achieving peace of mind, daydreaming and experiencing pride. It follows that utility should be: (a) broadly construed to include all hedonistic ends that are valuable; and (b) regarded as an essential part of good functioning.[40]

Sen does acknowledge the value of utility. In fact, he refers to being happy as a 'momentous functioning' that has 'importance on its own'. Happiness, he says, 'can certainly be seen as one of many capabilities of relevance to development' (Sen, 1984, p.513; 1985a, p.200). But Sen does tend to conflate utility as an object of value with achieving happiness or pleasure. Most of the time he appears to regard modern conceptions of utility (in terms of desire-fulfilment or choice) as little more than a problematic 'valuation device' (e.g. Sen, 1987, ch. 1; 1992, pp.54–5). In principle, the strength of a desire for object X provides a rough and ready guide to the value a person attaches to X. Of course, satisfying the *desire* for X (realising the utility or satisfaction that goes with X) can be just as valuable as the mere achievement of X itself. Desires carry intrinsic value in addition to providing a crude practical guide to the value of the object that allows the satisfaction of that desire. Other forms of satisfaction are not discussed in Sen's writings on well-being. In the Dewey Lectures Sen (1985a, pp.188–9) remarks that 'there are mental states other than being just happy, i.e. stimulation, excitement etc., which are of direct relevance to a person's well-being'. But this is all he has to say on the subject.[41]

Moreover, despite having recognised that utility has intrinsic value of its own, Sen devotes little attention to the realisation of this 'momentous' functioning in his accounts of well-being. Consider the hypothetical examples Sen puts forward to justify focusing on the evaluative space of *functioning* (see Figure 2.1 and Section 4 above). Utility barely gets mentioned, and when it does the implications for personal well-being are not spelt out. Sen does not explicitly say that consuming a loaf of bread can yield a great deal of pleasure and satisfy potentially desperate desires (especially if the person in question is starving or hungry). Nor does he acknowledge that these achievements make a separate and distinct contribution to the quality of life.[42] He simply points out that achieving important functionings such as 'moving around' on a bicycle yields utility (Sen, 1985, p.27), which is not always so (see above). In the two examples devised by Sen, utility is effectively divorced from the category of functioning and well-being is made completely dependent upon the latter, i.e. other non-hedonistic ends. This implies that utility has no real bearing on matters of personal well-being – a position that Sen himself does not maintain or wish to take.

There is another dimension to the problem. Commodities (bicycles and bread) contribute to well-being by facilitating certain achievements (moving around, avoiding calorie deficiency, etc.), which in turn generate utility. In these examples utility is portrayed as a by-product of human functioning (although elsewhere Sen recognises that utility itself is a valuable functioning). More generally we can observe that performing certain functionings of value (e.g. 'moving around') may have a positive or negative effect on utility (depending on contingent circumstances). We have argued that the utility consequences of these acts (and not just the acts themselves) have intrinsic significance for good living. Notice however, that utility may also have considerable *instrumental* importance for human functioning and well-being. Taking pleasure from some activity (e.g. riding a bicycle) helps to facilitate the realisation of other achievements (e.g. moving around). At the extreme a happy or content person with a positive attitude is likely to function much better than a manic depressive who has lost the will to get out of bed. Part of the problem then is that Sen does not sufficiently see that some of the functionings themselves come into being and depend intimately upon mental attitudes[43] (see Table 2.1).

In fairness, the two examples Sen constructs are designed to: (1) introduce the concept of functioning; and (2) illustrate the category's strengths vis-à-vis utility. In consequence, we would not expect Sen to devote much space to the significance of utility in these passages. But while Sen frequently maintains that utility (in terms of happiness or pleasure) is important, this achievement receives remarkably little emphasis in his writings on well-being and development. His work on well-being also says little about the heterogeneity of utility, which cannot be reduced to a single mental state such as happiness or pleasure. Sen is aware of these issues (e.g. Sen, 1980–81). So far he has focused on the physical condition and basic needs of the disadvantaged and deprived in his work on poverty, development and justice. But he has expressed an interest in the psychology and motivation behind choice. In a paper that deals with some of the methodological issues involved in description Sen remarks:

> The joys and suffering of human beings and their deprivations and fulfilments have interest of their own . . . It is this part of descriptive motivation that has been least well served by recent developments of utility theory, most notably by the theory of revealed preference. Focusing only on predicting behaviour, the richness of human psychology has been substantially ignored, refusing to see anything in utility or happiness other than choice. (Sen, 1980a, p.362)

Moreover, in a footnote tucked away in an early paper, Sen (1984, p.335, n.16) writes that 'utility . . . [itself] can be given some room within the general approach of capabilities'.

Some of Sen's followers, on the other hand, have adopted what they believe to be a less Utilitarian and more Aristotelian position. For example, although Martha Nussbaum includes 'being able to have pleasurable experiences' on her list of functional capabilities (Nussbaum, 1995, p.83),[44] she refuses to make pleasure a separable functioning on the grounds that it supervenes human activity:

> According to EN X [Aristotle, Nicomachean Ethics, Book X] pleasure supervenes upon the activity to which it attaches, like the bloom on the cheek of a healthy young person, completing or perfecting it. Here pleasure is not identical with activity; but it cannot be identified without reference to the activity to which it attaches. It cannot be pursued on its own without conceptual incoherence, any more than blooming cheeks can be cultivated in isolation from health and bodily fitness with which they belong. Still less could there be a single item, pleasure, that is separable from all the activities and yielded up by all of them in differing quantities. (Nussbaum quoted in Crocker, 1995, p.155)

In contrast to the Utilitarian approach however, which ultimately reduces the concept of well-being to a single category ('utility', defined in terms of some mental condition, such as pleasure, happiness or desire), Sen's framework can comfortably accommodate the entire range of objects that make up a good life (Sen, 1992, pp.43–4, 53–5). In particular, well-being is defined in terms of functionings or states of a person, which make it possible to include categories that cover both mental and physical states. The capability approach can therefore handle complex notions of well-being (like the ones described above) very easily by treating different mental states as examples of valuable functionings. In comparison, Utilitarianism tend to conflate utility with a single mental state (such as happiness or desire) and neglects non-hedonistic objectives altogether. Sen has emphasised the importance of basic physical functionings such as being adequately nourished, achieving good health, and avoiding premature mortality. He has also pointed to the value of some more sophisticated social achievements such as self-respect and taking part in the life of the community (e.g. Sen, 1992, p.5). In practice, however, a diverse range of complex social and mental functionings such as being happy, relaxing, having friends and an active social life, achieving self-respect, being fashionable and possessing status make a phenomenal contribution to a good life style (see Table 2.1). A more substantial account of the psychology of well-being is developed in Chapter 4.

6.2 Resources and Functioning

Apart from the fact that people typically differ in their capacity to convert a given bundle of commodities (and characteristics) into intrinsically valuable achievements we can observe that:

- Many commodities share similar characteristics and can therefore be used to facilitate the *same* functionings[45] (see Table 2.1). This does not mean that a person can get by without access to a reasonably *diverse* range of resources. Man cannot live on bread and water alone. A *balanced* diet is required to be properly nourished. Moreover, even a hungry person may eventually fail to take pleasure from the consumption of bread (or rice) if s/he repeatedly has little else to eat. The same can be said about other commodities and their use(s). For example, good quality clothing helps to facilitate being fashionable and achieving status. But in order to adequately realise these ends a person may require a good job, decent house and fast car (among other things). In short, a person needs a *combination* of inputs before s/he can achieve specific functionings satisfactorily.[46]

- It is unlikely that any combination of relevant inputs will do. Some items appear to be necessary (but not by themselves sufficient) for good functioning. For example, even a person who possesses protective clothing still needs solid, well-insulated and properly heated housing to ensure adequate shelter from the forces of nature. More fundamentally, a person cannot manage without water or salt if s/he wants to go on living. It is possible that some of these essential inputs are endowed with *intrinsic* value (see Chapter 4, Section 6), and should therefore count as examples of important functionings. Sen is reluctant to acknowledge this possibility (see Section 2). In the following chapters, an effort is made to identify some of the most essential inputs for good functioning. The question of whether or not these items possess some intrinsic value in addition to considerable instrumental significance is ultimately left open.

- Commodities are not the only things that facilitate important functionings. We have already seen that some functionings depend intimately upon mental states. This is only the tip of the iceberg. In more general terms we can observe that many activities (beings and doings) themselves have considerable *instrumental* importance. Playing football, watching television and drinking beer are all examples of activities that promote valuable achievements (Table 2.1). Many important functionings are derived from recreational activities and various forms of interaction with family and friends. Religious and educational activities can also facilitate worthwhile ends[47] (see Chapter 4). In this respect many human activities share the characteristics of resources (broadly construed), in the sense that these 'beings' and 'doings' *also* represent necessary inputs for good living.[48] In consequence, it is difficult to know how to classify these items in Sen's system.

- Finally, in many cases, the link between specific characteristics of a good and a particular functioning is less robust than Table 2.1 suggests. Some characteristics clearly facilitate more than one functioning, while some achievements ultimately depend on more than one commodity characteristic.[49]

6.3 Negative Functionings

Another difficulty with Sen's approach relates to the treatment of *negative* functionings. Sen does not discuss the very real possibility that some achievements may actually reduce well-being (see Table 2.1); and it is not entirely clear how his system is supposed to deal with these harmful functionings. One possibility is to exclude all intrinsically bad 'beings' and 'doings' from the concept of the human good. This approach does not seem to be practical or desirable. For example, there is no such thing as a *completely* healthy diet. Moreover, today's knowledge of healthy eating may turn out to be quite wrong. In practice, it is not possible to achieve *pure* functioning. A person may also be compelled to give up many of the good things in life in order to avoid the bad things. Losing weight, for example, is often achieved at the expense of adhering to a strict diet and forgoing the satisfaction and pleasure derived from the consumption of things like chocolate cake, ice cream and Coca-Cola. So even if all of the intrinsically bad 'beings' and 'doings' could be successfully purged from a person's life, there is no guarantee that the results will add up to a good life.

A more realistic and plausible approach (that Sen would probably endorse) is to attach negative weights (reflecting the degree of badness) to harmful functionings,[50] rather than to strike them from the system altogether. This has the advantage of permitting individuals to get the most out of life by allowing each person to maximise his or her net well-being.

Table 2.1 Some Examples of Commodities and Activities, their
Characteristics and the Functionings they can help to Facilitate

Commodity/Activity	Characteristics	Functionings
1. Coca-Cola (and other soft drinks)	* low in protein and fat * high in carbohydrates/ sugar * provides for liquid needs * clean, safe and hygienic * medicinal properties * yields utility * fashionable product * social drink	* some nourishment * provides energy, but like all sugary drinks can rot teeth * meets liquid needs, quenches thirst * avoid ill-health * relieves stomach ache, wind, diarrhoea * provides 'a simple moment of pleasure' * feeling of being 'transported' to the West. * being fashionable * facilitates social activities
2. Clothing	* basic/ ordinary clothing * good quality clothing * yields utility	* protection from the elements * avoid embarrassment * being smart, attractive and fashionable * achieve status * achieving happiness
3. Good housing	* solid, well constructed, properly insulated, spacious, clean and hygienic, etc. * yields utility	* shelter from the elements * physical security/ safety * self-respect and privacy * peace of mind * feel proud, achieve status * being in good health * achieving happiness
4. Playing sports	* exercise * learning skills * social activity * yields utility * team work * contest * facilitate status and prestige	* physical fitness * acquiring skills * enhancing social life * pleasure * develop team spirit * love of competition * achieve status and prestige
5. Watching sports	* yields utility * restful and relaxing * social activity * observe rules, tactics and new techniques	* enjoyment, excitement and anticipation * fulfils desire for competition and gambling * dream of being a sports star * facilitates relaxation * facilitates social life * learn about rules, tactics and new techniques

Continued/....

Table 2.1 (cont.)

Commodity/Activity	Characteristics	Functionings
6. Television and cinema	* educational?	* learn new things * satisfy curiosity * misleading/ undermines moral values
	* yields utility	* pleasure and entertainment * escapism (takes you away from reality) * facilitates daydreaming and imagination
	* recreational	* avoid boredom and mischief
	* social activity	* facilitates social life.
7. Alcohol and tobacco	* relaxing	* facilitates relaxation * relieves depression, calms nerves * drown sorrows and forget problems
	* yields utility	* pleasure * satisfies (urgent?) desires
	* social activity	* facilitates social interaction, e.g. dancing
	* bad for health (in large quantities)	* harmful to health
	* potentially anti-social	* jeopardises personal relationships * leads to crime and violence
8. Advertising	* provides information	* facilitates buying products * promotes choice (but some advertising is misleading)
	* promotes economic activity	* facilitates economic activity (e.g. sales, market expansion, competition and profit)
	* yields utility	* pleasure, entertainment and amusement * dream of future

7. THE IDENTIFICATION OF FUNCTIONINGS AND DANGER OF PATERNALISM

As it stands, Sen's framework has considerable 'cutting power' (Sen, 1993, p.33). Development is about the things people manage (and have the potential) to 'do' and 'be' – even if these doings and beings happen to include some hedonistic and material ends. A fuller account of development however, requires the identification of important functionings and capabilities.[51]

Sen claims that certain functionings such as being well-nourished and being in good health simply are valuable and 'must be intrinsically important for the wellness of [a] person's being' (Sen, 1992, p.40). One of the most diverse lists of valuable functionings and capabilities put forward by Sen includes being able to 'live long, escape avoidable morbidity, be well-nourished, be able to read, write and communicate, take part in literary and scientific pursuits and so forth' (Sen, 1983, p.754; 1985, p.46). But while there is probably a broad consensus about including achievements like living long and being well-nourished in an account of development, it is unlikely that all people will agree that reading and writing (not to mention participating in literary and scientific pursuits) are desirable or *valuable* aspects of a good life style (see also Sugden, 1986). Thus, it is possible to argue that there is an element of paternalism in Sen's system. Ultimately, someone must decide: (1) how people should function; and (2) what people need to function properly.

The problem here is not with Sen's conceptual framework itself, but with the *potential* for its misuse and abuse. Much depends on how Sen's system is developed and applied. Some followers of Aristotle – most notably Martha Nussbaum – believe that 'there is just one list of functionings (at least at a high level of generality) that do in fact constitute human good living' (Nussbaum, 1988, p.152; 1993). This is a very bold and controversial position to take. But it can be defended and is not necessarily untenable *as long as*: (1) a democratic methodology is developed and properly employed to gauge the values of ordinary people; and (2) an effort is made to respect the (informed) judgements of *all* people (see Chapter 3).

Sen has 'no great objection' to going down this road, but is reluctant to endorse a unique list of functionings and capabilities as objectively correct (Sen, 1993, p.47). Sen is concerned that such a list 'may be tremendously over specified', and he does not seek to develop or subscribe to a comprehensive theory of the good. In fact, the design of Sen's framework deliberately leaves space to accommodate divergent views of the good life (see Sen, 1985, ch. 7). He does not want to risk compromising the influence and reach of his approach by endorsing a 'complete evaluative blueprint' (Sen, 1993, p.47). Instead, Sen argues that his framework can be extended in other ways 'which also have some plausibility' (ibid.).[52]

At times, however, Sen does appear to endorse a common set of values and subscribe to the existence of a broadly universal development ethic. In one paper he argues that while the commodity requirements for certain capabilities may vary greatly between different communities (making the poverty line *relative* in the space of commodities), there is considerably less variation in the capabilities different people and societies seek to achieve through the use of these commodities (Sen, 1984, essay 14). Elsewhere he is remarkably optimistic about the chances of reaching an agreement concerning the ordering of functioning vectors (life styles): he believes that the intersections of different people's rankings are 'typically quite large' (Sen, 1985, pp.54–6). In particular, Sen advises us that:

> In the context of economic development, there might well be considerable agreement as to what functionings are valuable, even though there might be disagreement on the relative values to be attached to the different functionings. (Sen, 1988, p.18)

Ultimately however, Sen leaves the concept of the good largely unspecified, although he does point towards a few isolated examples of intrinsically valuable functionings and capabilities (see Table 3.1 below). Some commentators have urged Sen to be 'more radical . . . by introducing an objective normative account of human functioning . . .' (Nussbaum, 1988, p.176), while others have argued that the open-endedness in Sen's list of functionings is, in many ways, his 'Achilles heel' (Qizilbash, 1998, p.54).

In Chapters 3 and 4 we will see that it does appear to be possible to construct and defend a broadly shared development ethic. By drawing on the values of some ordinary poor people, an attempt is made to draw up a first approximation of the most central human functionings and capabilities. Before proceeding with this task however, it is prudent to reflect more fully upon the risk of paternalism. Sen and Nussbaum both try to avoid this potential problem by leaving scope for pluralism. Freedom and choice are regarded as a central feature of development (see Nussbaum, 1995, pp.94–5; Sen, 1992, ch. 3.5). Hence their concern with capability rather than just bare achievement. Sen insists that

> The good life is partly a matter of genuine choice, and not one in which a person is forced into a particular life – however rich it might be in other respects. (Sen, 1985, p.39)

For Nussbaum and Sen the role of the state is to enhance freedom and choice by providing the necessary resources to promote good human functioning. Each person is left with the freedom *not* to function in certain ways if s/he wishes (Nussbaum, 1995, p.95). This seems reasonable. But the amount of room their respective approaches really leave for genuine choice between different life styles is unclear. For example, Sen could be interpreted as *insinuating* that we all value a common set of basic functionings, even if we choose different mixes.[53] This suggests that some possible life styles cannot be chosen by rational agents pursuing the human good. Ultimately however, Sen argues in favour of the supremacy of freedom and choice. His system is required to respect the evaluations of all individuals in the event of a *genuine* disagreement about the value of certain achievements. Nussbaum's position is more disconcerting. She leaves room for a different kind of pluralism. Her theory of the good is defined in sufficiently 'vague' terms to allow each of the central human functionings to be realised in a variety of different ways (see Chapter 3). The problem is that Nussbaum goes on to contend that 'much is ruled out as inappropriate to full humanity' by this [her] vague list of functionings (Nussbaum, 1990, p.235). This requirement may have to be dropped if Nussbaum is serious about avoiding the charge of paternalism and maintaining a flexible development ethic that can be revised in line with local assessments of human values.[54]

Of course, not all concepts of the good try to accommodate the values and attitudes of ordinary people. Some moral theories and political philosophies seek instead to impose a pre-defined set of values from above. Consider, for example, the kind of ethical imperialism practised by Neo-Marxist intellectuals such as Paul Baran and Vance Packard. In the 1960s these thinkers argued that a large part of capitalist output is 'wasteful', 'useless' and perhaps even 'positively destructive' in terms of catering for 'genuine human needs' (Baran and Sweezy, 1966, chs 5, 11 and appendix; Packard, 1961). Activities alleged to be particularly wasteful include expenditure on advertising (and the sales effort in general[55]), and the growth of the Finance, Insurance and Real Estate sectors of the economy.

On closer inspection, however, it is by no means certain that these activities are as 'wasteful' or 'destructive' as Baran and Sweezy contend. Some kinds of advertising may be harmful and abusive insofar as they condition ('brainwash') consumers to purchase particular brands of products and pay relatively high prices, but many forms of advertising play a much more 'constructive' role.[56] Advertising can provide useful information and enhance the freedom of choice between genuine alternatives. Paul Samuelson (1961, p.138) also cites evidence from a Gallup Poll that suggests many people actually 'like advertising' and do not necessarily 'believe all they hear'.[57]

Moreover, advertising may effect utility levels indirectly. The reality is that consumers would not derive as much pleasure from the consumption of certain products if advertising and the use of sophisticated imagery were not behind those products. This is especially true of the high-quality advertising of recent times. Encouraging people to 'eat, sleep and drink' Coca-Cola and serving the drink in high-quality bottles and cans with a colourful and distinctive logo adds to the enjoyment of the product. Some modern forms of advertising (e.g. slogans like 'a Mars a day helps you work, rest and play') may be misleading, but they are not comprehensively manipulative insofar as consumers gain utility.

The Finance, Insurance, Real Estate, and Legal Service industries also use up huge amounts of resources. While it is probably possible to simplify the functions and hence the costs of these industries, even Baran and Sweezy

(1966, p.140) acknowledge that at least some of the resource utilisation of these sectors should count as 'necessary costs of producing the social output'. Any society based on the division of labour and the exchange of products requires some kind of banking and financial system. And as far as Insurance and Real Estate is concerned, a staff of supervisory and service workers is clearly a necessary minimum. Finally, even in the most rationally conducted economies there would be at least some need for financial settlements between enterprises and for the services of solicitors and lawyers rendering legal aid to people or helping settle controversies between economic units (ibid.).

These activities have much greater significance than Baran and Sweezy admit. In a capitalist society the services of lawyers and solicitors are required to defend property rights. And the defence of private property rights, as Adam Smith (1776) and, more recently, Douglas North and Robert Thomas (1973) have shown is essential for the development of capitalism. Spending on law and order is also necessary to protect people from personal attacks and to guarantee basic freedoms. This expenditure cannot be dismissed as wasteful. In fact, the welfare of many poor people would benefit substantially from greater spending on the effective enforcement of civil liberties through the rule of law (see Chapter 4). Baran and Sweezy however, have no practical interest in upholding law and order or protecting private property. Their objective is to undermine the capitalist mode of production by encouraging revolution.

Expenditure on supposedly 'wasteful' activities such as marketing and corporate expansion may also add to the level of effective demand in the economy and boost output and employment. Baran and Sweezy are predictably hostile to this kind of reasoning. In their view such expenditure paves the way for further rounds of unproductive spending (Baran and Sweezy, 1966, pp.126–7). They are also concerned that the growth of such expenditures may help to prop up monopoly capitalism (ibid., pp.111, 123–5), which is viewed as an ailing and undesirable mode of production. This is why Baran and Sweezy (like the post-war Marxists they inspired) try to dismiss the economic and social achievements of modern capitalism. In a strongly worded passage they argue that the nature of economic growth and technical change under monopoly capitalism leads to the social and economic stratification of the working class, permitting the more advantaged 'skilled' and 'white collar' workers to catch up with the 'middle classes' and 'corporate rich', who have incomes large enough to participate in rounds of 'discretionary spending' and indulge in the consumption of luxury items (such as cars and boats) which are not necessary to live life in comfort (ibid., pp.127–8).

However, there is plenty of evidence to suggest that capitalism has advanced the position of the working class. Of course, we can always object to the social and economic stratification and gross inequalities that often accompany capitalist development (and with justification). But capitalism has – in the long term at least – systematically raised the wages and living conditions of the working class (Mitchell, 1998, table B.4). Even the poorest of the poor have benefited. If development is primarily about reducing (absolute) poverty rather than dealing with income inequalities (see Fields, 1980), then the form of capitalist development Baran and Sweezy want to criticise must have some value.

Baran and Sweezy think otherwise. Economic growth, increasing affluence and rising consumption are all shunned once capitalism begins to mature. Conspicuous consumption ('discretionary spending') is effectively ruled out as an element of the good life. The only spending that counts is spending on 'genuine human needs' (Baran and Sweezy, 1966, p.349). And these needs do not include things like cars and boats, fashionable and expensive clothing, television or national defence (ibid., pp.127, 344, 347). At one point Baran and Sweezy manage to mention 'the slums that surround us' and the 'rock and roll that blares at us' in the same breath, and maintain that both are equally harmful to the 'welfare and all round development of man' (ibid., p.139). Most people, however, would probably want to object and say that television, cars, fashionable clothing, pop music and perhaps even national security are desirable components of a good life for *them*, if not for Baran and Sweezy (see e.g. Tables I.6 and II.9).

But Baran and Sweezy argue that the function of leisure undergoes a change in capitalist society: it becomes less about the recreation and the revival of mental and psychic energies by engaging in 'genuinely interesting pursuits', and more about 'killing time' which leads to 'grinding debilitating boredom' (Baran and Sweezy, 1966, p.346).

[Leisure] no longer signifies doing what a person wants to do, as distinct from doing, at work, what he must do; to an ever increasing extent it means simply doing nothing. And the reason for doing nothing is partly that there is so little that is genuinely interesting to do, but perhaps even more because the emptiness and purposefulness of life in capitalist society stifles the desire to do anything. (ibid.)

But reading Baran and Sweezy leads to the conclusion that listening to the radio, watching television, going to the cinema and even socialising with friends all constitute ways of doing nothing. These activities, they insist, 'do not make undue demands on the intellectual and emotional resources of the recipient'; their only purpose is to provide 'fun', 'relaxation' and 'a good time', i.e., 'passively absorbable amusement' (ibid., p.366). The same is said to be true of 'being a sports fan', which 'does not involve participation in any activity or acquiring any skill' (ibid., pp.346–7). But even if this were true, it would not automatically follow that people do not desire or value these kinds of pursuits. In fact, it is precisely because things like watching television, going to the cinema, and being a sports fan are fun and relaxing (and do not make large demands on the intellectual and emotional resources of the consumer), that most people tend to value these activities (see Table 2.1). In contrast, Baran and Sweezy paint a picture of a joyless and monotonous life of reflection, discovery and intellectual pursuit, in which everyone would presumably spend their free time discussing philosophy, visiting art galleries and watching opera. If progress towards such a society constitutes development for the likes of Baran, Sweezy and Packard,[58] it is doubtful that it will for the majority of people.

NOTES

1. There are more sophisticated versions of the commodity approach, such as Rawls's list of 'social primary goods', Dworkin's call for equality of resources (broadly construed), and the emphasis on meeting basic needs. These approaches push us in the general direction of human capability – but do not go far enough (Sen, 1984, essays 13 and 20; see also Crocker, 1992). In the following discussion I will focus on the crude version of the commodity approach.

2. The UNDP (1997) estimates that 2.6 per cent of people in developing countries are disabled (ibid., table 13). This figure is probably low. I can recall reading that the World Health Organisation estimates that as many as 10 per cent of the world's people are disabled in some way. (I have been unable to corroborate this statistic.) I have used the figure of 2.6 per cent and the UNDP's (1997, table 22) estimate of the total population in developing countries in 1994 (4,326 million people), to calculate that as many as 112.4 million people in the developing world alone are disabled.

3. John Broome (1991) has taken issue with Sen on the use of 'utility' and Sen (1991) has responded.
   Sen (1985, p.24; 1992, p.54) is aware that some forms of philosophical utilitarianism – such as those based on informed preferences (see Qizilbash, 1998, part III), the objective realisation of desired states (e.g. Griffin, 1986), and reinterpretations of utility as 'usefulness' or the human 'good' (see Broome, 1991) – depart significantly from standard utilitarianism and, in many ways, resemble the capability approach.

4. John Stuart Mill (1859, p.140) pointed to the lack of 'parity' between one source of utility and another.

5. According to Sen, Welfarism demands that 'the goodness of states of affairs must be judged entirely by the goodness of the set of individual utilities in the respective state of affairs'. Utilitarianism imposes the stricter requirement that 'the goodness of any set of individual utilities must be judged entirely by their sum total' (Sen, 1982, p.278).

6. Sen (1982) contends that either of these adjustments entails rejecting Welfarism. This is because Welfarism requires that pleasures and desires 'must be weighed only according to their respective intensities, irrespective of the source of [utility] and the nature of the activity that goes with it' (ibid. p.363). In principle, I can see no reason why this requirement could not be dropped within a welfare inspired framework. Welfarism could be refined to discriminate against offensive tastes and recognise the heterogeneity of utilities whilst retaining an exclusive focus on mental states.

7. Taylor (1982) criticises utilitarian reduction for not paying sufficient attention to the diversity of goods that guide moral judgements. Space needs to be made for other

incommensurable goals such as personal integrity, liberation, rationality and the virtue of charity (ibid., pp.133, 135).

8. Sen repeatedly makes this point (e.g. Sen, 1984, pp.308–9, 512; 1985, p.21; 1985a, p.191; 1992, p.55). See also Crocker (1992, p.602), Nussbaum (1990, p.213; 1995, p.91; 2000, ch. 2), Qizilbash (1998, pp.61–2) and various papers presented at the WIDER Quality of Life conference (Nussbaum and Sen, 1993). Jon Elster (1982) has discussed the general question of adaptive expectations.

9. The evidence presented in Chapter 4 only provides equivocal support for this supposition.

10. Two discussions of variations in the nutritional requirements of different people include Dasgupta (1993) and Osmani (1992).

11. Sen would also require a just concept of development to promote capability equality (see Sen, 1980; 1992). He is also aware that there is a distinction between development broadly defined (to include economic progress), and improvements in the quality of life (see Sen, 1983; 1988).

12. For example Sen (1985a, p.200) says: 'The central feature of well-being is the ability to achieve valuable functionings [i.e. capabilities]'. Compare this with the references cited in the first paragraph of this section and the quotation below.

13. The following pages draw heavily on people's responses to questions about the value of (and motives for) consuming food, riding bicycles, drinking Coca-Cola and so on. Note that the responses of ordinary poor people (those most likely to be concerned with basic achievements) should yield a reasonably sympathetic appraisal of Sen's approach, as it is primarily concerned with aspects of poverty, equity and need. The tables referred to in the text below can be found in the Annex.

14. The examples in Table 2.1 have not been selected on an ad-hoc basis. Nor are they meant to impose some sort of bias. They are merely intended to help pave the way for making the capability approach operational by filling some gaps and exposing certain complications that can be overcome. The examples in Table 2.1 are not exhaustive. Nor is it likely that all people or societies would want to endorse them. However, the fact that significant numbers of people in our survey areas value these capabilities implies that any credible account of human development ought to be able to handle them.

15. Sen also considers the example of rice. But the rice example turns out to be the same as the bread example, in that both goods are said to exhibit the same characteristics and functionings.

16. A bicycle was the quintessential 'basic needs' good in Maoist China.

17. In poor countries labourers often have to cycle long distances on poor quality bicycles and roads to get to and from work.

18. Some people also pointed out that travelling by car is more comfortable, more convenient, saves time, is safer and avoids having to use unreliable public transport or unruly taxi services.

19. These examples can be queried. A loaf of bread is of little use to a person who suffers from a serious allergy to wheat (at least for promoting health). Moreover, in some social contexts (e.g. Christmas in England) a bowl of rice may be inappropriate for entertaining family and friends. The capability approach dispenses with these difficulties by focusing on potential achievements.

20. The failure to adopt a healthy diet could reflect weak will power. There is, however, no guarantee that a person will not genuinely value certain meals over more healthy alternatives.

21. APU (1996) charts Coke's continuing success in developing countries, and reports on the official launch of Coca-Cola Beverages Pakistan. From 1980 there has been a rapid expansion in the consumption of Coca-Cola and soft drinks in China (see Nolan, 1995, p.5). See Nolan (1999) for an extensive discussion of Coca-Cola.

22. Sugar free coke is also very successful, but much less nutritious. Our fieldwork findings also confirm this contention (see Tables II.11 and II.11.A).

23. It is not my intention to imply that soft drinks are more harmful than many other products, such as sweets and chocolate. Taking sugar in tea and coffee or consuming too much bread can also 'harm health'.

24. The average Coca-Cola label includes a list of ingredients and a free phone information line, but does not tell the consumer if the product is high or low in protein, energy, carbohydrates and fat, etc. Interestingly, the labels on diet Coca-Cola bottles includes this information.

25. The hygiene and quality of small scale soft drinks products in poor countries are often questionable. In contrast, the minimum hygiene and quality standards for all of Coca-Cola's products and plants are set internationally (Nolan, 1995, pp.15, 32). Growing concern about the health and quality standards of soft drinks in China prompted the government to adopt 'Coca-Cola's quality standards as the norm for the whole soft drinks industry' (ibid., p.15).

26. In a survey of more than 1,000 Korean consumers by the Choongang Ilbo newspaper, 'Coca-Cola emerged as the leading top-of-mind product in the country' (APU, 1996, p.3).

27. When asked, several respondents were reluctant to endorse the value of using Coca-Cola to be fashionable or enhance their status (Table II.11). These objectives however, were openly endorsed by more than two-fifths of teenagers, young adults (aged 20-34) and men.

28. A detailed discussion of these two items is presented in Chapter 4.

29. I am reliably informed that some of these activities were common in Britain during the Second World War and lasted at least until the suspension of rationing in the early 1950s. It was also common to dye old clothes and sew lace collars and cuffs into shirts and blouses.

30. Sen does mention the value of 'being able to fulfil one's requirements for clothing' and, following Adam Smith (1776), emphasises the importance of 'appearing in public without shame'. In recent lectures Sen implicitly relates the capability approach to identity (see Sen, 1999a; 2001).

31. Watching sport is important for people of all ages and is considered presently.

32. Some popular sports such as cricket, golf, snooker and darts involve little physically challenging exercise.

33. While I neglected to ask about this item in my surveys, it was clear that most respondents probably would value the development of a team spirit.

34. The motive for avoiding physical exercise matters. Some of the people we interviewed did genuinely not value the capability to participate in sports. Others however, preferred not to take part in physically challenging activities because they were 'too old', 'lacked energy' or were in 'ill-health'. Some people complained about the lack of opportunities for playing sports.

35. John Wells (1977, p.273) found that the poorest households in the city of Sao Paulo typically allocate 'a higher proportion of expenditure to the acquisition of household goods and appliances' such as televisions and radios, than the richer ones did.

36. In some cases choosing to exercise certain capabilities (e.g. escapism) might be a symptom of poverty. I owe this insight to Mozaffar Qizilbash.

37. One Coloured woman however, stated that she did not watch television because this would mean having 'to go to other people's houses to watch'.

38. Most people would probably weigh the satisfaction and relaxation derived from watching television or going to the cinema more highly than their estimate of its educational value in their account of what makes a good life. This is almost certainly why the majority of ordinary people tend to spend more time watching movies, sport, soap-operas, comedy and sitcoms than watching the news, current affairs programmes and documentaries. None of the people we interviewed expressed concern about the social consequences of watching violent or sexually explicit programmes. But two or three people did reject the value of watching television on the grounds that TV is 'bad for the eyes' and 'misleading'. One person also observed that 'there are no good programmes'.

39. Some respondents also claimed not to understand advertising or complained that it interrupts their television programmes.

40. There is a vast literature of empirical research in the field of psychology that examines utility conceptions across cultures (e.g. Diener and Suh, 2000). However, 'there is an unfortunate lack of awareness of the more subjective and psychological studies in development circles' (Alkire, 2002, p.183). For an introduction to this literature see Alkire (2002).

41. However, in an early paper Sen (1980–81) proposes 'viewing utility primarily as a vector

(with several distinct components) and only secondarily as some homogenous magnitude'. Although he recognises that such an approach has the advantage of yielding 'a significantly richer descriptive account of a person's well-being' than the secondary view (ibid., p.193), he is primarily interested in considering the moral arguments for using the vector view to evaluate states of affairs.

42. By this I do not mean to imply that utility is generated independently of other functionings. The point is that whatever utility flows from a set of functionings makes an intrinsically valuable contribution to a person's well-being. In Table 2.1 I have recorded utility as a separate characteristic (and functioning) for each item. This is because utility is inextricably bound up with most (if not all) doings and beings: it is impossible to specify the precise nature of the relationship between each functioning and utility, which depends upon personal circumstances and typically varies between people and over time. For example, while I may derive a good deal of pleasure from cycling through the streets of Cambridge in my free time, the migrant labourer, who is compelled to cycle long distances to work every day, may derive a considerable degree of dis-utility from riding his bicycle.

43. I owe the final point in this paragraph to Gay Meeks who has helped clarify my thoughts on some of these matters.

44. 'Being able to have pleasurable experiences, and to avoid non-necessary pain' features much less prominently in the latest version of Nussbaum's list of central human capabilities. Instead of occupying its own distinct space (as in previous lists), the ability to achieve pleasure and avoid non-beneficial pain is treated as an 'add on' to the description of the cognitive capacities and senses of human beings (Nussbaum, 2000, pp.78–9).

45. Sen is aware that different commodity bundles can promote the same human functionings. He refers to this as a 'many-one correspondence' between combinations of goods and services and given capabilities (Sen, 1984, pp.513–4).

46. Of course it is commodity fetishism (rather than access to the necessary material things for good living) that typically bothers critics of resource based accounts of well-being.

47. Of course, there is a material dimension behind some of these activities. A person needs a football to play football, a television to watch television, and so on. On the other hand, a person does not need any material goods in order to achieve important functionings such as being loved or cared for.

48. Recently, Sen (1999, ch. 2) has discussed the instrumental role of freedom (human capabilities) in development.

49. Housing, for example, must be (1) constructed from solid materials and (2) properly insulated before it can guarantee adequate protection from the elements. (Heating may also be required.)

50. Sen believes these weights should be determined by the values of the people in question.

51. Sen (1987, pp.29–31) distinguishes between two related exercises: the (1) identification and (2) ranking of valuable functionings. I shall have little to say about the latter in what follows. On this and related issues (including the evaluation of capability sets) see Sen (1985, chs 5-7). See also Basu (1987), Clark (1996), Crocker (1995, pp.178–80), Griffin (1986, part II), Muellbauer (1987), Sugden (1986; 1993) and Saith (2001).

52. See Sen (1990, p.46) for a brief account of possible extensions of the capability approach.

53. This is a harsh interpretation of Sen's position. Sen does not claim people value a common set of functionings. He merely hints that further investigation would probably reveal that this is the case (e.g. Sen, 1988, pp.18–20). Sen certainly does not support the view that people ought to live in accordance with a set of independently defined functionings (see Nussbaum and Sen, 1989).

54. Nussbaum strives to achieve both of these objectives (see Chapter 3).

55. Other strategies associated with the sales effort include product differentiation, planned obsolescence and frequent model changes. See Packard (1961, part II).

56. The term was originally coined by Alfred Marshall. See Samuelson (1961) and Table 2.1 for a brief summary of the pros and cons of advertising.

57. It has also been pointed out that as a by-product of advertising expenditure, consumers have access to a private press and a choice of many radio and television programmes.

58. Not all revolutionaries practice the values they preach. For example, while Mao had a

profound influence on the lives of millions of people in communist China, he did not always choose to lead the kind of life style he advocated. In particular, he avoided the call for manual labour. Further examples of the contradiction between Mao's philosophy and actual life style can be found in Roxane Witke's (1977) biography of Comrade Chiang Ch'ing. It is not practical to pursue these issues here.

ADDENDUM: THE CONCEPT OF CAPABILITY

The distinction between functioning (bare achievement) and capability (opportunity) is important and probably deserves more attention than Sen provides. Cohen (1993), Crocker (1995, pp.157–64), Gasper (1997), Kanbur (1987), Nussbaum (1988, pp.160-172) and Williams (1987) have helped to clarify the concept of *capability* – particularly vis-à-vis *functioning*.[1] I do not want to dwell upon the concept of capability for long. But it is worth noting that Sen (1992, p.41) refines the notion of capability to incorporate *genuine* choice with *substantial* options.[2] The goodness of a capability set should be evaluated in terms of the *quality* as well as the quantity of available opportunities (Sen, 1985, p.69; 1993, pp.34–5). (There also seems to be a case for assessing capability sets in terms of the *diversity* of possible choices.)

The idea of *responsible* choice is also central to the relevance of the capability approach (Sen, 1992, ch. 9.9). For example, Sen accepts that it might be better to concentrate on the *outcome* (functionings achieved) if intelligent choice is complicated by uncertainty (ibid., p.149; see also Kanbur, 1987). The same applies if social conditioning makes a person lack the courage to choose to live in a particular way. In these cases the person's predicament 'can scarcely be dismissed on the grounds of personal responsibility' (Sen, 1992, p.149). But if a responsible person 'wastes' his or her opportunities or 'takes a risk and ends up losing the gamble' no unfair outcomes may be involved (ibid., pp.148–9).

This raises the issue of whether *all* capabilities entail the opportunity to choose. It is not difficult to think of examples of important capabilities (such as being able to live long and avoid illness) that do not appear to involve a meaningful notion of choice (see Williams, 1987).[3] A person cannot always choose to cheat death, avoid flu or breathe unpolluted air.[4] Moreover, many capabilities, as Sen has observed, depend upon public action and policy rather than individual choice. However, the elimination of chronic hunger, epidemics and other maladies through public policy can still enhance the 'effective' freedom to live as one 'would value, desire and choose' (Sen, 1992, pp.64–9).[5]

Moreover, Sen does not conceptualise freedom in terms of effective powers only. In fact, he acknowledges 'the special significance of negative freedom' for the capability approach (Sen, 1992, p.87). Capability failure can stem from the violation of personal rights as well as the absence of positive freedoms (Sen, 1985a, lecture 3). But in marked contrast to Isaiah Berlin (1958), Sen is primarily concerned with positive liberty – the freedom to do and be certain things.

On the other hand, Sen's concept of capability should probably pay more attention to the internal powers, skills and other traits *possessed* by the person (see Crocker, 1995; Gasper, 1997). These personal powers are developed in childhood, maintained and exercised in maturity, and decline or are lost in old age (Nussbaum, 1988, pp.160–172). More importantly, having these internal powers is necessary for *exercising* freedom and choice, and for achieving good human functioning. Consider the example Williams (1987) provides of the deranged man who 'sings all the time'. The madman's singing 'is not an expression of the capability that we normally associate with singing, which involves, among other things, the capability [internal power] of not singing' (ibid., p.96). Nor can it count 'as an example, in the relevant sense, of functioning' (ibid., p.97).

It is harsh to conclude that Sen 'restricts capabilities to opportunities' (Crocker, 1995, p.162). Sen clearly does tend to characterise capabilities in terms of possibilities and options for action. But he does seem to regard personal powers and traits as more than a *means* to freedom and good living. Crocker forgets that Sen contends that internal powers and skills such as moving about, reflective choice and literacy are examples of *intrinsically* valuable capabilities (see Chapter 3, Table 3.1).

It follows that the actual capacity to function requires both the realisation of internal powers and skills, and the presence of external material and social conditions that provide rich opportunities for good living (see also Nussbaum, 1990, p.228). For example, bicycling requires that the cyclist has the internal skill to ride, access to a bicycle, and no social conditions that hinder cycling (such as a high risk of being hijacked and forcibly deprived of the bicycle). There may be a case for inserting a category between Sen's concepts of 'functioning' and 'capability' that more adequately captures the significance of personal powers and *real* opportunities. We could call this intermediate category 'actual abilities to function'.[6] This does not represent a substantial departure from Sen's capability approach. While Sen often refers to opportunities (without further clarification) his approach is intended to focus 'on the real freedoms actually enjoyed, taking note of *all* the barriers...' (Sen, 1992, p.149).

NOTES

1. Sen (1987; 1992; 1993) has responded to some of the issues raised by these commentators.
2. More freedom to make trivial and costly decisions (such as choosing from a growing range of washing powders) may indeed 'make one's life more wretched' (Sen, 1992, pp.59, 62–4). Sen has also broadened his concept of freedom to include goals and values that go beyond (but do not necessarily coincide with) the pursuit of personal well-being. See his distinction between 'agency' and 'well-being' freedom (see Sen, 1985a; 1992, ch. 4).
3. Even the capability to live longer may promote some choices by providing more time to 'end life' (Sen, 1987, p.111) or decide to carry on living (Crocker, 1995, p.164).
4. Choosing to realise some capabilities may involve large opportunity costs. Hence the example Williams (1987, p.99) provides of the Los Angeles resident who has to move away from the city to breathe unpolluted air. It follows that a person's opportunities should not be viewed in isolation. Instead we need to focus on 'sets of co-realisable capabilities' (ibid., p.100; see also Sen, 1987, p.109).
5. Notice that 'effective' freedom does not necessarily entail an increase in the freedom to choose from a given number of options (see Sen, 1992, pp.67–8). For example, now that Smallpox has been eradicated (thanks to a global vaccination campaign in the late 1960s and 1970s by the World Health Organisation) we cannot catch the disease, even if we so choose. Nor does 'effective' freedom involve being able to directly operate the 'levers of control'. In fact, '[m]any freedoms take the form of our ability to get what we value and want, without the levers of control being *directly* operated by us' (ibid., p.64).
6. David Crocker (1995, p.168) originally proposed this category.

3. Towards A Theory of the Good Life

1. INTRODUCTION

Sen has been criticised for not supplementing his framework with a substantial list or taxonomy of human functionings and capabilities (Doyal and Gough, 1991, p.156; see also Chapter 2). The aim of this chapter is to help fill this gap by injecting some empirical content into Sen's analytical framework. This task entails developing a *theory of the good* to formerly identify the relevant 'functionings' and 'capabilities' (dimensions of development) in question. Several different lists of human functionings and needs can be found in the literature (see Alkire and Black, 1997; Braybrooke, 1987; and Section 6 below). Unfortunately however, none of these schemes are without problems.

In general it is possible to distinguish between 'thin' and 'thick' (or 'full') theories of the good.[1] Thin theories, like Rawls (1971), are 'confined to the enumeration of all purpose means to good living' (Nussbaum, 1990, p.217), and typically leave final ends unspecified.[2] While this kind of approach has the advantage of preserving a rich context of choice for individuals, it provides relatively little insight into the content of development. In contrast, 'thick' theories of the good deal with the identification of important ends across all spheres of human life. In other words, these theories are concerned with the totality of human functionings and capabilities that make up a good life. Clearly, the nature of our project demands the enumeration of a full theory of the good. Favouring a thick conception of the good,[3] however, opens the door to some potentially grave objections from the liberal and relativist camps. These objections include the charges of:[4]

(1) Prejudicial Application: Any determinate conception of the good that is supposed to have some normative moral and political force – no matter how equitably and comprehensively designed – can be used to exclude the powerless and discriminate against the disadvantaged. (Aristotle himself excludes women, manual labourers, farmers and slaves from his system of political distribution on the grounds that none of these people are fully fledged human beings with the natural capability to achieve 'eudaimonia', i.e. live a flourishing life.[5])

(2) Importing Metaphysical Elements: Any substantial conception of the good runs the risk of trying to import extra-historical and extra-experiential metaphysical truths (which, it is argued, do not exist, or if they do exist, are not in fact knowable). These metaphysical elements are likely to be the subject of much controversy, and in consequence make it impossible to achieve a political consensus about the content of development.

(3) Overlooking Historical and Cultural Differences: Any attempt to specify the dimensions of the good life cannot hope to take adequate account of the historical and cultural differences between different people and societies. Different people and cultures, it is said, understand human life and perceive development in a variety of different ways.

(4) Neglects Autonomy and Choice: Any thick conception of development is objectionably paternalistic in the sense that it tends to discriminate either in favour of, or against, certain life styles (bundles of functionings) people might want to choose.

There is however at least one 'thick' conception of the good that not only fits naturally into Sen's analytical framework but also has the potential (with some adjustment) to meets all four of these criticisms. I am referring to Martha Nussbaum's *Thick Vague Theory of the Good* (TVTG), which is discussed and evaluated below.

2. TOWARDS A CONCEPTION OF THE GOOD

Martha Nussbaum's objective is to provide an Aristotelian account of the human good which will proceed and serve as a base for considering the responsibilities and structures of a just political system. She begins by developing a radical methodology, which anticipates and tries to deal with the four core objections raised by the liberal and relativist camps (points 1–4 in Section 1 above). I shall consider the main features of Nussbaum's methodology before describing her theory of the good in detail.[6]

2.1 Nussbaum's Methodology

Nussbaum emphasises several distinct methodological points. In response to the first objection cited above, Nussbaum concedes that thick conceptions of the good can be unjustly and prejudicially applied to minority groups (Nussbaum, 1992, p.226; 1995, pp.62, 96–8). However, she points out that this objection does not undermine the conception of the good in question itself, but the moral status of the agent(s) who seek to abuse its application (Nussbaum, 1992, p.226). In order to reduce the scope for discrimination Nussbaum flatly rejects the practice of 'capability testing' (which has a long history of abuse) and advocates proceeding on the assumption that all human beings have acquired the basic capabilities (ibid., p.228; 1995, p.102). This procedure helps to eliminate one of the most popular justifications for discriminating against women and minority groups.

In response to the second objection often levelled at thick conceptions of the good Nussbaum claims that her approach is *not* metaphysical on two grounds: first, it is not externalist in the sense 'that it is not a theory arrived at in detachment from the actual self understandings and evaluations of human beings in society'; second, neither is it a 'theory peculiar to a single metaphysical or religious tradition' (Nussbaum, 1990, p.217). Instead, Nussbaum describes her theory as 'internal' in the sense that it draws on human history and experiences, and 'essentialist' in the sense of offering an evaluative yet revisable conception of the good (Nussbaum, 1990; 1992; 1995).

Furthermore, Nussbaum's approach 'is not intended to deny that the items it enumerates are to some extent differently constructed by different societies' (objection 3) (Nussbaum, 1995, p.74). In fact, Nussbaum recognises that there are very real differences between different cultures and societies. For this reason, Nussbaum's 'thick' conception of the good is deliberately 'vague'. Her list of valuable capabilities is extremely general and 'allows in its very design for the possibility of multiple specifications for each of its components' (ibid., p.95). The Aristotelian proceeds in this way on the grounds that it is better to be vaguely right than precisely wrong (Nussbaum, 1990).

A vague conception of this kind 'can be expected to be broadly shared across cultures' (Nussbaum, 1990, p.206). The objective 'is to be as universal as possible' (ibid., p.217), 'to focus on what is common to all, rather than on the differences . . . and to see some capabilities and functionings as more central, more at the core of human life, than others' (Nussbaum, 1995, p.63). Nussbaum calls for 'an intercultural ethical inquiry' (Nussbaum 1990, p.206), in an effort to forge an international political consensus (Nussbaum 1995, p.74; see also Nussbaum, 1993).

This consensus, however, is only acceptable if it is achieved by following certain 'reasonable procedures' (Nussbaum, 1995, p.74–5). For example, Nussbaum allows 'explicitly for the possibility that we may learn from our encounters with other human societies to recognise things about ourselves that we had not seen before . . .' (ibid., p.74). In particular, this process can facilitate *internal* criticism of traditional values and even lead to the 'rejection of some of them' (Nussbaum and Sen, 1989, p.317). In this way an internal inquiry that is genuinely rational and critical can yield clarity and guide societies towards 'what actually are, for them, the most central values' (ibid., pp.312–3). Insofar as these inquiries yield truth and objectivity (as Nussbaum like Aristotle before her believes) we can expect different cultures and societies to move towards an international political consensus.

Nussbaum also makes an effort to deal with the charge of paternalism (objection 4) by providing scope for plural and local specification. The possibilities for plural specification stem from conceptualising development at a high level of *generality* which 'leaves a great deal of latitude for citizen's to specify each of the components [functionings] more concretely, and with much variety, in accordance with local traditions, or individual tastes' (ibid., p.94). Closely linked to this is the idea of local specification. Nussbaum observes that societies may also choose between a wide range of potential options for promoting a particular capability (Nussbaum, 1990, p.249; 1995, p.94). In fact, the Aristotelian should recognise that a good way of promoting a given end in one part of the world may be completely ineffectual in another. Therefore, the selected strategy must take account of local traditions, and circumstances, and should be chosen in consultation 'with those most deeply immersed in those traditions' (ibid.).

2.2 Nussbaum's Thick Vague Theory of the Good

Nussbaum (1990; 1992; 1995) advocates using this kind of methodology to provide an account of the most important human functionings and capabilities. She begins by asking the question: 'what makes a given life human?' More specifically, what are the defining characteristic activities (doings and beings) associated with the human form of life?[7] (Nussbaum, 1990, pp.218–9; 1995, pp.72–3). According to Nussbaum her investigation 'proceeds by examining a wide range of self interpretations of human beings from different times and places' (but see Section 5),[8] and *suggests* that people from different cultures and societies share a common view of the general features of human life (ibid., pp.73–4; Nussbaum, 1990, pp.218–9). A 'first approximation' of this consensus constitutes the first level of the TVTG or what Nussbaum refers to as the 'constitutive conditions' of the shape of the human form of life. Briefly, according to Nussbaum (1995, pp.76–80),[9] the human form of life is characterised by:

1. Mortality (all humans face, are aware of, and have an aversion to death).

2. The human body (we all live our lives in bodies of a certain kind which exhibit certain possibilities and vulnerabilities: specifically, we all need food and drink, require shelter, have sexual desires, and need/desire mobility).

3. The capacity for pleasure and pain. (Experiences of pleasure and pain, and an aversion to the latter, is common to all human life.)

4. Cognitive capability. (All human beings have sense perception, the ability to imagine and the ability to think.)

5. Early infant development. (All human beings experience helplessness, need and dependence in early life; these common experiences influence their desires and emotions.)

6. Practical reason. (All human beings (try to) evaluate, choose and plan a conception of the good life.)

7. Affiliation with other human beings. (All human beings 'live with and in relation to others', and value that form of life.)

8. Relatedness to other species and to nature. (Human beings are dependent on, and owe some respect and concern to, other species and nature.)

9. Humour and play. (All forms of human life make room for some kind of recreation and laughter.)

10. Separateness. (Each human being is 'one in number' and follows a separate path from birth to death.)

11. Strong separateness. (Each human being has his or her own peculiar context and surroundings, i.e. objects, places, history, particular friendships and relationships, etc.)

Nussbaum emphasises that this is a working list, 'put out to generate debate', and can and should be revised accordingly (Nussbaum, 1990, p.219; 1995, p.80). The list is also heterogeneous, 'for it contains both limits against which we press and powers [capabilities] through which we aspire' (Nussbaum, 1990, pp.219, 224).[10] More importantly, Nussbaum insists that level 1 only constitutes a 'minimal conception of the good'. Any life that fails to meet the criteria is judged to be 'too lacking, too impoverished to be human at all' (Nussbaum, 1995, p.80).

The second level of Nussbaum's conception of the human being attempts to sketch a vague and general outline of those 'functional capabilities' that, together, make up the dimensions of a *good* human life. This list draws inspiration from Aristotle and is based on the conception of human existence discussed above in the sense that the level 1 list is taken to be the starting point for elaborating a set of higher and more specific (though still general) functional capabilities.[11] (While this could be either a list of valuable *functionings* or valuable *capabilities* Nussbaum, like Sen, chooses to view development in terms of the latter.)

Nussbaum (1995, pp.81–86) identifies two distinct 'thresholds', or levels of human functioning, which correspond to the two lists mentioned above. Briefly, she claims that a life that lacks the ability to achieve any of the functionings on the first list is too deprived to be considered human; similarly, any life that lacks one or more of the capabilities associated with the second list, 'no matter what else it has, will fall short of being a *good* human life' (ibid., p.85).[12]

Nussbaum argues the second list is the one to focus on. For the Aristotelian, the role of government and the task of public policy is to move people across the level 2 threshold, since 'we don't [just] want societies to make their citizen's capable of achieving the bare minimum' (Nussbaum, 1995, p.81). In other words, the state should ensure that every person is able to achieve a good human life if s/he so desires. This is contentious. In fact, most traditionalists would probably want to argue in favour of a minimal role for the government. The state should act only as a safety net to ensure that each individual can achieve the necessary minimum for basic subsistence. (At best, this probably only corresponds to something like Nussbaum's level 1 threshold.) The responsibility for being able to achieve anything more (such as a 'flourishing life'), lies with the individual his or her self and not with the state.

In contrast, development itself must be about crossing Nussbaum's second threshold. The concept of human development can hardly be restricted to the bare minimum required before a given life can be recognised, with confidence, as human. So even if Nussbaum's second list is not thought to provide appropriate criteria for public policy, it does still specify those higher functionings and capabilities that generally make up the dimensions of a good life.

Table 3.1 presents the second level of the TVTG. The practice of grafting Sen's own scattered remarks onto Nussbaum's list of 'functional capabilities', and of labelling the items included in level two with the names of Aristotelian 'virtues' has been adopted.[13] I have compared and discussed the merits of Nussbaum and Sen's lists of human capabilities elsewhere (Clark, 1998; see also Crocker, 1995).[14] For the purpose of the following discussion it is sufficient to note that: (1) every item in Table 3.1 is regarded as a separate component which is 'distinct in quality' and of 'central importance',[15] and this strictly limits the trade-offs that it is reasonable to make (Nussbaum, 1995, pp.85–6); and (2) all of the items in Table 3.1 are related to each other in many different and complex ways. For example, the Virtues of Separateness are related to all other virtues: whatever a human being does, that being does as a separate and distinct entity, 'tracing distinct paths through space and time' (Nussbaum, 1990, p.225).

Table 3.1 Nussbaum and Sen's list of 'Functional Capabilities'

1. Virtues in Relation to Mortality
(a) N&S: 'Being able to live to the end of a human life of normal length' (see also Sen, 1984, p.497; 1985, p.75; 1992, p.125); 'not dying prematurely' (see also Sen, 1988, p.13; 1992, p.39).
(b) N: 'Being able to be courageous' (Nussbaum, quoted in Crocker, 1995, p.225).

2. Bodily Virtues
(a) N&S: 'Being able to have good health' (see also Sen, 1984, p.513; 1985, p.46; 1985a, p.197; 1992, pp.39–40).
(b) N&S: 'Being able to be adequately nourished' (see also Sen, 1982, p.367; 1984, p.513; 1987, p.16; 1993, p.21).
(c) S: 'Capability to be free from hunger' (Sen, 1984, p.376; see also Sen, 1985a, p.217; 1989, p.773; 1992, p.66).
(d) N&S: 'Being able to have adequate shelter' (see also Sen, 1982, p.367; 1984, p.513; 1985, p.73; 1990, p.46).
(e) S: The power to fulfil one's requirements for clothing (Sen, 1982, p.367; 1984, p.281; 1985, p.73; 1992, p.110).
(f) S: Being able to keep warm (Sen, 1984a, p.86).
(g) N: 'Having opportunities for sexual satisfaction'.
(h) N: 'Having opportunities for choice in matters of reproduction'.
(i) N&S: 'Being able to move from place to place' (see also Sen, 1982, p.367; 1982a, p.20; 1984, p.281; 1988, p.15; 1990, p.44).

3. Virtue of Pleasure
(a) N&S: Being able to 'have pleasurable experiences' (see also Sen 1985a, p.200; Sen 1984, p.513; 1985, p.15; 1992, p.39).
(b) N: 'Being able to avoid unnecessary and non beneficial pain, so far as [is] possible'.

4. Cognitive Virtues
(a) N: 'Being able to use the [five] senses'.
(b) N: 'Being able to imagine, think, and to reason'.
(c) S: Being 'acceptably well informed' (Sen 1985a, p.199).
(d) S: Being able to read, write, count and communicate (Sen, 1984, p.497; 1984a, p.85; 1989, p.773; 1992, p.125).
(e) S: Being able 'to take part in literary and scientific pursuits' (Sen, 1983, p.447; 1984a).

5. Virtues of Affiliation I (Compassion)
(a) N: 'Being able to have attachments to things and persons outside ourselves'.
(b) N: 'Being able to love, to grieve, to experience longing and gratitude'.

6. Virtue of Practical Reason
(a) N&S: 'Being able to form a conception of the good' (see also Sen and Williams, 1982, p.13).
(b) S: 'Capability to choose' (ibid., p.13; Sen, 1992); 'ability to form goals, commitments, values' (Sen, 1985a, p.218).
(c) N&S: 'Being able to engage in critical reflection about the planning of one's own life' (see also Sen, 1985a, p.218).

7. Virtues of Affiliation II (Friendship and Justice)
'Being able to live for and to others, to recognise and show concern for other human beings, to engage in various forms of social interaction'.
(a) N: 'Being capable of friendship' (Nussbaum, 1990, p.233); and
S: 'Being able to visit and entertain friends' (Sen, 1985a, p.199; see also Sen, 1984a, p.86).
(b) S: 'Being able to participate in the community' (Sen, 1985a, p.199; see also Sen 1982, p.367; 1984, p.514; 1990, p.44; 1992).
(c) N: Being able to participate politically (Nussbaum, 1990, p.233) and be capable of justice (Nussbaum, 1988, p.163).

8. Ecological Virtue
(a) N: 'Being able to live with concern for and in relation to animals, plants and the world of nature'.

9. Leisure Virtues
(a) N: 'Being able to laugh, to play, to enjoy recreational activities'.
(b) S: Being able to travel and go on vacation (Sen, 1985, p.46).

10. Virtues of Separateness
(a) N: 'Being able to live one's own life and nobody else's'.
(b) N: 'Being able to live in one's very own surroundings and context'.

11. Virtue of Self-respect
(a) S: 'Capability to have self-respect' (Sen and Williams, 1982, p.20; see also Sen, 1984, p.337; 1984a, p.85; 1990, p.44; 1992, p.39).
(b) S: Capability 'to appear in public without shame' (Sen, 1985a, p.199; see also Sen, 1984, pp.333–7; 1987, p.104; 1990, p.44; 1992, p.110).

12. Virtue of Human Flourishing
(a) N: 'Capability to live a rich and fully human life, up to the limits permitted by natural possibilities' (Nussbaum, 1990, p.217).
(b) S: 'Ability to achieve valuable functionings' (Sen, 1985a, p.200; 1992, ch. 4).
(c) S: 'Being wise and contented' (Sen, 1987, pp.26–7).

Note: 'N' and 'S' stand for Nussbaum and Sen respectively.

Source: Nussbaum (1995, pp.83–5) unless otherwise stated.

3. SOME GENERAL METHODOLOGICAL CONCERNS

While Nussbaum's approach provides a starting point for thinking about the concept of development, it is possible to raise some general concerns about her style of essentialism and methodology. While some of these concerns can be dealt with relatively easily, others seem to be serious enough to justify substantial revisions. Interestingly, most of these concerns are linked to the four objections Nussbaum claims to transcend (see Section 1 and 2.1 above).

The fist of these concerns relates to the charge of prejudicial application. Wolf (1995, p.106) argues that an approach based on the concept of the human being (in contrast to an approach based on the notion of personhood) is more susceptible to sexism and speciesism. The risk of sexism stems from the fact that the idea of the human being is in part a biological one, and because gender is a biological fact, the possibility of different kinds of human beings with different natures, needs and capabilities, naturally arises. In fairness however, the charge of sexism goes against the spirit and letter of Nussbaum's writings. Her work is not only extremely critical of those who deny equality to women, but also argues in favour of a single norm for human functioning, i.e. a single conception of the good that applies equally to both men and women (see Nussbaum, 1995, pp.96–104; see also Annas, 1993).[16] In fact, Nussbaum justifies the decision to base her conception of the good on the notion of the human being by arguing – in marked contrast to Wolf – that it is much harder to discriminate arbitrarily against women (or any other oppressed members of the species) by denying their humanity than by denying their status as a person.

On the other hand, Nussbaum's approach is probably more vulnerable to the charge of *speciesism*, i.e. the neglect or disregard for non-human forms of life. So far Nussbaum has not responded to this criticism but, in defence, she could point towards her ecological virtue (item 8 on the level 1 and the level 2 list), which incorporates 'concern' and 'respect' for other species.

Some of the other potential difficulties associated with Nussbaum's approach however, cannot be dealt with so easily. Most of these problems stem from her style essentialism and are related to objections 2–4. Firstly, there is a difference between trying to characterise 'human existence' and 'good living', and attempting to *literally define* these concepts. Nussbaum claims her project is concerned with the former, and for good reasons (see Section 2.1). But at times her language and style of essentialism suggests that she is actually pursuing the latter project.[17] Consider Nussbaum's two thresholds for *human* and *good* human functioning. If these thresholds are interpreted in the literal sense, then each item recorded on the list in question is deemed to be essential (and together sufficient) for achieving human and good human functioning respectively. These are strong claims. For example, a glance at the level 1 list indicates that a being would not count as human if s/he were blind, deaf or crippled! In reality however, it is not difficult to imagine such a being living not only a human life, but a good human life, of a sort; for the inability to function in these ways is compatible with the development of talents, the acquisition of virtues and the achievement of a wide range of (other) worthwhile ends, as the lives of Stephen Hawking, Stevie Wonder, Beethoven and many others have shown (Wolf, 1995, pp.107–8).

Nussbaum's strong style of essentialism also risks exposing her approach to the charge of paternalism. For instance, each item on the first list is associated with a strong assertion of the following kind: 'all human beings . . .' achieve function X. This is uncomfortably close to saying that all human beings *should* strive to achieve the ends associated with level 1 functioning. Anyone who fails to live up to these expectations is judged to be non-human. But it is conceivable that a rational person may value the freedom to choose a life style that does not conform to Nussbaum's criteria for human functioning.[18] For example, contrary to Nussbaum's claims, a person *may not* choose to live a life 'with and in relation to others' (violating level 1's item 7), or 'regard a life not lived in affiliation with others to be a life not worth living' (Nussbaum, 1995, p.78). In fact most, if not all, cultures and societies have their fair share of hermits, eremites and monks (among others), who choose, in line with their personal preferences, to live their lives in solitude and isolation. Similarly, some people deliberately choose a life style that makes little room for recreational activities (violating level 1's item 9) or pays very little respect to the surrounding environment (violating item 8). Eric Fromm has even suggested that some people may actually want to escape from the kind of freedom associated with item 6. It follows that not all of the items on Nussbaum's list should be regarded as *strictly* universal.

The second level of Nussbaum's conception of the good, on the surface at least, seems to fare a lot better on this count. For a start, level 2 consists of a list of functional *capabilities* (rather than bare achievements), which implies an element of choice. The importance of choice is explicitly emphasised by Nussbaum (e.g. Nussbaum, 1990, pp.238–9; 1995, pp.94–5). Furthermore, the notion of capability and the idea of choice are now reflected in a much weaker, flexible and plausible language of essentialism. (Compare the grammar of the first list, e.g. 'all people . . .' with the grammar of the second, e.g. 'being able to . . .').

However, despite these reassurances, it is still possible to raise some legitimate concerns. The crux of the problem is that Nussbaum's general approach still gives the distinct impression that individuals *ought* to function in the ways specified in Table 3.1. First, Nussbaum's theory of good human functioning seems to be characterised by the implicit assumption that all *able* human beings *will* (freely) choose to realise the specified capabilities; for on Nussbaum's conception, to choose otherwise is to settle for a less than good life style. However, while it is probably true that all capable individuals will choose (in line with their preferences) to achieve certain functions (such as being properly nourished, moving around or using sense perception[19]) realistically, the same cannot be said of some of the other items in Table 3.1 as the examples just referred to clearly show.

In fairness, the methodology devised by Nussbaum is designed to counter the charge of paternalism. In particular, her account 'is meant to be both tentative and open ended' (Nussbaum, 1995, p.75; and Section 2 above). This important methodological point needs to be emphasised (Wolf, 1995, p.109) and strictly adhered too. On balance however, this procedure does not seem to be consistent with Nussbaum's style of essentialism; in particular it is inconsistent with her rigid and insensitive conception of the two thresholds for functioning and with her assertion that trade-offs between the items in Table 3.1 should be strictly limited on the grounds that 'each is of central importance' (among other things). For these reasons it is plausible to argue that Nussbaum's theory of the good is 'internally inconsistent' in the sense that several of the concepts employed come into conflict with one another.

Other tensions can also be found between Nussbaum's general approach (style of essentialism) and the methodology she advocates and claims to employ. For example Wolf (1995, p.109) observes that her

> . . . language of essentialism tends to suggest that in constructing an account of the human good, we are engaged in a project that, at least in principle, will eventually be both *universal* and *complete*, in need of no further revisions or exceptions. (My italics)

This is in marked contrast to the methodology Nussbaum expounds which is tailored to the enumeration of a *working* conception of the good and encourages continuous dialogue between cultures in an attempt to capture and continuously refine a shared development ethic. By definition such an account cannot be complete or strictly universal.

On balance, much of Nussbaum's methodology – unlike her essentialism – appears to be worth preserving. First, there are well-known philosophical reasons for believing that a *complete* and *strictly* universal account of the good is unlikely to be attainable (see Braybrooke, 1987, esp. chs 2.2, 2.3 and 3.7). And second, any attempt to construct such a conception is likely to be objectionably paternalistic insofar as it neglects the values and preferences of potential dissenters. *It follows that Nussbaum's concept of development should not be regarded as strictly universal or complete (in line with her essentialism), but as broadly universal, necessarily incomplete and open to revision, which is much more realistic and consistent with the kind of methodology she advocates.*

4. ADJUSTING THE METHODOLOGY

To respond to the above criticisms by reducing Nussbaum's conception of the good to a list of even more basic and essential functions would overlook the value and purpose of her entire project. For the idea that these ends are of general value to people from different cultures, places and times is not discredited by acknowledging that some individuals have managed to live fulfilling lives without one or other of these capabilities (Wolf, 1995, p. 108), or by recognising that some people and cultures may not value or desire a particular item (or items) featured on Nussbaum's lists.

One possible way forward, which has been suggested by Susan Wolf (1995), is to view Nussbaum's two lists not as standards or 'tests for the humanity or quality of individual lives', but 'as a basis for assessing communities' and for devising 'a set of needs and goals' for informing public policy (ibid., p.108). While proceeding in this way overcomes the problems associated with Nussbaum's rigid and inflexible thresholds for functioning, it makes no allowance for variations between the preferences and values of people *within* the boundaries of specific communities. In fact, focusing on the community as a whole directs attention away from individuals in general and dissenters in particular.

Methodological individualism however, is an important feature of Sen's conceptual framework: development is ultimately about what each individual person can do and be.[20] The value of this approach is reflected in Sen's studies of sex-bias in poverty and famine, which underline the importance of analysing the allocation of resources and basic capabilities among different individuals (or groups of individuals).[21] Several of the items in Table 3.1 appear to presuppose the superiority of individualism over communitarianism. Consider, for example, Nussbaum and Sen's concept of Practical Reason, which entails being able to use internal deliberative powers to plan and direct one's own life. The same goes for Nussbaum's notion of Separateness, which includes certain 'guarantees of non-interference' in the private sphere of life and a range of personal freedoms (Nussbaum, 1995, p.85).

There is, however, a way forward that can address many of the problems associated with Nussbaum's general approach while retaining the emphasis upon individualism. This involves *weakening* Nussbaum's language and style of essentialism so that the items and thresholds associated with level 1 and level 2 functioning are interpreted in a much more liberal and flexible way.[22] Such an approach does not automatically judge a person lacking one of the capabilities associated with level 1 functioning to be less than human. This flexibility also provides latitude for respecting the preferences and choices of dissenters without judging the life style of these people to be less than good. For instance, we can recognise that a hermit choosing to live in isolation or a priest deciding to forgo sexual activity can still live a good kind of life. In contrast to Wolf's proposal, favouring this new weaker style of essentialism helps to eliminate the problem of paternalism. In addition, introducing an element of flexibility into Nussbaum's framework enhances the prospects for cross-cultural sensitivity which was previously confined to the possibilities for plural and local specification.

In order to support the weaker and more flexible style of essentialism advocated above it is necessary to revise and augment some aspects of Nussbaum's methodology. The crux of the problem is that Nussbaum's methodology, like her essentialism, tends to neglect the very real possibility that individual dissenters may exist *within* specific cultures and traditions. By placing a firm emphasis on inter-cultural dialogue and on the importance of forging an international development ethic, Nussbaum's methodology seems to entail the unrealistic assumption that *all* members of specific cultures and societies share the same preferences and values. This oversight invites paternalism.

Ideally, the call for cross-cultural discussion needs to be supplemented with a firm(er) commitment to *local* dialogue. Of course, Nussbaum and Sen (1989) do acknowledge the importance of internal discussion. Self diagnosis for groups located in a particular local space (which is informed by external values) is seen as the appropriate mechanism for formulating a list of generally valuable capabilities (ibid., p.320). But at times Nussbaum and Sen's efforts to encourage critical reflection by confronting local traditions with foreign values seems to underplay the importance of internal discussion and the priority of local values and attitudes. The crux of the problem is that Nussbaum and her followers judge some local traditions and cultural values to be morally objectionable, particularly from the standpoint of gender justice (see Nussbaum and Glover, 1995, pp.11–15 and part IV; see also Chen, 1995; and Nussbaum and Sen, 1989). By calling for the internal criticism and rational assessment of these values (Nussbaum and Sen, 1989, p.300), and encouraging the process of 'value rejection' in traditional societies, Nussbaum and Sen have raised some concerns regarding the imposition of Western culture.[23] Providing a genuinely *internal* dialogue is established however, and local values are ultimately respected (as Nussbaum and Sen intend), these concerns can be dismissed. This does not necessarily undermine the normative force of Nussbaum and Sen's approach. There is nothing to stop local people appealing to external values to criticise gender differences and other practices that may, after careful deliberation, be considered objectionable or unjust. Nevertheless, the logic of this approach requires that we must ultimately accept any *genuinely rational* assessment of values local people see fit to provide.

These remarks are broadly consistent with the spirit of Nussbaum's project. While her approach is designed to confront local traditions with external values, Nussbaum (1990, p.236–7) denies that it is paternalistic in the sense that it 'simply tells distant people what wisdom requires' (Dworkin, 1985). Instead, it seeks to 'direct reflection' about some of the most pressing issues in the developing world by confronting participants with 'a map of possibilities', encouraging dialogue about those possibilities, and then, after deep and imaginative reflection, asking local people 'what they would choose' (Nussbaum, 1990, p.237).

5. NUSSBAUM'S THICK VAGUE THEORY OF THE GOOD IN PERSPECTIVE

This brings us to the TVTG itself. Nussbaum claims to provide a first approximation of human and good human functioning that can serve as the foundation for elaborating an international development ethic (see Section 2.2). But Nussbaum does not arrive at this approximation 'by examining a wide variety of self interpretations of human being in many times and places' (Nussbaum, 1995, p.73). Instead, her conception of the human being turns out to be almost exclusively based on the myths and stories of Ancient Greek culture and on the writings of Aristotle in particular.[24] This leaves the TVTG in a fairly vulnerable position. Liberals and Relativists could argue that:

(1) The TVTG does not draw directly on human experience but is in fact confined to the myths, legends and stories of ancient history. In

consequence, Nussbaum's theory may unknowingly end up importing extra-experiential and extra-historical elements after all.

(2) By confining her investigation to the myths and stories of Greek antiquity, Nussbaum is unable to sufficiently demonstrate the general applicability of her theory across time and space.

(3) Drawing primarily on Aristotle's account of human flourishing does not constitute a sufficient foundation on which to base even 'a first approximation' of an international development ethic. Such a conception is unlikely to have much practical relevance for modern civilisation or today's developing countries (as Nussbaum intends). It is simply not realistic to expect a theory originally intended to describe a life style of virtue and leisure for a privileged minority of affluent Greeks (who lived and died more than two thousand years ago) to apply to the great mass of poor people living in Africa, Asia and Latin America.

(4) Any attempt to apply Nussbaum's TVTG (as it currently stands) therefore runs the risk of imposing Aristotelian style 'virtues' on local traditions. What is required is a systematic study of human values across cultures and societies. Such a study may well reveal that different people and societies subscribe to distinct and perhaps divergent sets of values.

These potential objections strike at the foundations of the TVTG. Nussbaum does not provide any *direct* evidence to support the idea that people share a universal set of values. The TVTG may indeed describe many of the most central human capabilities. But Nussbaum does not demonstrate that different cultures and societies really do subscribe to this development ethic. There are at least four broad possibilities (see Box 3.1). Human values may be: 'Universal' or 'Relative' and 'Aristotelian' or 'Non-Aristotelian'. Some tentative suggestions as to where different moral theories stand in relation to this dichotomy are summarised in Box 3.1.[25] Most 'thick' theories of the good fit naturally into the bottom right quadrant. Possible examples of moral theories that subscribe to universal values that might be described as Non-Aristotelian include philosophies that emphasise the pursuit of happiness and the priority of negative freedom. Some accounts of non-virtuous functioning and immoral forms of conduct also fit into this category. A well-known example is Hobbes's view of human nature and morality, which portrays man as a self-seeking egoist driven by the desire for conflict, power and war. Some modern forms of Utilitarianism and moral theories that emphasise the 'priority of the right' seem to fit into both the top left and bottom left quadrants of Box 3.1. These theories typically permit individuals to pursue a diverse range of potentially different interests that may or may not include some 'virtuous' objectives.

Box 3.1 A Typology of Human Values and Development Ethics

	Particularism (Relative Values)	Universalism (Non-Relative Values)
Non-Aristotelian Values	The fictional Callicles and Thrasymachus portrayed in Plato's Dialogues, who rejected traditional rules of moral conduct and concluded that the rational way to live is to pursue one's own interests and power, acting unjustly if one can get away with it. Some modern forms of Utilitarianism and moral theories that demand the 'priority of right'.	John Stuart Mill and Isaiah Berlin's emphasis on negative freedom. Classical Utilitarianism (the pursuit of pleasure and avoidance of pain). Hobbes's egoistic view of human nature and morality.
Aristotelian Values	Conduct based on Hume's concept of 'Sympathy' (concern for other people's feelings of happiness and misery); or Sen's notion of 'Commitment' (selfless acts that may or may not coincide with personal utility and well-being).	Nussbaum's TVTG. Sen's examples of intrinsically valuable capabilities. Griffin's list of Prudential Values. Most Basic Needs approaches to development.

In order to throw some light on the relevance of the categories in Box 3.1, a substantial part of this book is devoted to a systematic study of human values in two distinct communities. In particular an attempt will be made to confront the TVTG (and some of the theories discussed in the following section) with the views of some ordinary poor people (see Chapter 4). Notice that Nussbuam's unscientific 'story telling' methodology is rejected at this stage in favour of a more reliable approach that involves conducting fieldwork to gauge directly the preferences and values of poor people themselves.

6. SOME REFLECTIONS ON THE THICK VAGUE THEORY OF THE GOOD

So far this chapter has outlined one of many possible lists of functional capabilities and has proposed, criticised and revised a methodology that is particularly well suited for the task of confronting that conception of the good with local attitudes towards development.

Before proceeding with this task however, it is appropriate to pause and consider the normative content and structure of Nussbaum and Sen's list of functional capabilities. How does Table 3.1 compare with some of the other lists that have been advanced in the development studies, economics and philosophy literatures? In addressing this question, the following remarks draw on a range of alternative conceptions of the good, including the schemes presented by Alkire and Black (1997), Allardt (1993), Braybrooke (1987, chs 2 and 7), Brock (1993), Carr-Hill (1986), Dasgupta (1993), Doyal and Gough (1991), Erikson (1993, table 1), Griffin (1986, ch. IV), Klasen (1997), Max-Neef (1992, esp. tables 7.1–7.6), Miles (1992, esp. pp.292–9), Rawls (1971; 1982; 1988), Streeten (1981; 1984), and the UNDP (1992).

One of the most striking conclusions relates to the sheer amount of common ground most of these lists share. In fact the extent of overlap between the items on each of these lists is fairly remarkable, especially if we take account of the fact that several of these conceptions were devised with different countries (or regions) in mind or for very different purposes. These preliminary considerations go a long way towards vindicating Nussbaum's approach and imply that a broadly universal list of functional capabilities based on a cross-cultural consensus is probably attainable.

However, the theoretical and normative content of Nussbaum and Sen's list needs to be scrutinised much more thoroughly. Do all of the items included in Table 3.1 really belong there? Have Nussbaum and Sen adequately described those that do? Are any important human capabilities missing from their list? The objective of the list, as we have seen, is to record those functionings and capabilities *thought* to contribute to a good form of human life. With this objective in mind an attempt can be made to provide an intuitive answer to these questions.

None of the items in Table 3.1 seem to be obvious candidates for elimination at this stage – given the apparent scale of the consensus in the academic literature. However, there does seem to be considerable scope for spelling out most of the items on Nussbaum and Sen's list in greater detail. In particular, the Virtues of Separateness and Affiliation need to be clarified and discussed. (On balance, this task can be accomplished without compromising the methodological requirement for 'vagueness'.) Moreover, it is possible to identify two or three potentially important omissions in Table 3.1. In particular, Nussbaum and Sen's list of functional capabilities neglect the need for physical security and economic resources, which may have some intrinsic value in addition to considerable instrumental significance. Their conception of the good also seems to pay insufficient attention to the value of participating in socially meaningful activities such as employment, homemaking and child rearing (although recreational activities do receive an all too brief mention). These apparent 'omissions' are considered in turn before an effort is made to clarify some of the functional capabilities recorded in Table 3.1.

It is widely recognised that physical security is an essential component of personal autonomy and well-being (Carr-Hill, 1986; Doyal and Gough, 1991, pp.212–4).[26] The most common threats to physical security and survival stem from: (1) the breakdown of law and order and subsequent exposure to violence; (2) the risk of being injured at home, at work or at play; and (3) the fear of arbitrary interference from the state with human rights and personal liberty (Carr-Hill, 1986). It follows that personal safety, or being able to avoid violence, physical harm, and injury should occupy a central place on Nussbaum and Sen's list.

Nussbaum and Sen's list also overlooks the importance of access to economic resources such as income and wealth, and goods and services, which have traditionally received a great deal of attention from development economists. The decision to exclude these items probably reflects their desire to keep attention firmly focused on the category of 'functioning' (rather than commodities) and is justified on the grounds that material things only have instrumental value. Nonetheless, it is important not to underestimate the instrumental value of economic resources. In fact, some basic goods such as nutritional food, clean water, clothing, sanitation and fuel for cooking and heating seem to be an indispensable part of *any* life. Without a given quantity of at least some of these essential inputs a person will not be capable of achieving many of the intrinsically valuable functionings on Nussbaum and Sen's list, and may eventually cease to function altogether. Most commentators also mention the importance of adequate housing and access to medical and health care as additional necessary inputs for healthy functioning. Education also plays an important role by helping to expand the limits of the cognitive capabilities and by developing the capacity for practical reason. It follows that basic goods like these, which are *necessary inputs* for achieving intrinsically valuable functionings, deserve a central place in any conception of the good that aims to be as complete as possible.

There is also a case for including some less basic commodities and luxury goods. Access to consumer durables such as cars, bicycles, radios, televisions, refrigerators, washing machines, vacuum cleaners, electric irons and kettles, cookers and telephones have featured prominently in much of the literature (e.g. Klasen, 1997; UNDP, 1992; Wells, 1977). While there is no 'one to one correspondence' between any of these inputs and the functional capabilities in Table 3.1, consumer durable goods do make an extremely useful contribution to good living. These goods provide the means to expand a person's capability to function in most, if not all, of the specified ways. Among other things consumer durables reduce domestic chores, improve health and create new opportunities for recreation and satisfaction.

The possession of some discretionary income and luxury goods is also an essential determinant of self-respect in most cultures and societies (see Chapter 4). Income and wealth together with certain luxury and consumer durable goods also have instrumental significance for achieving status, influence and power. While individuals often strive to achieve these ends, these functionings do not appear in Nussbaum or Sen's account of the good (perhaps because these goals are not considered to be virtuous enough).

Commodity command may also have some intrinsic value. Clean water, fuel for cooking and heating, quality housing and education among many other things may be valuable ends in their own right. In a recent paper Stephan Klasen (1997, p.10), a former student of Professor Sen, asserts that these items do possess intrinsic value. (Klasen does not explain why clean water, firewood, quality housing and education qualify as ends in themselves.) Ultimately however, it is very difficult to establish whether or not these things are endowed with intrinsic value (see Chapter 4, Section 6). The instrumental significance of material goods however, is sufficient to make these items a necessary addition to any practical development ethic.

Nussbaum and Sen's inventory of human capabilities can also be criticised for not explicitly mentioning the importance of being able to participate in certain meaningful social activities such as paid employment, subsistence work, managing the household, caring for siblings and studying (see Doyal and Gough, 1991, pp.184–7).[27] Taking part in any of these activities has the potential to be intrinsically valuable in addition to facilitating other important functions. (For example, having a job may be a worthwhile end in itself if it helps give life meaning and substance – as Marxist ethics implies it will.)

While these activities can have either a positive or negative impact on *personal* well-being, *all* are necessary if groups and societies are to survive and flourish (see Doyal and Gough 1991, ch. 5). In consequence, most people are obliged to fill at least one of these social roles for a substantial part of their lives. It follows that any practical development ethic that is supposed to apply to most ordinary people needs to consider the impact of these activities on personal well-being.

In this context, a lot of attention has been paid to the importance of good working conditions for the quality of life. Specifically: (1) the physical and mental demands of work should not be excessive; (2) the work environment must be non-hazardous (i.e. reasonably free from the threat of injury and disease) and of a reasonable quality (e.g. not to noisy or hot); and (3) the kind of work itself should not be de-skilled, excessively repetitive, or boring (see Allardt, 1993; Doyal and Gough, 1991; Erikson, 1993). In fact, a wide range of research indicates that opportunities for control, skill use and variety in the work place typically contributes to well-being (Doyal and Gough, 1991, pp.199–200) and also provides the means for further self-development (Braybrooke, 1987, ch. 7.35). For these reasons 'satisfying work' is yet another candidate for inclusion in Table 3.1.

Nussbaum and Sen do of course recognise that economic resources, gainful employment and physical security are vital for doing and being. In fact, Sen has developed a theory of *entitlements* that takes account of these factors, which explains why disadvantaged groups of people sometimes fail to achieve basic functionings such as being adequately nourished and free from hunger (Sen, 1981; 1987a; 1999, ch. 7). For her part, Nussbaum (1990, p.228) has argued that the task of politics is to identify, for each individual, the *requirements* for good human functioning in each of the areas described in the TVTG. According to Nussbaum, these requirements include access to economic resources (such as a limited amount of money, healthy air and water, education and training, adequate housing and comprehensive health care), security of life and protection from assault, and a scheme of labour relations (ibid., pp.228–34).

The problem is that Nussbaum does not develop these ideas. In one paper she manages to describe the TVTG without making any substantial references to economic resources, employment and physical security (see Nussbaum, 1995, pp.67–80, 83–5).[28] This is probably because Nussbaum like Sen, only wants to include ultimate ends and objectives in her account of the good. But it is likely that personal safety and worthwhile forms of employment qualify as examples of intrinsically valuable capabilities. There are also reasons for thinking that at least some economic resources may be valuable ends in their own right (see Chapter 4, Section 6).

I shall now turn to the specification and clarification of the items featured in Table 3.1. Most of the functional capabilities endorsed in the first three categories of Table 3.1 are relatively uncontroversial. The ability to live long lives, avoid ill health and achieve happiness are generally accepted as valuable components of a good life. It is, however, possible to place a large question mark next to Nussbaum's 'capability to be courageous' (item 1b). While a courageous act may be noble it can have grave consequences for personal well-being. There is also a case for adding the need for 'sleep and rest' and 'exercise' to the list of Bodily Virtues[29] (item 2). Happiness is also an extremely important aspect of well-being, *even though* it is overlooked in most objective accounts of the good life (including the majority of schemes cited above[30]). The value of happiness however, has been widely recognised since ancient times and, in the eighteenth century, found expression in the writings of Jeremy Bentham whose famous slogan 'the greatest happiness of the greatest number' sums up the essence of Classical Utilitarianism.[31]

It is also worth making one or two brief remarks about the Cognitive Virtues and the closely related Virtue of Practical Reason. Both of these items overlap with Max-Neef's (1992, pp.206–7) categories of 'understanding' and 'creativity'. While neither the capacity to understand or the capability to be creative are explicitly present in Table 3.1, Nussbaum and Sen's scheme does include some of the constituent elements of each.[32] However, many core components of understanding and creativity are not present in Nussbuam or Sen's conception of the good. Capacities such as 'receptiveness' and 'discipline' (which contribute to understanding) and 'passion', 'determination' and 'boldness' (which contribute to creativity) as well as 'curiosity', 'intuition' and 'rationality' (which are necessary for both) are absent. Most of these missing items closely correspond to (or could supplement) Rawls's (1971) inventory of 'natural assets', which includes natural talents and abilities as well as capacities like motivation and conscientiousness (ibid., pp.72–4). On balance, there seems to be a *prima facie* case for making some provision for natural assets in a working conception of the good. However, it is possible to object to the inclusion of 'rationality' on the grounds that it is not one of the objects that makes up a good life; instead, it merely allows us to identify the things that constitute a good life (Griffin, 1986, p.67).

This brings us to the Virtues of Affiliation (categories 5 and 7 in Table 3.1). There is a case for adding access to the 'care and support' of other people (Carr-Hill, 1986, p.303) to item 5, since *being loved*, is just as important as the ability to love. In addition it is possible to add the Aristotelian style virtues of toleration, passion, generosity, appreciation and sharing (Max-Neef, 1992, table 7.1; Nussbaum, 1993, p.246) to the capability for love and grief (item 5b). Deep personal 'reciprocal relations of friendship and love' (Griffin, 1986, p.69) are generally thought to rank among the most fundamental aspects of well-being (Carr-Hill, 1986, 6.4),[33] and the ability to entertain friends (item 7a) and take part in the life of the community (item 7b) supplement this function.

A more fundamental objection can be raised about the specification of Nussbaum's 'ecological virtue'. Living in harmony with nature (item 8) places clear restrictions on the kind of life style (bundle of functionings) a person is permitted to choose, and can interfere with his/her capability (opportunities) to promote personal well-being. For example, living with concern for the environment could entail forgoing the opportunity to use a car (in order to help reduce pollution) but might make other aspects of life (such as travelling to work) more difficult. This helps to explain why much of the quality of life literature has focused on what the environment can do for individuals rather than on what individuals can do for the environment.[34] In particular, attention has been directed towards atmospheric pollution and resource depletion, as well as access to clean water and sanitation.[35] Of course, much of the economics and environmental literature does recognise that some potential gains in economic growth and consumption levels may have to be sacrificed if development is to be sustained (Dasgupta, 1993, ch. 10; World Bank, 1992).

A lot also remains to be said about leisure (item 9) and free time which both receive very little attention in Table 3.1. Under the heading of recreational activities, 'which involve a good deal of variation amongst the people of even the richer countries . . .' (Sen, 1985, pp.46–7), one could investigate the importance of holidays and travelling (ibid., p.46), as well as playing games, watching television, and going to pubs and parties (Max-Neef, 1992, table 7.1). The ability to absorb, appreciate and enjoy nature (Allardt, 1993; Griffin, 1986) and 'respond to forms of beauty' (Griffin, 1986; Wolf, 1995, p.110) may also be of value in many societies. These pursuits may facilitate more general and universal functions such as relaxing, daydreaming and remembering which are not included in Table 3.1. There may also be a case for adding the capability for 'adventure' (Braybrooke, 1987, p.248) to Table 3.1.

The problem is not just that Nussbaum's development ethic says little of substance about the importance of recreation. It is more fundamental than that. Level 2 of the TVTG is supposed to describe, in general terms, the character of a *good* human life. The level 1 criteria for basic human functioning is said to serve as the starting point for elaborating this account of higher capabilities. But while level 2 puts forward a more specific and robust description of human capabilities, it does not appear to add much of substance to Nussbaum's theory of the good. Most of the capabilities recorded on the second list represent nothing more than a condensed but more concrete version of the areas of life described in the first stage of the TVTG.[36] It is difficult to see how Nussbaum (and others) manage to associate these schemes with two fundamentally different levels of human functioning.[37] Both levels appear to describe the same set of 'beings' and 'doings'. No new capabilities are introduced, and the existing items do not appear to be re-defined in a way that makes them obviously 'higher'.

Nussbaum's 'Virtues of Separateness' are probably more in need of discussion and clarification than any of the other categories in Table 3.1. The notion of Separateness consists of the liberty to 'rule one's own life' (Friedman and Friedman, 1980), which involves freedom from external interference with one's own affairs (Berlin, 1958; Mill, 1859). Personal autonomy however, also incorporates certain basic rights of equal citizenship. These include civil and political liberties such as the right to vote, be eligible for public office and freedom of speech and assembly along with the right to hold private property (for example see Dasgupta, 1993; Rawls, 1971, p.61 and ch. 4). It also incorporates equality of opportunity, the idea that no person should be prevented from occupying a particular position (or occupation) in society on the grounds of certain arbitrary characteristics such as gender, colour, race or religion (Friedman and Friedman, 1980, ch. 5; UNDP, 1992, p.31).[38] Finally, personal autonomy is also thought to consist of physical security (discussed above), certain mental and cognitive capacities including the ability to choose (item 6b) and a substantial dose of self-respect (item 11a).

Individual autonomy is widely recognised as one of the most important aspects of development (e.g. Doyal and Gough, 1991, esp. ch. 4),[39] and has often been regarded as the most fundamental aspects of a good life (e.g. Berlin, 1958; Brock, 1993; Dworkin, 1985; Friedman and Friedman, 1980; Mill, 1859; Nozick, 1974; Rawls, 1971).[40] The irony is that it is in this very area that Nussbaum and Sen's own list of functional capabilities is relatively weak. In fairness however, Nussbaum (1990; 1995) does acknowledge that her conception of the good needs to be supplemented with a more extensive list of personal liberties. She also makes it clear that such a list should include 'certain guarantees of non interference' in the personal sphere of life, freedom of speech and association, and equal employment rights (Nussbaum, 1995, p.85).[41]

In general, Nussbaum is less sympathetic to private property rights. At times they seem to implicitly enter her conception of the good: for example, Table 3.1's item 5a refers to the capability to be able to have attachments to *things* as well as to persons. At other points in her writings however, Nussbaum rejects the idea of an *absolute* right to property on the grounds that it may stand in the way of promoting good human functioning (Nussbaum, 1990, p.231). For Nussbaum, the integrity of personal property

> . . . is always up for negotiation in connection with the interpretation of the other capabilities, since personal property, unlike personal liberty, is a tool of human functioning rather than an end in itself. (Nussbaum, 1995, p.85)

This is a fairly radical view that ordinary people may want to reject. At the very least, most individuals would probably agree that the *ownership* of things like housing, televisions and cars is preferable to only having the right to *use* these resources.

This brings us to the final two categories in Table 3.1: the Virtues of 'Self-respect' and 'Human Flourishing'. Neither of these items appear to need revising. The final category can be excluded from the revised conception of the good on the grounds that it is composed of all the other items recorded in Table 3.1. However, it is worth noting that the 'ability to achieve valuable functionings' is an important component of personal autonomy and helps provide the necessary latitude for each individual to pursue his or her own conception of the good life (at least within the boundaries specified in Table 3.1). On the other hand, the notion of 'being wise and contented' provides insight into the kind of life style Sen seems to value. At times some notion of virtuous functioning appears to be lurking behind the TVTG. This may explain the absence of potentially important achievements (vices?) such as being successful and achieving status and power.

Table 3.2 presents a summary of the revised and clarified version of Nussbaum and Sen's development ethic. I shall refer to this as the *Augmented Theory of the Good* (ATG). For clarity each of the 'virtues' discussed above has been grouped under one of four headings in Table 3.2: (A) physical capabilities; (B) mental well-being and intellectual development; (C) relating and interacting; and (D) personal autonomy and freedom. These headings are arbitrary and have been included for convenience. It should be noted that it is not necessarily my intention to endorse these categories. I have also included a list of essential inputs for human flourishing (the starred categories in Table 3.2). These items deserve a central place in a practical development ethic irrespective of whether they possess intrinsic value. Table 3.2 should be regarded as nothing more than a *theoretical* approximation of the good. The real test is to confront this list with the views of ordinary poor people.

Table 3.2 The Augmented Theory of the Good

(A) Physical Capabilities

1.   Capability to live a long life and avoid premature death (see also BK; CH; DG; IM; PS; SK; UN).

2.   Bodily Capabilities
(a) Being able to have good health (see also BK; CH; DB; DG; EA; IM; MN; PD, PS, p.337; RE; SK; Streeten, 1984).
(b) Being able to be adequately nourished (see also DB; DG; IM; PD; PS, p.337, SK; UN; Streeten, 1984).
(c) Capability to be free from hunger (see also PS, p.337).
(d) Being able to have adequate shelter (see also CH; DB; IM; MN; Streeten, 1984).
(e) The power to fulfil one's requirements for clothing (see also CH; DB).
(f) Being able to keep warm (see also DB).
(g) Having opportunities for sexual satisfaction (see also CH; DB; MN;

Soper, 1993, p.123).

(h) Having opportunities for choice in matters of reproduction (see also DG; IM).

(i) Being able to move from place to place (see also BK; IM; JG RE).

(j) *Being able to sleep and rest* (BK; DB).

(k) *Being able to exercise* (DB).

2* *Essential Inputs:*

(a) *Access to basic necessities, including: (i) nutritional food, (ii) clean water, (iii) clothing, (iv) sanitation, and (v) fuel for cooking and heating* (CH; DB; DG; IM; MN; PD; PS; SK; Streeten, 1984; UN).

(b) *Access to adequate housing* (see PD).

(c) *Access to medical and health care* (DG; EA; IM; MN; PS; RE; SK).

(d) *Access to the appropriate means of transportation* (Soper, 1993, p.123; SK).

(B) Mental Well-being and Intellectual Development

3. Capacity for Pleasure and Pain

(a) Being able to have pleasurable experiences (see also Friedman and Friedman, 1980, p.2; JG).

(b) Being able to avoid unnecessary and non beneficial pain, so far as [is] possible (see also JG; Rawls, 1988, p.257).

4. Cognitive Capabilities (Understanding, Knowledge and Skills)

(a) Being able to use the [five] senses (see also IM; JG).

(b) Being able to imagine, think, and to reason (see also BK; DG, pp. 60–61, 122; IM).

(c) Being acceptably well informed (see also CH; DB; DG, p.181; JG).

(d) Being able to read, write, count, and communicate (see also BK; DB; DG, pp.181–5; JG; PD; UN).

(e) *Being able to use (other) basic skills and abilities* (CH; DG, pp.181–5; MN).

(f) Being able to take part in literary and scientific pursuits (see also CH; MN; PS, p.337; UN).

4a. *Other Natural Capabilities (or 'Natural assets')*

(a) *Capability to be creative* (MN).

(b) *Capacity for receptiveness, curiosity and intuition* (MN).

(c) *Capacity for discipline, determination and motivation* (JR, pp.72–4; MN).

4* Essential Inputs:
(a) Access to education (DB; DG; EA; IM; PD; PS; RE; SK; Streeten, 1984; UN).

(C) Relating and Interacting

5. Opportunities for Affiliation I (Compassion)
(a) Being able to have attachments to things and persons outside ourselves (see also BK; CH; DB; DG; EA; IM; RE).
(b) Being able to love, to grieve, to experience longing and gratitude (see also CH; JG; MN); and the *capacity for toleration, passion, generosity, appreciation and sharing* (MN; see also Nussbaum, 1993, p.246).

5* Essential Inputs:
(a) Access to the care and support of family and friends (BK; CH; IM; MN).

7. Opportunities for Affiliation II (Friendship and Participation in Society) 'Being able to live for and to others, to recognise and show concern for other human beings, to engage in various forms of social interaction'.
(a) Being capable of friendship (see also CH; DB; DG; EA; MN; RE); and being able to visit and entertain friends.
(b) Being able to participate in the life of the community.
(c) Being able to participate in certain meaningful social activities (DG, pp.184–7; see also BK; CH; DB).

7* Essential Inputs:
(a) Being able to obtain and participate in employment (BK; CH; EA; IM; MN; PS; RE; SK; UN).
(b) Access to good working conditions (DG; EA; RE).
(c) Opportunities for control, skill use and variety in the work place (DG; IM; MN).

8. Interaction with the Environment
(a) Being able to live with concern for and in relation to animals, plants and the world of nature (see also CH; DG, pp.143–6, 242–4; EA; IM; MN).
(b) Being able to live in a clean environment (DG, pp.200–201, 219, 241 260); and *being able to breathe unpolluted air* (IM; Soper, 1993, p.127; Sen, 1987).
(c) Capability to avoid noise pollution (CH; IM).

9. Opportunities for Recreational Activities
(a) Having opportunities for free time (DB; IM; MN; Rawls, 1988, p.257;

Soper, 1993, p.127).

(b) Being able to laugh, to play, to enjoy recreational activities (see also BK; DB; EA; IM; MN; RE).

(c) Being able to relax, daydream, and remember (MN).

(d) Being able to absorb, appreciate and enjoy nature (EA; JG).

(e) Being able to 'respond to forms of beauty' (JG; Wolf, 1995, p.110).

(f) Capability for adventure (DB, p.248).

9* Inputs Worthy of Investigation:

(a) Being able to travel and go on vacation (see also DB; IM RE).

(b) Being able to play games (BK; MN).

(c) Being able to watch television and go to the cinema (MN).

(d) Being able to go to pubs, clubs and parties (BK; MN).

(D) Personal Autonomy and Freedom

6. Capacity for Practical Reason

(a) Being able to form a conception of the good (see also AB; DG, p.64; IM).

(b) Capability to choose (see also AB; BK; DG, p.67; EA; IM; JG); ability to form goals, commitments, values (see also MN).

(c) Being able to engage in critical reflection about the planning of one's own life (see also AB; IM).

10. Separateness (Negative Freedom and Civil and Political Rights)

(a) Being able to live one's own life and nobody else's; *freedom to 'rule one's own life'* (Friedman and Friedman, 1980).

(b) Being able to live in one's very own surroundings and context; freedom from external interference with one's own affairs (Berlin, 1958; Friedman and Friedman, 1980; Mill, 1859), including:

(i) Physical security (personal safety): being able to avoid violence, physical harm and injury (CH; DB; DG; IM; PS; RE; Soper, 1993, p.127; SK).

(ii) Political rights (right to vote, hold public office, freedom of speech and assembly) (DG; IM; JG; JR; PD; PS; RE).

(iii) Equality of opportunity and social mobility (Friedman and Friedman, 1980, ch. 5; IM; MN; UN).

(iv) Right to hold private property (JR; UN).

11. Self-respect

(a) Capability to have self-respect (see also Goulet, 1971; IM; JR; MN; Rawls, 1982; 1988).

(b) Capability 'to appear in public without shame' (see also Smith, 1776, Vol.2, pp.399–400, 405).

12. Capability to Function (Positive Freedom).
(a) Ability to achieve valuable functionings (see also Goulet, 1971, pp.91–4; Lewis, 1955, pp.420–424).

12* Essential Inputs:
(a) Access to economic resources including, (i) income and wealth and (ii) goods and services (see DG; EA; IM; JG; JR; PD; Rawls, 1982; 1988; RE).
(b) Access to discretionary income (IM), and luxury and consumer durable goods such as: (i) cars, (ii) bicycles, (iii) radios, (iv) televisions, (v) refrigerators, washing machines, irons, kettles, cookers, vacuum cleaners, and (vi) telephones (see IM; SK; UN; Wells, 1977).

Note: the numbering of the main categories (1–11) and most of the sub categories (a, b, c, etc.) correspond to the groupings used in Table 3.1. New items are in italics.

Key: AB= Alkire and Black (1997); EA= Allardt (1993); DB= Braybrooke (1987); BK= Brock (1993); CH= Carr-Hill (1987); PD= Dasgupta (1993); DG= Doyal and Gough (1991); RE= Erikson (1993); JG= Griffin (1986); SK= Klasen (1997); MN= Max-Neef (1992); IM= Miles (1992); JR= Rawls (1971); PS= Streeten (1981); UN= UNDP (1992).

Source: Table 3.1 unless otherwise indicated in the text.

NOTES

1. See Nussbaum (1990, pp.208–17) and Rawls (1971, pp.92–3 and ch. 7).
2. In recent years Rawls's theory of the good has become thicker as he has revised and extended his list of primary goods (e.g. Rawls, 1982; 1988). Some libertarians however, have put forward much thinner notions of the good. For example, it has been argued that Nozick's (1974) system only consists of constraints (in the form of rights) and endorses no final goals whatsoever (including rights). On this see Sugden (1993, pp.1958–61). Soper (1993, p.116) cites a very different distinction between 'thin' and 'thick' theories of need.
3. Nussbaum (1990) advances some additional reasons for favouring a 'thick' account of the good.
4. These objections have been discussed at length by Nussbaum (1992; and 1995, esp. pp.67–72). She provides an excellent guide to the literature and a useful bibliography. See also Doyal and Gough (1991, part 1), Dworkin (1985), Nussbaum (1988; 1990; 1993) and Soper (1993).
5. See Nussbaum (1988, esp. pp.156, 165–6, 171, 173).
6. Relatively little is said about Nussbaum's (interpretation of Aristotle's) conception of justice, social democracy and political distribution in the following discussion. On this see Nussbaum (1988; 1990; 1995). See also Crocker (1995).
7. Nussbaum locates the human form of life between the type of functioning connected with

animals and plants and the kind of activity attributed to immortal gods and other imaginable anthropomorphic creatures.

8. Nussbaum's inquiry is really concerned with the way in which ancient myths and stories interpret the human form of life.

9. See also Nussbaum (1990, pp.219–24; 1992, pp.216–20; 1993). Nussbaum's strong language of essentialism is preserved in the presentation of this list and will be discussed below.

10. Nussbaum recognises that human limits (as well as capabilities) constitute an important part of the good life. For 'human life, in its general form, consists of an awareness of these limits plus a struggle against them . . . It is a characteristic of human life to prefer recurrent hunger plus eating to a life with neither hunger nor eating; to prefer sexual desires and its satisfaction to a life with neither desire nor satisfaction . . .' (Nussbaum, 1995, p.80; 1990, p.224). Braybrooke (1987, 7.34) also points to the need for some 'antagonistic features of life'.

11. This represents a shift from Nussbaum's (1990, pp.224–5) position: originally level 2 of the TVTG was regarded as a first attempt to 'specify vaguely certain *basic* functionings that should, as constitutive of human life, concern us' (ibid., p.224, my italics). In short, the list was meant to 'provide a minimal theory of the good' (ibid.).

12. On moving from a human life to a good human life and the problems associated with identifying the corresponding thresholds see Nussbaum (1995, pp.81–2).

13. Here I follow David Crocker (1995, pp.174–7). The interested reader might like to compare Table 3.1 with Crocker's own list. Notice that Table 3.1 is an updated, revised and extended version of Crocker's original list. Some more recent versions of Nussbaum's list have appeared since this book was written (most notably, Nussbaum, 2000, pp.78–80). These lists are largely the same as the one under discussion and, if considered, would not greatly affect the analysis or conclusions presented here.

14. Strictly speaking, of course, Sen does not develop a theory of the good or put forward a systematic list of generally valuable capabilities (although he often makes brief references to examples of intrinsically valuable functionings and capabilities). While I frequently refer to Nussbaum and Sen's 'development ethic' in the following discussion, many of the criticisms I shall make only apply to Nussbaum and her TVTG, and not to Sen and his capability framework.

15. At times Nussbaum seems to give priority to the 'Architectonic functionings', i.e. the Virtues of Practical Reason and Affiliation. See Nussbaum (1988, pp.179–84; 1990, pp.204–7).

16. Nussbaum does not overlook biological differences between the sexes. Following Plato she argues that such differences in no way require, or even suggest, 'a life long differentiation of functions' between men and women (Nussbaum, 1995, p.100). Nussbaum's conception of the good also makes an effort to promote women's autonomy in the area of human reproduction by introducing level 2's item 2(h) which is not present in Aristotle's original theory of human flourishing.

17. See also Crocker (1995) and Wolf (1995).

18. Of course, not all of the items on Nussbaum's list permit a very meaningful notion of choice (e.g. item 1) and some do not allow any meaningful scope for choice at all (e.g. items 5, 10 and 11). Some of these items are probably best described as functionings (bare achievements) rather than capabilities (opportunities). The distinction between these two categories was briefly discussed in Chapter 2, Addendum.

19. It is conceivable that there may be one or two exceptions: for example, the hungry faster or the malnourished hunger striker.

20. Hence Sen's (1980) call for equality in the space of human capabilities. More recently Sen (1992) has acknowledged that the case for equality should be assessed in the light of 'aggregative concerns' (efficiency considerations).

21. On these issues see Sen (1984, esp. essays 15, 16 and 18). See also Sen (1981; 1985, pp.82–104; 1987a; 1992; 1999).

22. Crocker (1995, pp.172–3) argues a much more plausible interpretation of Nussbaum's first threshold would say something like: the more the central functionings on the first list 'are

irremediably missing, the less confidence we have in calling a creature human'. Presumably, Crocker would accept that a similar reinterpretation must also apply to Nussbaum's second threshold. Nussbaum however, makes it clear that she does not intend either of her thresholds to be interpreted in the weaker sense. In some rather disturbing remarks she provides some examples of lives that, in her opinion, do not qualify as human. These examples include just about everything from living in a permanent vegetative state to the absence of mobility that makes speech as well as movement from place to place impossible (see Nussbaum, 1995, pp.81–2). These remarks may not be consistent with Nussbaum's proposal for avoiding prejudicial application (objection 1 above).

23. Some critics have overreacted. In a strongly worded email circulated around academic institutions in India and the UK, Smita Jadeja (1999) claims that Sen's 'contempt for Hindu realities, Hindu people, Hindu institutions and Hindu communities and Hindu families makes him a false prophet and false saviour'. Jadeja's commentary offers nothing in the way of reasoned argument or corroborative evidence to support these (or other) accusations.

24. See especially the references Nussbaum (1990) cites in footnotes 52–65. Two exceptions seem to be level 1's items 5 and 8. Nussbaum gives the credit for the former to Freud and Melanie Klein. Erik Allardt receives the credit for the latter. More recently, Nussbaum has claimed that the latest version of her list (which is essentially the same as the one considered here) is derived from 'years of cross-cultural discussion' (Nussbaum, 2000, p.76). This is simply not the case. On this see Clark (2001) and Section 2.2 below.

25. The examples in Box 3.1 are only meant to illustrate how different moral theories can be categorised. Few moral theories slot neatly into a given quadrant. There is scope for arguing about where to locate some of the ethics placed in Box 3.1. For example, some Aristotelians may object to categorising negative freedom as 'Non-Aristotelian'. Moreover, acts performed out of 'sympathy' for other people could be categorised as Non-Aristotelian if they are not based on fine motives, e.g. giving to charity to get into heaven.

26. See also Braybrooke (1987, section 2.2), Erikson (1993), Klasen (1997), Miles (1992) and Streeten (1984).

27. Sen does frequently mention the value of being able to 'take part in the life of the community'.

28. Some brief and trivial references are made to the provision of education, adequate housing, and women being able to seek employment outside the home.

29. The list could be expanded even further to include bodily functions such as eating and procreation, not to mention the need for hygiene and to excrete (Braybrooke, 1987; Brock, 1993; Doyal and Gough, 1991; Max-Neef, 1992). However I shall refrain from doing so to keep the list manageable. All these items can be derived from the functional capabilities already included in Table 3.1. See Braybrooke (1987) on derived needs.

30. Apart from Nussbaum and Sen (who underplay the importance of happiness) the only exception cited in the references above is Griffin (1986, p.67) who speaks of 'enjoying pleasurable experiences'.

31. The Utilitarian objective was also captured in the United States Declaration of Independence, which ranked the pursuit of happiness alongside the fundamentally important rights to life itself and liberty. More recently, Thomas Jefferson's inalienable rights to 'life, liberty and the pursuit of happiness' have been echoed by Friedman and Friedman (1980).

32. Clearly, items 4(b) to 4(e) in Table 3.1 are all important components of understanding. In addition, Max-Neef's notion of a 'critical conscience' (which he lists as an important component of understanding) seems to share some common ground with item 6(c), although the latter is construed much more narrowly than the former so that it only relates to critical reflection in 'the planning of one's own life'. Creativity is less well represented in Table 3.1, though Nussbaum and Sen's list does include the capacity to imagine (item 4b) which is clearly an essential ingredient of creative activity.

33. The importance of personal relationship and contacts also features in the work of Allardt (1993), Brock (1993), Doyal and Gough (1991), Erikson (1993), Griffin (1986) and Max-Neef (1992).

34. Allardt (1993), for example, proposes a scheme for 'measuring predicaments in the biological and physical environments of individual citizens' (ibid., p.90).
35. See Allardt (1993), Dasgupta (1993), Doyal and Gough (1991), Miles (1992), Todaro (1995, ch. 10) and World Bank (1992).
36. In one of her earlier papers Nussbaum states that the purpose of the second stage of the TVTG is to specify, in general terms, the basic functionings that constitute human life (Nussbaum, 1990, p.224). But in later papers the same level 2 list is said to describe a good human life (see Section 2.2).
37. Des Gasper (1997, p.295) wants to insert an intermediate category, 'a missing middle', that represents 'a sketch not of minimal humanness or of "flourishing" but of a decent minimum'. Ironically, Nussbaum's two lists may already describe this missing middle. What is required is a distinct account of basic and good human functioning.
38. This component of personal autonomy is fairly contentious and is therefore put forward more tentatively. Some Marxists have dismissed the idea of equality of opportunity as nothing more than a bourgeois right to inequality. Tawney (1931) for example, talks of 'equal opportunities for becoming unequal'. Rawls (1971, ch. 2), on the other hand, has put forward the case for fair equality of opportunity.
39. See also Allardt (1993), Erikson (1993), Griffin (1986), Max-Neef (1992), Miles (1992). The UNDP (1992, box 2.2) provides a useful checklist of 'political freedom' indicators.
40. In a well-known passage John Stuart Mill contends 'the sole end for which mankind are warranted, individually or collectively, in interfering with the liberty of action of any of their number is self protection. That the only purpose for which power can be rightfully exercised over any member of a civilised community, against his will, is to prevent harm to others. His own good, either physical or moral, is not a sufficient warrant. He cannot rightfully be compelled to do or forbear because it will be better for him to do so, because it will make him happier, because in the opinion of others to do so would be wise or even right' (Mill, 1859, p.13).
41. Sen also recognises that negative freedom has 'some intrinsic importance of its own, in addition to its instrumental role in the pursuit of positive freedom' (see Sen, 1985a, p.219). However, there are powerful elements in Sen's writings that play down the importance of rights vis-à-vis positive freedoms (e.g. Sen, 1982a; 1985a, lecture 3). Qizilbash (1996a, p.1211) argues that '[t]here is little room for [negative freedom] in . . . [Sen's] account of development'.

4.   Perceptions of Development

1. INTRODUCTION

This chapter has two objectives. The first is to investigate how poor people perceive a good life. A search through the abstracts of Cambridge University's copyright library, the archives of SOAS and SALDRU, and two electronic databases ('BIDS' and 'EconLit') revealed no records of any study or investigation that dealt specifically with this issue.[1] In consequence, a decision was taken to administer a questionnaire to collect the necessary information. This proved to be an extremely profitable exercise, which provides some interesting and potentially unique insights into the concept of development.

The second objective involves using the data collected in the field to evaluate some abstract concepts of development. This entails confronting some of the theoretical concepts of development described in previous chapters with the values, hopes and expectations of poor people *themselves*. How realistic and how relevant are these concepts? In particular, we will focus on Nussbaum and Sen's development ethic and the augmented list of 'functional capabilities' described in the last chapter (i.e. Tables 3.1 and 3.2).

This chapter is organised as follows. Section 2 describes the fieldwork and some of the problems encountered during the administration of surveys. Section 3 reflects on some of the practical and methodological problems we addressed. Section 4 presents an analysis of the survey results (which is supplemented with data from poverty studies conducted in other regions). Section 5 draws out the implications of our findings for some contemporary development ethics. And Section 6 provides some concluding remarks.

2. THE FIELDWORK

In March 1998 several in-depth interviews were conducted in two impoverished South African communities located in the Province of the Western Cape. A total of 157 personal interviews were completed in a rural village called Murraysburg (located deep in the Karoo), and a semi-urban squatter camp known as Wallacedene (situated approximately 30 kilometres from the centre of Cape Town).

2.1 Questionnaire Design

The questionnaire was divided into two parts that dealt with untutored and tutored responses respectively. In the first half of the interview respondents were asked to specify, in order of priority, the five most important aspects of a good life. A series of questions designed to uncover the reasons and motives for valuing some of the most frequently mentioned items were then put to respondents. The second part of the interview consisted of a set of similar questions, which, instead of being left open, asked respondents to evaluate a specific set of capabilities. The questionnaire schedule[2] is reproduced in the Annex.

2.2 The Surveys

Two teams of experienced interviewers supplied by the South African Central Statistics Service (CSS) were assembled for a training session held at the University of Cape Town organised by Mr Dudley Horner and myself. Both teams worked under the guidance of a fieldwork supervisor.[3]

While random sampling techniques were applied in both survey areas, some difficulties were encountered due to the lack of reliable maps and demographic statistics at the time of our surveys. In Murraysburg a map was obtained from the town clerk but appeared to overlook some important recent developments, including the rapid growth of a squatter camp on the outskirts of the village. Demographic information was obtained from Mr Isaac Dokter the local representative of the Reconstruction and Development Programme (RDP), the community nurse and the school principal, but these statistics did not strictly agree with one another.[4] The absence of reliable maps and demographic information made it difficult to identify enumerator areas or to calculate a sample interval. In consequence a visual inspection of the entire village was made. We then took a decision to visit every 35th household beginning from a random point in the village.[5] Interviewers did their best to select the person interviewed at each house on a random basis while allowing for the race, age and gender skew of the population.

No demographic statistics were available for Wallacedene at the time of the survey.[6] Using a map supplied by the CSS, the township was divided into 35 enumerator areas. Each enumerator area (EA) contained between 15 and 30 houses. A decision was taken to administer either two or three questionnaires in each EA (depending on the number of houses in the EA).[7] Sample intervals for each EA were calculated by dividing the total number of houses in the EA by the number of questionnaires allocated to that area. The first house selected in each EA was chosen randomly. Interviewers then proceeded to visit every nth household, where n represents the sample interval.

The interviews themselves lasted between one and two hours. Several households were revisited in order to give the respondent a chance to rest or to collect missing data. There were no refusals and only one substitution was made. The majority of interviews (73%) were conducted in the respondent's first language.

2.3 The Sample Characteristics

A total of 157 people over 12 years of age made up the survey sample. The sample was divided between the two fieldwork sites and included roughly equal numbers of men and women (see Table 4.1). In both locations the sample consisted of relatively more young people than old people. (Seventy-three percent of the survey sample were younger than 35 years.) The racial breakdown was 42% African, 53% Coloured and 5% White. (Virtually no Asian people live in either survey area (see SSA, 1999).) Nearly all of the people interviewed spoke Afrikaans (61%) or Xhosa (35%). The rest were English, Zulu or Sotho speakers.

Table 4.1 Characteristics of the Survey Sample (Total no. of Respondents)

	All	Murraysburg	Wallacedene
Men	70	39	31
Women	87	41	46
African	64	9	55
Coloured	82	63	19
White	8	8	0
No response	3	0	3
Aged 12–19	50	39	11
Aged 20–34	65	19	46
Aged 35–59	31	13	18
Aged 60 plus	11	9	2
Total	157	80	77

Source: Fieldwork database

The majority of survey respondents were clearly poor. Forty percent of individuals reported that they received less than R250 per month from all (cash) income sources. Almost half of the survey respondents received no more than R300 each month. Only a quarter of the sample received more than R800 per month.[8] This compares with an average monthly per capita (cash) income of R820 in the Western Cape as a whole in 1993 (PSLSD, 1994, table 13.1.2).[9]

Just under a quarter of the sample (24%) were in full time education and approximately one-fifth (18.5%) were housewives or pensioners. Thirty-two percent were unemployed and 13% worked in the formal sector of the economy. The remaining 11% worked in the informal sector participating in a range of temporary, casual and semi-permanent activities such as working as labourers, selling food or clothes and char work. Of respondents aged 14 plus 55.2% had achieved at least eight years of formal schooling and 37.5% of those aged 16 or over had completed ten years of schooling.[10] But one-fifth of the survey sample had failed to complete five years of schooling and could therefore be regarded as functionally illiterate.

The majority of rural respondents lived in brick housing requiring attention with rough and unfinished exteriors. There were also some wood and iron structures and the occasional wood and iron extension to existing houses. (The new RDP housing had not been completed at the time of our survey.) Most urban informants lived in poor quality shacks constructed of corrugated iron and waste materials. The majority of houses we visited were small and had no more than two or three rooms. Several of the more affluent houses were well furnished and most had access to electricity and clean water although adequate sanitation and refuse collection was sometimes a problem. Many of the households we visited seemed to posses a radio and several also had a television set.

These numbers do not adequately convey the true extent of economic and social inequality in the two survey areas. While 40% of the survey sample received an income of less than R250 per month, those with a formal sector job typically earned several thousand rands each month. (The top 10% of the survey sample earned between R1,800 and R7,000 per month. Furthermore, while a fifth of the survey sample was effectively illiterate and only half had achieved eight years of schooling, 7.6% had passed Matric (twelve years of schooling) and a further 6.1% held a diploma or degree.

2.4 The Analysis of the Results and Adequacy of the Survey Sample

The fieldwork findings have been broken down by location, gender and age to explore how perceptions of development differ between: (1) the rural and urban poor; (2) men and women; and (3) the young and old.[11] This approach helps to provide a richer and more detailed assessment of Nussbaum and Sen's development ethic by subjecting their list of human capabilities to a fairly demanding test. Can their theory of the good cater for the expectations of a diverse range of poor people that live in two very different communities and have different preferences, experiences and problems?

Some brief remarks about the adequacy of the survey sample are in order. Neither of the sampling techniques described above is ideal. Unfortunately, given the time and resources available it was not possible to conduct a systematic survey of either fieldwork site to establish accurately the numbers and precise whereabouts of different groups of people prior to the administration of the questionnaire. In particular, the following shortcomings should be noted:

- The sample is not properly balanced between the two fieldwork sites. Recent demographic statistics show that Wallacedene is more than four times the size of Murraysburg in terms of population and dwellings (SSA, 1999). This is not a serious limitation since our real objective is to compare and contrast the responses of rural and urban people.

- The sample drawn in Wallacedene does not accurately reflect the composition of the local population. In particular, it is skewed against men (compare Table 4.1 with the statistics cited in n.6 of this chapter). This is partly because the statistics required to design a balanced sampling procedure were not available at the time of our survey. In addition, enumerators were sometimes forced to interview whoever happened to be at home (instead of returning to the household at a later date if the preferred candidate was unavailable) due to a lack of time and money. The fact that the majority of interviews were conducted on workdays helps explain why urban men are under represented.

- A more serious limitation concerns the inclusion of an insufficient number of informants over the age of 60 in the Wallacedene sub sample (see Table 4.1), which makes it difficult to draw firm conclusions from our survey for this group of people. This was partly the result of some sloppy sampling techniques employed by some of our less experienced interviewers. It also reflects the fact that the vast majority of township residents were migrant labourers of working age (or their partners and children) that had ventured to Wallacedene in search of gainful employment.

On the other hand, the sample drawn includes a sufficient number of men and women and enough respondents of different ages for separate analysis.

The survey sample also includes a small number of respondents living in female-headed households and some disabled people who typically constitute the exceptionally poor (unless they receive a state grant) and usually face a particularly narrow and restricted range of opportunities.

3. BACKGROUND AND METHODOLOGY

Investigating perceptions of development among the poor poses some potential difficulties. An impoverished person may lack the necessary knowledge or experience to imagine many aspects of a good life. In addition, the wants, expectations and aspirations of the disadvantaged may be crushed by the harsh realities of life. A poor person may learn to take pleasure in small mercies and to desire nothing more in order to avoid bitter disappointment (see Chapter 2.3).

These remarks imply that a survey which seeks to investigate perceptions of the good among the disadvantaged and deprived is unlikely to yield a very meaningful set of results. It is not my intention to dispute the doctrine of false consciousness. The thesis itself is not implausible and some evidence can be found to support it (see Chapter 2, Section 3; and Bottomore, 1983).[12] But accepting this does not necessarily mean our approach is ill conceived. At the very least it is possible to take some precautions.

One important set of safeguards concerns the careful selection of the two survey sites, and the country in which they are located. South Africa has one of the most unequal distributions of income of any nation in the world (May, 2000; RDP, 1995). In this country, perhaps more than any other, aspects of the first world and the third world are visible in close proximity. Thus, even the poorest and most deprived South Africans are explicitly faced with at least one possible vision of a good life. This is especially true of our fieldwork sites, which are both clearly poor by national standards but happen to be situated in one of South Africa's richest provinces (see Section 2.3).

In addition, neither survey site is isolated from the rest of South Africa or cut off from the world in general. Television in particular has played an extremely important role in shaping local attitudes and preferences by projecting potential images of the good life directly into the shacks of our informants. These images reflect a variety of different life styles not only in South Africa but also in developed countries themselves (not to mention a diverse range of other cultures and societies around the world). Even those people who rarely watch television or venture beyond the boundary of our survey areas are directly exposed to some graphic visions of development. In both locations socio-economic inequality is high. While the majority of people are deprived, the few successful people who have prospered are highly visible. Everybody knows of the man in the village fortunate enough to own a car.

Precautions can also be built into the design of the questionnaire schedule itself and the methodology employed in the field. One possibility is to confront local people with a specific conception of the good life (such as Table 3.1 or 3.2), and then to encourage independent and critical reflection before requesting a personal assessment of that theory from each respondent. At times,[13] this seems to be precisely what Martha Nussbaum is advocating:

> [The Aristotelian approach] . . . is an invitation to participate in a reflective adventure. And the claim is that the 'thick vague conception' is only as valuable and as lasting as its role in guiding such adventures. The parties are provided with a map of possibilities, or rather initiated into a dialogue about such a map – and then, after imaginative reflection, they are asked what they would choose. (Nussbaum, 1990, p.237)

Such an approach can help to inform individual preferences without lapsing into paternalism so long as independent and internal criticism are encouraged, and external values are *not* thrust upon participants. In fact, the real drawback with this procedure emanates from other quarters. Insofar as this project involves devising a questionnaire schedule composed of closed items – as it seems it must – it places unacceptable restrictions on the range of possible responses informants can provide, and risks overlooking a lot of potentially important information. As one distinguished anthropologist puts it 'to use this [kind of] technique is fatal, because the research becomes strait-jacketed . . . [I]t is the affairs of which one had no inkling before one went to the field that really matter' (Polly Hill, 1984, p.3).

While the procedure described above will allow respondents to reject the particular concept of development put to them, it will *not* permit them to provide a very meaningful critique of that concept or allow them to suggest an alternative. Reverting to a questionnaire based on open questions however is problematic for different reasons. The preferences of ordinary poor people may not be a reliable point from which to start, because such preferences are endogenous and may not reflect a fully informed or rational assessment of the objects that make a good life for them.

Combining these two approaches however, does seem to provide a way forward. This entails designing a questionnaire schedule composed of open and closed items, which invites respondents to put forward their own conception of a good life *before* confronting them with some pre-defined notion of well-being (i.e. Table 3.2). Such an approach combines the advantages of the two methods described above. It also provides some useful insights into the nature and scope of social consciousness in the survey areas. If respondents begin by advancing a simplistic notion of development that lacks ambition, but systematically raise their expectations of the good life after some alternatives are suggested to them, we may want to conclude that these people were deluded by false consciousness.

This did not appear to be the case. Most of the people interviewed – despite often lacking formal education – had clear ideas about the things their lives lacked and the problems facing their community, not to mention the things they wanted the authorities to do about it (see Section 4.3 below). This intense form of political consciousness, which is not uncommon at the bottom of South African society, has roots in the struggle against apartheid. The majority of people we interviewed had little trouble imagining a substantially better life style.[14] These remarks imply that it is reasonable to focus on the responses to open-ended questions. However, there is some evidence to suggest that respondents may have used the survey as an opportunity to further a narrow range of political interests. Informants were selective in terms of the preferences they chose to declare (see Section 4.3). Comparing these findings with the responses to tutored questions and evidence from other studies helps to restore some balance.

Asking about preferences can be problematic for other reasons. There is no guarantee that respondents will reveal their true preferences. Instead, informants may try to impress the interviewer or provide the expected response to a given question. Respondents may also attempt to conceal preferences of a humiliating or embarrassing nature. Some insights can be gleaned by looking directly at human behaviour and patterns of consumption. But in some cases *values* do not match preferences or actual choices. Desiring an object and valuing an object are two very different things. We have therefore used budget data and behavioural information sparingly, and only as a supplement to our survey findings or where it is likely that respondents may not have been entirely open and frank with us. In most cases however, there is no evidence to support the contention that respondents were dishonest.

An alternative approach (which is popular in the field of anthropology) is to send the researcher into a particular community with the objective of integrating his-or-herself into that society. By living and actively participating in that community, the researcher can gain unique insights into the activities, attitudes and culture of local people. This approach was ruled out by budget and time constraints. It may also have been difficult (but not impossible) to persuade predominately Black and Coloured South African communities to accept a White English male as an ordinary member of their society. (I am reliably informed that some English anthropologists have managed to achieve this goal.) But even if this approach had not been ruled out by practical concerns, there would still be doubts about the relevance and suitability of this methodology for the task in hand. Many of the issues we need to explore are purely hypothetical from the standpoint of poor people, and cannot be directly observed by the anthropologist or picked up from budget surveys. By definition, poor people are not able to participate in many of the activities (beings and doings) associated with development.

4. ANALYSIS OF THE FIELDWORK FINDINGS

The results of my fieldwork have been summarised in a set of well over one hundred and fifty statistical tables. While I have drawn on all of these tables, only a small selection is cited in the text and reproduced in the Annex. The discussion that follows is supplemented by referring to a range of different studies that deal with aspects of poverty and living conditions from specific times and places (e.g. Breman, 1996; Iliffe, 1987; Moller, 1996; Wilson and Ramphele, 1989).[15] Almost as much can be learned about the concept of development from a careful study of these inquiries as from the survey findings themselves.

4.1 The Priorities of Life

Table I.1 provides an ordinal ranking of the top 30 aspects of a good life based upon the subjective opinions of informants living in Murraysburg and Wallacedene. According to these people the three most important aspects of a good life are: (1) jobs, (2) good housing and (3) an education. The value of these items was repeatedly emphasised in both survey areas. Access to jobs and good housing were spontaneously mentioned by more than half of all informants; and more than two-fifths of respondents cited the importance of an education.[16] In addition, the majority of people that mentioned these items ranked them highly, i.e. as either their first or second development priority (see Figure 4.1).

A particularly high premium was placed upon jobs and good housing in Wallacedene. Over 70% of respondents living in the township mentioned these two items. More than half of the respondents that mentioned the value of a good job described this item as the most important aspect of a good life. In Murraysburg more emphasis was placed upon an education (Table I.1.1). The greater emphasis on housing in Wallacedene probably reflects the relatively poor quality of dwellings and harsh living conditions in the township.

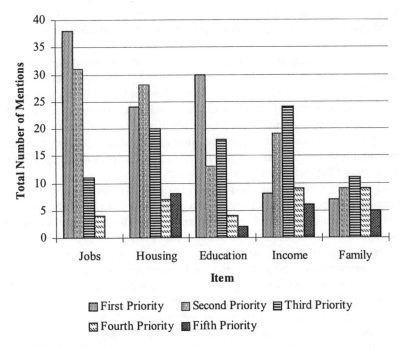

■ First Priority ▦ Second Priority ⊟ Third Priority
▨ Fourth Priority ▤ Fifth Priority

Source: Fieldwork database

Figure 4.1 The Top 5 Aspects of a 'Good Life' in Murraysburg and Wallacedene

Interestingly, women attached considerably more weight to jobs than men in both survey areas (Table I.1.2). Relatively more women (57.5%) than men (48.6%) mentioned the value of a good job. More importantly, a substantially larger proportion of women (88.0%) than men (44.1%) nominated employment as one of the top two aspects of a good life. Among other things, this probably reflects the particularly narrow range of employment opportunities for women in developing areas, their increasing demands for personal autonomy, and the relatively precarious situation faced by a large number of lone women who lack the support of a husband, partner or other male relative.[17]

Education was the single most important item among the youth (12–19 age bracket) but was displaced by jobs and housing among young adults (20–34 age bracket) and the middle-aged (35–59 age bracket). The value of education fades into relative insignificance for those in the oldest age group (60 plus age bracket) who were approaching the end of their working life or had already retired. Jobs were rated relatively highly by those of working age, and by younger members of the labour force in particular. The emphasis placed upon housing however, does not appear to vary much with age (Table I.1.3).

Access to 'adequate', 'regular' or 'better' income also featured prominently in many respondents' perceptions of a good life. In fact, this item received almost as many mentions as 'education', although it was not rated as highly. The majority of those who mentioned the value of income also expressed a preference for other items, which were ranked above it (Figure 4.1). However, in contrast to jobs, housing and education, access to income commands a steady level of support from men and women of all ages in both survey areas (Tables I.1.1–I.1.3).[18]

All of the remaining items in Table I.1 lag a fair way behind jobs, housing, education and income. But the value of a good family, a Christian life style,[19] good health, sufficient food and happiness were all frequently mentioned. Several respondents (usually the young) also pointed to the value of good friends and the importance of owning a car or a business. These items were closely followed by the desire for 'understanding' and harmony between people, the support of family and relaxation. A handful of respondents also mentioned living in a good area, personal safety, nice clothes, having children, respect, sport, marriage and independence.[20] Most of these items were emphasised by specific groups of people (see Tables I.1.1–I.1.3).

At this stage it could be argued that the prospects for Nussbaum and Sen's development ethic look bleak. None of the top four items in Table I.1 are included in Nussbaum or Sen's lists of intrinsically valuable capabilities. While neither Nussbaum nor Sen deny the importance of jobs, good housing, education or income (at least on instrumental grounds) the absence of these items in Table 3.1 does represent a striking omission. These aspects of life not only received a lot of support from both the rural and the urban poor in our survey, but were also systematically ranked above all other potentially valuable capabilities. Moreover, there are reasons for believing that these findings can be generalised. For example, a recent survey of Kwa-Zulu Natal found that jobs, better wages and housing were among citizens' top four priorities for improving living conditions – although education lagged behind in fourteenth place (Moller, 1996, p.23 and table 2). Later in the survey however, it is revealed that ordinary people, once explicitly asked, considered 'education and training' to be the single most important item on a list of expert defined development goals (ibid., p.26 and table 5).[21] These findings indicate that jobs, housing, income and education should be included in the ATG (i.e. Table 3.2).

Critics could also point out that only a third of the items in Table I.1 are actually included in Nussbaum and Sen's conception of development. For example, in addition to the top four items discussed above, living a religious life, access to food, owning a car or business, relaxation and living in a good environment (among other things) are not explicitly referred to. In fairness however, most of these items can be derived from the capabilities that are present in Table 3.1. In contrast, the ATG fares a lot better: the only really prominent omission is the capability to live a religious life (Table I.1's item 6).

It can also be argued that the capabilities advanced by Nussbaum and Sen are not rated particularly highly in Table I.1. The most popular item that is represented in their scheme ('belonging to a good family') only achieves fifth place in Table I.1, and lags a long way behind the top four perceived aspects of a good life as Figure 4.1 shows. In fact, closer inspection reveals that this item was only mentioned by a quarter (26.1%) of respondents. A related line of attack entails pointing to the fact that some of the capabilities included in Nussbaum and Sen's development ethic do not earn a place in Table I.1.

Finally, it might be observed that several of the items in Table I.1 received the bulk of their support from fairly specific groups of people. (For example, the value of living a good Christian life style was mentioned almost exclusively by rural women in the youngest and oldest age groups.) This casts doubt on the feasibility of constructing a broadly universal account of the good life (even at a very high level of abstraction) that rests on a consensus between different groups of people. If broad agreement cannot be achieved within specific cultures and societies the possibility of successfully forging an international development ethic that stretches across cultures and traditions must be extremely limited.

These objections may appear compelling. But there are reasons for thinking that this line of attack is misleading and ultimately unjustifiable. To begin with we need to consider why respondents value the items recorded in Table I.1. It is possible that some of the things in Table I.1 may be required in order to facilitate other valuable ends; and that these ends may turn out to be the very functionings and capabilities described by Nussbaum and Sen. Some evidence can be found to support this hypothesis (see Sections 4.2 and 4.4). Factors that are linked to the design of the survey must also be taken into account. For practical reasons it was only possible to ask each respondent to nominate up to five things that, in his or her opinion, contribute to a good life. In total a large number of different items were mentioned during the surveys.[22] But this does not necessarily imply that perceptions of the good life differed radically between respondents. In fact respondents appear to have selected up to five items from a common set of fundamental ends.[23] The fact that each person could only nominate up to five items from a potentially large bundle of fundamental ends helps to explain why so many items in Table I.1 *appear* to command the support of a small proportion of people.

But this does not explain why some items received more emphasis than others. I shall endeavour to show that the items respondents chose to emphasise were determined by a range of practical considerations and political objectives (see Section 4.3). It is not a coincidence that certain things in Table I.1 were mentioned by groups of people with similar interests and problems.

4.2 The Objects of a Good Life

The results presented so far must not be viewed in isolation. We need to consider the *motives* for valuing the items in Table I.1. This will help to throw further light on the things the poor ultimately value.

4.2.1 Jobs

The single most important reason for valuing a good job in both survey areas was to 'earn money' or acquire a 'good income' (Table I.2). This goal was mentioned by more than two-thirds of all survey participants without any prompting from interviewers. Half of all the people questioned stated that earning an income was *the* most important reason for valuing employment. This reflects the fact that the able-bodied among the poor can often escape extreme poverty by becoming wage labourers (Breman, 1996, ch. 1; Iliffe, 1987, p.114).

The value attached to the *earning power* of a good job is remarkable. In total more than four times as much weight was attached to income than to the next most popular item in Table I.2. In addition, respondents mentioned a range of items closely linked to income, which included facilitating expenditure, acquiring various goods and services, achieving economic security and improving the quality of life (see also Section 4.2.4 below).

Respondents were also aware that a good job provides the means to achieve many of the ends they associated with a good life style (i.e. Table I.1). Acquiring reasonable housing, adequate food and clothing, supporting family and friends, and achieving happiness were important reasons for valuing a job. Several people also nominated confidence, self-respect, peace of mind, pursuing a challenge, learning new things and being able to plan for the future and help others as examples of valuable capabilities promoted by a good job. Some important reasons for wanting a good job also reflect the desire for personal autonomy among young adults. These aspirations were usually expressed in terms of a demand for 'independence', 'self-sufficiency' or capacity to 'earn [one's] own money'.[24] Several respondents also mentioned the value of having a good job to achieve less virtuous ends such as status, respect and pride (see Table I.2).

Few respondents spontaneously acknowledged the value of good working conditions, job security and social mobility.[25] These things are important features of a good job and make an enormous contribution to the overall quality of life. It is worth pausing to consider why. In South Africa, as in other developing countries, employment opportunities among the poor are typically restricted to casual work in the informal sector of the economy.[26] The impact of informal employment arrangements on the quality of workers lives is well documented in Jan Breman's studies of the Indian poor. In a recent book, which draws on more than thirty years of fieldwork experience in and around South Gujarat, Breman (1996, pp.133–40) describes some of the appalling working conditions that typically characterise a range of informal occupations. These horrifying descriptions defy summary, but Breman does note that 'independently or in combination, heat, cold, dampness, noise, dust and stench are noticeable risk factors' (ibid., p.135). The threat that these and other factors (such as poor hygiene and the presence of toxic chemicals) can pose to health in terms of exposing workers to disease and physical injury is very real (for example see Wilson and Ramphele, 1989, pp.77–81). In many cases employers do not take adequate precautions or wilfully neglect the welfare of their workers. A notable example is the case of the South African foundry manager who explained: 'We found that the hot metal bounces off of people's sweat better so we don't supply them with aprons' (ibid., p.80).

Many occupations in the informal economy are also physically exhausting and place excessive demands on workers. Breman (1996, pp.114–5) observes that:

During my fieldwork I repeatedly met people who found it impossible to continue in the brickworks, cane cutting, quarries, or salt pans. They simply could not keep up with the killing work tempo, were unable to cope with work during the night or for more than twelve hours at a stretch, and suffered too much from the abominable conditions in which they were forced to live and work. It was easy to see from their experience that complaints were by no means always due to weak physical stamina or to unsuitable age, i.e. either too young or too old. Some people had literally fled from such work because they obviously lacked the mental toughness that would enable them to acquiesce to the demands of the production process.

Workers in the informal sector of the economy also generally lack job security and effective legal protection. At best, work in the unregulated economy is semi-permanent. Most workers have to be content with temporary or seasonal assignments. The labour process is subject to discontinuity and life alternates, often unpredictably, between work and idleness (ibid., pp.5, 144). Pay is by piecework rather than a regular wage. In consequence, incomes are often uncertain and workers are compelled to work excessively long hours whenever the work is available.[27] Breman also reports that wages are often not paid until dismissal and are sometimes withheld or reduced on false grounds to maintain discipline in the workforce (ibid., pp.20, 149). If production is disrupted for *any* reason (e.g. because of a power cut, breakdown of machinery, or temporary lack of raw materials) the workforce is unlikely to be paid (ibid., p.129). Workers are also frequently dismissed without notice or compensation for: (1) a fall in production; (2) reduced output on the part of the worker; (3) absence due to illness; (4) displacement in favour of newcomers; and (5) for disinclination to grant leave (especially for long distance migrant labourers to return home and visit family) (ibid., pp.69–70, 85, 127).

These considerations explain why informal workers in low and middle income countries *prefer* the switch to a formal contract that incorporates the security of a regular wage and various forms of protection, which are backed up by legal regulation (Breman, 1996, pp.11–12; World Bank, 1995). In his discussion of the Indian poor Breman observes that

> . . . a fixed weekly or monthly wage paid without fail, is a resource that goes a long way in improving one's chances of a reasonable life. To that extent the value attributed to *Pagar* (regular salary) is reminiscent of that given to land in the agrarian way of life. (ibid., p.32)

But informal labour arrangements continue to dominate the world economy. Moreover, the entire life of workers in informal occupations is increasingly geared to the demands of the job. Life styles have become increasingly regulated by time[28] and workers are often forced to migrate to towns and work long hours. This kind of existence can jeopardise personal relationships and break families (see Morifi, 1984; Wilson and Ramphele, 1989). Such life styles are also detrimental to the worker's own welfare. Migrants often have to travel to work in the early hours of the morning before working a full day. As the pattern repeats itself, labourers are left thoroughly exhausted and drained by the experience, as David Goldblatt's classic photograph of the sleeping migrant labourer on the 2.30 KwaNdebele night bus shows (see Badsha, 1986, p.35; reprinted in Clark, 2000a, p.18). Such scenes graphically capture the importance of two fundamental capabilities often denied to informal workers: the value of adequate sleep and rest.

The only real alternative to informal work facing the majority of poor people is no better. Unemployment can only offer the prospect of extreme poverty, and often generates loneliness, frustration, despair and feelings of worthlessness (Wilson and Ramphele, 1989, ch. 4). The following two statements were recorded for the Second Carnegie Inquiry into Poverty and Development in Southern Africa:

Unemployment brings three difficulties: sickness, starvation and staying without clothes. (Unemployed women cited in Wilson and Ramphele, 1989, p.96)

You feel really sick when you haven't got a job. It's there in the bottom of your stomach. You think that something's eating you . . . The days are so long. I don't know what to do with myself anymore. (Unemployed man in Cape Town cited in Wilson and Ramphele, 1989, p.96)

The value of good job opportunities and formal working arrangements were confirmed in our surveys of Murraysburg and Wallacedene. When specifically asked, almost all respondents indicated that regular employment and good safe working conditions were 'essential' or 'valuable' aspects of a good job (Table II.2). In fact these items were rated almost as highly as acquiring an income (Table II.2.A). Reasonable working hours, amicable relationships with employers, the opportunity to live at home (with family) and job satisfaction were also deemed to be important features of a good job. Respondents also endorsed the value of self-respect and opportunities for advancement (Tables II.2 and II.1). The latter is often restricted in poor countries. Social mobility typically depends upon capital, skills, vertical contacts, patronage, and good fortune, which the most disadvantaged groups in society lack (see Breman, 1996; Wilson and Ramphele, 1989, chs 3–4).

The vast majority of survey participants also agreed that a good job helps to give life meaning and substance (Table II.2), but this capability was not ranked as highly as the ends described above (Table II.2.A). In consequence, it is fair to say that a good job was primarily valued on instrumental grounds in Murraysburg and Wallacedene. Acquiring status, influence and power from a good job were also regarded as valuable ends by a clear majority of respondents. Yet, a substantial number of dissenters (approximately a third of all respondents) considered these objectives to be unimportant, and these items were consistently ranked below the other pre-defined ends we asked people to evaluate (see Table II.2.A).

These findings do not appear to be completely consistent with the responses provided to open-ended questions. One of the reasons few respondents spontaneously mentioned the value of items like job security, good working conditions and job satisfaction reflects the fact that the majority of people we interviewed were not actually in the market for a job. In addition many of those who were in the market for a job were either unemployed or had found a formal sector job. In short, only a very small proportion of the survey sample had direct experience of informal employment arrangements. In practice, the respondents that did spontaneously mention the importance of job security and opportunities for advancement tended to be those currently engaged in informal activities. The more affluent and better-educated respondents with comparatively good jobs usually mentioned the importance of job satisfaction and infusing life with 'meaning and substance'.[29]

4.2.2 Housing and living conditions

Housing and living conditions were poor in both survey areas. Several people responded to questions about the value of good housing simply by expressing the need for better or reliable housing. Some respondents insisted that 'good housing is a prerogative' or tried to convince us that 'the government should build more houses'.

The people we interviewed indicated that the single most important function of good housing is to provide *shelter* from the elements (Table I.3). This is one of the most basic and essential functions of reasonable housing. Without adequate housing and shelter the quality of life is seriously impaired (see below).

Almost as many respondents (particularly in Murraysburg) valued solid housing on the grounds that it provides physical security, safety and protection from danger.[30] The weight attached to this item was not anticipated (see Table I.3). None of the studies of housing problems in poor communities that I am familiar with discuss this function of housing (e.g. Morifi, 1984; Ntoane and Mokoetle, 1984; Wilson and Ramphele, 1989). But the people we interviewed ranked the importance of secure housing almost as highly as the requirement for shelter.

In poor communities physical security is often threatened by crimes of violence and property theft. Housing lacks even the most basic security precautions such as locks on doors and windows. In fact, the poorest houses usually lack front doors and proper windows to put the locks on in the first place. Few of the better quality houses are built from materials that would present a potential intruder with much of a challenge.[31]

One township dweller also mentioned the fire hazard ('burning shacks') in overcrowded shantytowns. These settlements are typically composed of flimsy structures constructed from highly combustible waste materials such as cardboard and asbestos and are erected in close proximity to one another. Many of these informal settlements lack an adequate supply of water, so if a fire does occur, the consequences can be catastrophic. The risk of fire presents a serious threat to life in many slums and townships. Witness the graphic photograph on the front cover of the report for the Second Carnegie Inquiry into Poverty and Development in Southern Africa (Wilson and Ramphele, 1989). Another common threat to the security of slum dwellers stems from the risk of eviction. Many tenants squat illegally on land that does not belong to them or pay unreasonable rents. On occasions shacks have been completely demolished and the materials left over have been confiscated (Breman, 1996, p.71; Ntoane and Mokoetle, 1984, p.8).

Most respondents also placed a high premium upon the *quality* of housing and better living conditions. In particular, many people mentioned the desire for adequate living space and privacy, the importance of water and sanitation, and the value of a neat, clean and hygienic place to live. Good quality housing was also highly valued on health grounds. Several people also valued adequate housing for facilitating basic functions such as sleeping and resting (Table I.3). Some of our poorest respondents simply valued housing on the grounds that it provides a place 'to live' and 'keep possessions'. A small number of people also observed that good quality housing provides a place to receive and entertain family and friends.

These capabilities are important. Millions of people in low and middle-income countries live in substandard housing and wretched conditions. The world's housing crisis is well documented and, in South Africa, several good surveys of the living conditions and problems encountered by poor people are available.[32] These studies indicate that the poor and destitute generally share the sentiments expressed in Murraysburg and Wallacedene.

One of the most common complaints is that poor quality housing provides insufficient protection from the weather.

My furniture has been spoiled by the rain coming through the hole in my roof. I have no money to replace the roof. I am sick to death of watching my possessions being ruined and not able to stop it. When it rains, I do not feel like cleaning the house because everything is a mess, with water dripping and buckets all over the show. *Die mense wat dood is, is beter af as die wat soos ons lewe.* [The dead are better off than those who live like us]. (Poor woman in Cape Town cited in Wilson and Ramphele, 1989, p.130)

Many cases of rising damp, flooding in winter, and choking dust have also been reported. On a stormy or windy day fragile housing can fall apart or be swept away altogether leaving the poor with nowhere to sleep. Badly designed housing can also make life exceptionally hot in the summer and very cold in the winter. One study commissioned for the Second Carnegie Inquiry estimated that the mean internal temperature in shelters erected on the Cape Flats can range from 4.2 degrees Centigrade in the winter to 43.1 degrees in the summer (Wilson and Ramphele, 1989, p.130).

Another common set of complaints relates to overcrowding and the lack of space in low-grade housing. Many of these houses are extremely small and accommodate more than one family. Often people have to eat, sleep and wash in a single room. Countless complaints about the lack of privacy (especially for married couples), impossibility of having visitors, need for space for children to play, inconvenience of sharing facilities, noise, and friction between inmates have been documented. Morifi (1984) cites the case of Aunt Bettie, a 52-year old woman from Philipstown, who lives in a single room rondavel with her brother and bed-ridden mother. When Aunt Bettie wants to bath or get dressed she has to go to other people's places or her brother has to move out. This is what she has to say:

Ons moet maar kap-en-punt slaap want daar is nie genoeg plek nie. [We have to sleep head-to-toe because there is not enough space]. If people are living like this then they lose respect for each other. How can you respect each other when the mother, father and children are all sleeping together? If a person gets visitors he or she cannot receive them properly. You have to sit outside in the open with your visitors because there is no room in the house. You cannot even offer them a place to sleep if they need accommodation, because there is only one room. It is very humiliating. (Morifi, 1984, p.10) [33]

Finally, numerous complaints about the living environment and lack of physical infrastructure have been documented. These are important issues in poor communities. Poor areas often lack clean water and adequate toilets. In some cases there are reports of 'sewerage overflowing into the streets' and a 'constant foul odour' (Ntoane and Mokoetle, 1984, pp.9, 19). Refuse collection is usually poor or non-existent, and waste is often strewn around. Diseases such as cholera, typhoid and bilharzia often break out and, in some places, complaints of vicious rats, cockroaches, fleas and bugs have been reported. Other frequently quoted complaints in poor areas include the lack of access to electricity, transportation, proper roads, medical and health care, shops and other services. Although some of these issues were not spontaneously mentioned in Murraysburg or Wallacedene (for reasons discussed in Section 4.3 and 4.4) some deeper probing did reveal that nearly all the people we interviewed valued these items highly (Tables II.1 and II.3).

The survey result also shows that many respondents valued good housing in order to improve their state of mind as well as their physical condition. A large number of people pointed out that living in a good house would facilitate happiness and 'joy'. Some also said that living in a good house would 'feel good'. Others were more specific. In Murraysburg several people insisted that good housing would facilitate 'peace of mind' and relaxation. Urban residents were more likely to value a good house in order to *feel* safe and secure. Self-respect was another important achievement associated with a decent house (see Table I.3).

Many rural dwellers also valued good housing on the grounds that it improves family relations ('togetherness' or 'oneness'), while urban residents of working age wanted sufficient housing to avoid separation from their families. Some people also regarded a good home as essential for starting a family or bringing their children up properly. (A few even mentioned the importance of a good house for educating children, instilling discipline and teaching 'right from wrong'). Large numbers of people (especially women and young adults) wanted their own house. Some informants also replied that a house promotes independence and responsibility. On the other hand some respondents wanted a good house to gain status and prestige or to 'feel proud' (see Table I.3).

4.2.3 Education

By far the most important reason for valuing an education among all groups of people we interviewed was to obtain a good or better job (Table I.4). This objective was cited by just over half of all survey participants (53%) and was usually described as the single most important reason for seeking an education. Earning a good income lagged behind jobs in second place but still received strong support especially from the residents of Murraysburg. Both of these items received significantly more emphasis from women than from men. A good education was also regarded as a valuable source of 'security' and 'survival', particularly among young adults. Some respondents remarked that a good education ensures the successful acquisition of basic necessities such as food, clothing, and housing. In general, respondents were very optimistic about the benefits of education. Many informants reported that they valued an education because it leads to a good life and promotes happiness.[34]

These views are not confined to the people we interviewed. Breman (1996, p.30) reports that numerous conversations with some of the Indian poor revealed 'that most parents are fully aware of the importance of education as a precondition of a better life for their off-spring'. In general the poor are aware that education and training are especially effective ways of escaping poverty (see Morifi, 1984, p.19). The cruel dilemma facing the majority of the world's poor, however, is that getting a good education is difficult to combine with survival. In the words of one destitute South African woman:

Now . . . even Africans and Coloureds can work in the banks, the post office and fill other good paying jobs. But the problem with our people is that they cannot afford to keep their children at school, because if they do their family will starve and by the time the child has obtained his good paying job there will be no family left to enjoy the benefits. (Ouma [grandmother] Anna, Philipstown, cited in Morifi, 1984, p.19)

In recent years most African and Coloured families in Murraysburg have managed to keep their children in school until the age of 15. Compared with other rural areas this is a remarkable achievement. Villagers insisted that education, skills and qualifications improved future prospects (Table I.4). A large group of respondents in both survey areas also valued an education in order to 'be somebody', 'get somewhere' or achieve 'success'. As one of our informants succinctly put it 'an education always pays back'.

Acquiring knowledge and understanding were also important reasons for valuing an education in both survey areas (Table I.4). These objectives were supported by all groups of people and were rated almost as highly as earning good money. Learning to read, write and count also received a lot of emphasis, particularly from the rural poor, women and the elderly, i.e. those groups of people most likely to be illiterate.[35] A small minority of people even hinted that they valued education to improve the power of practical reason although few managed to articulate the idea clearly. Some informants stated that they valued education on the grounds that 'it helps you through life' or 'lets you do what you want'. More appropriate was the answer of one knowledgeable White schoolgirl who replied that a good education 'enables you to discriminate and make choices'.

Respondents also pointed out that an education could make a useful contribution to other aspects of life. For example, urban informants thought education could 'improve communication between people' and promote harmony in the family and community. Several respondents also felt that an education could facilitate independence and enhance self-respect. Some individuals even valued education on the grounds that it would make them a better person or improve their social life (Table I.4). Education was also valued for enhancing health, facilitating self-confidence, avoiding mischievous behaviour, and providing the necessary skills to help or teach others. A small minority of respondents mentioned capabilities like acquiring status, feeling proud, meeting better people and creating a competitive atmosphere.

Respondents were also asked to evaluate a set of pre-defined motives for valuing education. The results of this exercise confirm that education was valued for raising incomes and providing training and skills for jobs, as well as promoting knowledge, understanding and wisdom. None of the people we interviewed disputed the value of these ends (Table II.4). Learning to read, write and count and to develop the power of practical reason (defined as the ability to plan life and make choices) were also regarded as important motives for seeking an education by the vast majority of respondents. A significant number of informants (16.5%) however, openly declared that the capability to take part in literary and scientific pursuits has no place in their conception of a good life. A large proportion of respondents (up to 40% in Murraysburg) also expressed doubts about the value of status, influence and power.

Table II.4 also tends to confirm that education is of intrinsic value to poor people. Respondents did consider the 'pursuit of knowledge' and 'understanding' to be worthwhile ends. The ability to 'read, write and count' was also highly valued, but *not* primarily by the people (in the 19–65 age group) most likely to be seeking employment.

4.2.4 Economic resources

Among the most important reasons for valuing education and jobs in poor communities is to acquire a 'good income'.[36] Respondents valued money in order to 'buy things' and purchase basic necessities such as food and clothing (Table I.5). Money and resources were generally regarded as the route to a better life as well as a necessary means for survival. While some people simply asserted the importance of possessing money, others added that a good income would enhance the quality of their life. Rural dwellers in particular insisted that a good income is essential for providing economic security, purchasing necessities and securing their future. And a large number of adult men simply stated that you 'can't live' or 'cannot survive' without income.

The single most important reason for valuing income however was to support family and friends (Table I.5). This item was mentioned by over a quarter (27.4%) of survey participants and performed well among all groups of people. Several respondents specifically mentioned the value of using money to educate relatives, care for children, acquire food and clothes for their family, or to provide their offspring with a livelihood. While these sentiments are consistent with African humanism ('Ubuntu'[37]), most respondents reserved the emphasis on 'assisting others' for their own family and kin rather than for people in general. Moreover, once respondents had the chance to reflect more fully, there was some evidence of a change in attitudes. The majority of respondents that ranked supporting family and friends in first place appeared to change their mind when we asked them to rank this objective in relation to using income to improve living standards, purchase food and promote happiness (Table II.5.A).[38]

The evidence presented so far indicates that money is of considerable instrumental value to poor people. In poor communities a good income goes a long way towards improving the quality of life of the fortunate recipient and his or her dependants. By drawing on the fieldwork findings summarised in Table I.5 it is possible to be more specific. A substantial number of respondents (24.8%) stated that they valued income in order to acquire food. Many respondents also mentioned the importance of spending on housing, education and clothing. The importance of these items is reflected in expenditure surveys. SALDRU, for example, estimates that the poorest South Africans typically spend at least half of their budget on food (PSLSD, 1994, table 8.5). Housing, clothing and schooling have also been identified as important categories of expenditure.

Several respondents also mentioned the importance of using income to either avoid or pay-off debts. This is an important aspect of development in many poor countries. The destitute often fall into the habit of purchasing everyday items on credit or repeatedly borrow small amounts of cash from moneylenders at exorbitant rates of interest. Such practices often make a bad situation worse and tend to confirm Mary-Jane Morifi's (1984, p.3) observation that 'poverty is expensive'.

Of course the good life goes beyond the acquisition of basic necessities and mere survival. In recognition of this fact an effort was made to find out which goods and services respondents would most like to purchase if they were free from the financial constraints imposed by extreme poverty. The results of this exercise reveal that spending on housing and home improvements dominated most people's list of priorities[39] (Table I.6). This is because decent housing is expensive and the poor can only afford to spend a small proportion of their meagre income on this essential item.[40] Purchasing food, clothing and shoes, and investing in education were also nominated as important priorities. These sentiments reflect the extreme nature of poverty endured by the people living in the fieldwork areas.

Despite their extreme situation however, most respondents expressed equally strong preferences for purchasing a range of non-essential items (Table I.6). The desire to own a car was repeatedly mentioned by men and women in both survey areas. The prospect of owning a car is nothing more than a dream which epitomises popular perceptions of a good life for the poor. Most respondents agreed that having a car facilitates happiness. But the majority emphasised the value of using cars to move from one place to another more conveniently (Table II.13.B). This capability is particularly important in poor areas, which typically lack adequate public transportation. A car however, is also an extremely powerful and highly visible status symbol in poor communities.[41] Some of the people we spoke to were reluctant to admit to wanting a car to achieve status or respect. But several respondents did express a preference for a 'new car', which is not necessary simply to 'move around more efficiently'.

Saving money in banks, making investments and taking out insurance were also important priorities. Most poor people are not in a position to engage in any of these activities. While saving and insurance help to guarantee economic security, investments such as these also contribute to self-esteem and are perceived as an important part of 'being a person'. Purchasing quality furniture also turned out to be an important priority, particularly among women and rural dwellers. Items such as chairs, sofas and beds not only facilitate physical functions (e.g. resting or sleeping) but also promote important social and mental capacities such as avoiding shame, relaxing and entertaining friends. It is also worth noting that several young urban men expressed a desire to invest in their own business. This is a common ambition in poor areas that stems from a general lack of worthwhile job opportunities.[42] Most respondents also expressed a desire to purchase a wide range of consumer durable and luxury goods including fashionable clothing, holidays and travel, television, music centres, computers, general entertainment, gambling, motorcycles, watches and jewellery (see Table I.6).

Being able to acquire these things requires access to a certain amount of discretionary income. A large number of respondents recognised the importance of having money for personal autonomy. Frequent responses included using money to 'do the things you want' and for achieving 'independence', which was usually defined in terms of 'self sufficiency' or 'doing your own thing' (Table I.5). Another important reason for wanting money was to facilitate happiness. The desire to achieve status and prestige, gain respect and to better one's prospects ('get somewhere in life') also received a significant number of citations.

A small minority of respondents, however, chose to question the value of income and wealth. All of these people lived in Wallacedene and most were in the 20–34 age group. Some stated that money could not buy happiness or love. Others insisted that money 'does not last' or causes problems. One or two informants also claimed that having money is 'pointless if you don't know how to use it', or were concerned that everyone would want to know them if they were wealthy. Some even stated that it was wrong to possess money and wealth if you 'don't care about [poor] people'.

4.2.5 Food and clothing

Informants in Murraysburg and Wallacedene repeatedly mentioned food and clothes. The contribution that these two basic goods make to personal well-being is crucial and deserves separate discussion. Both these items play a broader and much more diverse role in terms of promoting human functioning than the standard basic needs and development literature suggests.

4.2.5.1 Food

Food is essential for human functioning. In many ways this is probably the most urgent of all human needs. All people must eat and drink on a fairly regular basis in order to survive. A person may live without shelter or even clothing for reasonably long periods of time (under suitable conditions) but not without food or water. Consuming a reasonable amount of nutritious food on a daily basis is also necessary for adequate (healthy) functioning. This is why the very poor are obliged to spend such a large proportion of their meagre incomes upon food (see Section 4.2.4).

Because food is so important and central to life simply asking people why this item has value is not very meaningful. A more subtle approach is required. Respondents were asked about the motives behind their actual choice of foods.[43] The single most important concern in both survey areas was to promote health (Table I.7). This objective was cited by two-fifths (43.3%) of respondents and was usually nominated as the principal reason for choosing between alternative baskets of food. Many poorer rural informants emphasised the importance of avoiding malnutrition or deriving energy, protein and vitamins from food. Some urban women mentioned the value of maintaining a healthy diet. The promotion of physical fitness (building 'a strong body') was also a concern, particularly among young urban adults of working age.

Some responses were indicative of the acute poverty endured in the survey areas. Many people mentioned the objective of 'avoiding hunger' or choosing wholesome foods that fill the stomach and satisfy appetites. Even more people (especially in Murraysburg) mentioned the importance of selecting cheap and affordable foods. Some informants stated that their ultimate objective is to purchase 'as much food as possible' with the money available to them. These are common characteristics of poverty. Insufficient income often forces poor people 'to eat an incomplete diet' that lacks protein and fails to include enough meat, milk, eggs and fish (Morifi, 1984, pp.17–18; Wilson and Ramphele, 1989, ch. 5). The following testimony is typical of the dietary habits of the poor:

> We only eat meat when I have the money to buy meat and that is only (afval), tripe, trotters etc. I always buy my meat cash. We only eat in the morning and in the evening. In the morning we eat pap [porridge] and coffee and sometimes bread, always homemade and in the evening we eat pap and meat, that is, if I have money to buy meat; otherwise we have to make do with cabbage, or tomatoes and onions. (Ouma [grandmother] Mitta, Philipstown, cited in Morifi, 1984, p.22)

Some of the people we interviewed reported that they were often forced to go hungry or to consume whatever food happened to be available (such as 'food left over from the previous day', food they managed to obtain from other people, or food supplied in aid packages).

But even among the very poor who live on the edge of subsistence there is strong evidence that food is valued for reasons not connected with health or survival. Almost half of all survey participants (49.7%) mentioned the value of selecting foods they enjoyed consuming. This objective was mentioned more often than the desire to promote health, although most respondents did not rate it as highly.[44] Several people also mentioned the objective of catering for their family's tastes and some urban dwellers expressed a desire to purchase luxury foods when affordable.

In addition, a high proportion of young rural people (in the 12–19 age bracket) expressed the importance of selecting popular foods with good trade marks. Some young men also expressed a preference for convenience foods. A significant number of urban people also emphasised the importance of choosing foods that facilitate social events or religious activities. (Some migrant workers mentioned a family feast that traditionally marks their return home after a long period of absence.)

Finally, a large number of people in both locations emphasised the importance of consuming good quality food, which is often difficult to obtain in impoverished areas. Rural respondents specifically mentioned the value of being able to obtain fresh vegetables and other foods. A small number of people also expressed a desire to purchase durable foods that last reasonably long periods of time. (Most of the people we interviewed lacked a refrigerator.) Some informants also expressed a preference for greater variety in their diet or to try new food products.

Table II.7 indicates that all the people we interviewed considered avoiding malnutrition, escaping hunger and achieving good health to be valuable capabilities facilitated by the consumption of food. Nearly all respondents also agreed that enjoying a tasty meal is important. But not all respondents (approximately one-quarter) placed a premium on 'convenience' foods or the value of using food to facilitate social events. It is also worth noting that all groups of people ranked avoiding hunger above being adequately nourished (Table II.7.A). This implies that the psychological effect of food deprivation on a person's well-being (i.e. feeling hungry) is just as important as the consequences for that person's physical condition (i.e. under-nourishment and ill-health).

4.2.5.2 Clothing

Clothing also facilitates important capabilities but is not quite as urgent as the need for food. The poor can and often do manage with relatively few clothes. One Black middle-aged man told us: 'I can walk in the same clothes for a week'. In contrast to the need for food, poor people spend only a small portion of their meagre incomes on clothing (e.g. PSLSD, 1994, table 8.5).

Possessing at least some basic clothing however, is an essential part of human life. In both survey areas respondents insisted that the 'body must be covered'. This was generally perceived as the most important function of clothing by all groups of people. Clothing is necessary to protect human dignity and preserve self-respect in all but the most primitive societies. A person 'cannot go naked'. A substantial number of people also mentioned the value of using clothes to protect their bodies from the elements. In particular, respondents cited the importance of keeping warm or cool (depending on the weather), and having access to items of clothing such as hats to avoid sun-burn (see Table I.8).[45]

The poor also valued quality clothing. Many urban dwellers and young adults in particular, indicated that the ability to look smart and presentable or neat and tidy were important objectives. Several people felt that clothes said a lot about a person or emphasised the need to comply with social protocol. In particular, respondents valued the capability to dress properly for church. Some individuals were concerned that others judged them by the state of their clothes. One Coloured girl admitted to wanting good clothes in order 'not to look poor', while a young African woman proudly reported that her clothes were 'up to standard'.

The importance of being able to dress in accordance with custom for reputable people, even of the lowest order, has been recognised for a long time. More than two hundred years ago Adam Smith wrote:

A linen shirt . . . is, strictly speaking, not a necessary of life. The Greeks and Roman lived, I suppose, very comfortably, though they had no linen. But in the present times, through the greater part of Europe, a creditable day-labourer would be ashamed to appear in public without a linen shirt, the want of which would be supposed to denote that disgraceful degree of poverty, which, it is presumed, no body can well fall without extreme bad conduct. Custom by the same manner, has rendered leather shoes a necessary of life in England. The poorest creditable person of either sex would be ashamed to appear in public without them. In Scotland, custom has rendered them a necessary of life to the lowest order of men; but not to the same order of women, who may, without any discredit, walk about bare-footed . . . (Smith, 1776, Vol.2, pp.399–400)

From these observations Smith concludes that under necessaries we should include not only those items of clothing (and other commodities) that nature makes necessary for survival, but also those things that 'established rules of decency have rendered necessary to the lowest rank of people' (ibid., p.400).

Many respondents also indicated that good clothes generate happiness and promote a feeling of well-being. In addition, large numbers of teenagers and women (among others) mentioned the value of using quality clothing to look good or beautiful. Township dwellers were more likely to mention the importance of having good clothes to look attractive to the opposite sex or impress people. Many people also emphasised the importance of having the right clothes to achieve a fashionable image or to fit in with their peers (see Table I.8). Only a small minority of middle-aged informants indicated that good clothes were no longer important to them.

4.2.6 Family and friends
Belonging to a good family and having reliable friends are also important aspects of development. The value of family and friends was repeatedly mentioned during our survey (see Tables I.1, I.3, I.5, I.6 and I.9–I.11).

Above all respondents emphasised the value of having access to the care and support of family and friends (Table I.9). While this 'functioning' can take many forms, most informants chose to emphasise the economic benefits of a good relationship with family and friends. In poor countries family and kin can constitute the main source of economic support for the poor. John

Iliffe's (1987) history of African poverty tends to confirm the importance of family and the kinship system in poor societies:

In several African languages the common word for 'poor' – umphawi in the Chewa language of modern Malawi, for example – implies lack of kin and friends, while the weak household, bereft of able bodied male labour, has probably been the most common source of poverty throughout Africa's recoverable history. (ibid., p.7)

Iliffe's observations are supported by numerous case studies which show that abandoned women and children left to fend for themselves, are among the most vulnerable in poor societies (e.g. Sender and Johnston, 1996; Standing, et al., 1996; and Wilson and Ramphele, 1989, ch. 9).

Many urban dwellers and young people also mentioned the importance of relying upon family and friends for advice and assistance with solving problems. Some rural people also emphasised the importance of being able to visit and socialise with family and friends. Respondents also valued opportunities to 'learn from' and 'exchange ideas' with their friends.

While some people mentioned the capability of loving each other, most chose to emphasise the value of being loved. In particular a good family and reliable friends were regarded as valuable sources of moral support and comfort. The strong emphasis on the importance of 'being loved' and achieving 'emotional security' among the poor is understandable. In an interview with Courtney Tower, Mother Teresa, who spent many years living and working among the exceptionally poor, observed that

. . . poverty is not just being without food. It is the absence of love . . . Often in big cities, big countries, people simply die of loneliness, unwanted, unloved, forgotten. This is a much more bitter poverty than the poverty not to have food. (Tower, 1987, p.170)

Urban people in particular expressed a desire 'not to be alone' or to share their life with family and friends. Some individuals simply wanted companionship or 'to talk to someone' (see Table I.9).

While access to the care and assistance of other people was highly valued in both survey areas, the emphasis was not restricted to receiving economic and emotional forms of support. A large number of respondents, particularly in Murraysburg, mentioned the importance of helping each other. Wallacedene residents were more inclined to express concern for sharing items such as food or providing for the needs of family and friends. These aspirations reflect the African tradition of 'Ubuntu'.

Several respondents indicated that a good relationship with family and friends facilitates happiness and enhances the quality of life. Yet the family is not a happy or harmonious institution. Poverty has a habit of generating stress and frustration, which undermines relationships. Often the poor seek refuge in the abuse of alcohol. The consumption of alcohol exacerbates tension in poor households and often leads to domestic violence and abuse. Many of the people we interviewed (particularly in Murraysburg) expressed the need for better 'communication' or 'understanding' among people or wanted to strengthen personal relationships with family and friends.

Fewer respondents than expected mentioned the value of falling in love or sharing their life with someone special. In particular, sexual fulfilment was not spontaneously mentioned in either survey area. Questions about the value of this activity caused some embarrassment and were often greeted with a dubious response. A large proportion of respondents either refused to answer or claimed that they did not value sexual satisfaction (Table II.1).[46] The fact that a social stigma is attached to unbridled sexual activity and community life in both survey areas is dominated by the heavy hand of the church may well have encouraged respondents to conceal their true preferences. In support of this supposition it is worth noting that the demographic information we collected shows that a large number of respondents were cohabiting. Yet nearly all unmarried respondents who turned out to be living with a partner gave their marital status as 'single' at the beginning of the interview. Only three people openly admitted to 'cohabiting'.

4.2.7 Religion and the church

No questions about the value of religion or the church were included in the questionnaire.[47] The value of being able to live a good Christian life and take part in church activities however, is evident from responses to open questions that dealt with other issues (see Tables I.1, I.7 and I.11). Religion and the church appear to be rated particularly highly by rural respondents (Table I.1.1). In fact, upon arrival in Murraysburg, community leaders invited our party to guess how many churches were in the village. Our best estimates turned out to be embarrassingly low. Locals took great delight and pride in telling us that their village boasts more than twenty different churches of various denominations.

According to one of our local contacts, the church performs at least three useful functions in Murraysburg. These include: (1) providing economic and emotional support in times of misery, deprivation and hopelessness; (2) acting as a sign of hope for the future; and (3) organising social activities (Dokter, 1996, pp.8–9). But while the church is clearly more than an instrument of spiritual salvation, many respondents still chose to emphasise the value of leading a good Christian life style.

4.2.8 Free time and recreation

Respondents also confirmed that free time and recreation are central to a good life. The most important reason for valuing free time and leisure was to facilitate relaxation. This item was spontaneously mentioned by more than half (52.2%) of all survey participants. Several respondents also cited the importance of sleep and rest or relieving stress and frustration[48] (Table I.10). These functions received the most emphasis from men and women between the ages of 12 and 34 who are typically under substantial pressure to make a contribution to the support of family and friends.

More surprisingly, nearly half of all respondents (44.6%) mentioned the value of using free time to improve health and physical fitness (Table I.10). This partly reflects the fact that the survey sample was skewed in favour of young people with a keen interest in sports. The promotion of health turned out to be an important reason for taking part in less demanding recreational activities as well. For example, consider some of the reasons put forward for consuming Coca-Cola and alcohol in Tables I.12 and I.15 (see also Chapter 2).

More than a third of survey participants (35.7%) also pointed to the value of achieving happiness and enjoyment. Several others either observed that recreation enhances the quality of life or facilitates a good life. Recreation provides the opportunity to 'do what you want' or 'like best' (Table I.10). Happiness makes a fundamental contribution to human well-being and development despite the fact that more weight is attached to other items in Table I.10. The relatively high regard for mental and physical aspects of health is partly a consequence of the harsh life styles respondents have to endure. Frequent exposure to illness, exhaustion, stress and worry almost certainly influenced the survey findings. Good health, relaxation and rest clearly are important human achievements. But it is worth noting that happiness commands a stable level of support from all groups of survey participants, which is not true of other capabilities. Happiness also appeared to gain some ground after respondents were specifically asked to reflect upon the value of some of these items and rank them in order of priority (contrast Table I.10 with Tables II.8 and II.8.A).

A striking feature of Table I.10 is the apparent lack of support for free time. This is probably because there is a tendency to associate the desire for free time with laziness, which is scorned in African culture. Yet more free time does seem to be an essential part of a better life style for many poor people. Migrant labourers – for example – are often forced to rise in the early hours of the morning to get to work and seldom return home before the evening. For countless numbers of people around the world, 'life is an endless cycle of sleeping and working' (Wilson and Ramphele, 1989, p.152). Several of our respondents expressed strong desires to spend more time with their family, children or friends. Some informants also mentioned the importance of having time to do the 'important things' in life or to be by themselves (see Table I.10).

In many cases however, the problem is one of having too much free time and very little to do. The majority of the poor are either unemployed or under-employed and usually lack access to basic recreational facilities such as swimming 'bathes' [pools], halls, children's playgrounds and sports fields (see Morifi, 1984, p.10; Wilson and Ramphele, 1989, p.132). One of the most striking findings of the Second Carnegie Inquiry into Poverty and Development in Southern Africa

> . . . is the extent to which, under the conditions prevailing in the small towns or dorps and in the rural areas . . . there is virtually nothing to do. There are no fields to till; no cattle to be tended. There is not the rich traditional social structure with the concomitant rituals of kinship and neighbourliness that is to be found in the anthropologists reports of earlier societies, fifty or even thirty years ago. Boredom hangs like a dark cloud. And closely associated with it despair. (Wilson and Ramphele, 1989, p.160)

Attempts to escape the boredom and despair of extreme poverty through alcohol abuse, 'dagga' [marijuana] smoking, sexual experimentation, and various forms of mischief that can lead to crime are common.[49] Several respondents expressed a desire for recreation in order to 'avoid boredom', 'keep occupied', 'provide a change of scene', and to escape 'mischief', 'trouble' and 'crime' (Table I.10).

Sport, music and dance, reading, church meetings and activities, socialising and watching television and going to the cinema were nominated as the most important recreational activities (Table I.11).

- *Sport.* Sport was regarded as the single most important recreational activity, and commanded support from all groups of people. Sport was especially popular in Murraysburg and among younger men. Respondents mentioned the value of a wide range of different sports including football, rugby, netball, tennis, athletics, cricket, and volleyball. Less active and entertaining sports such as chess, cards and darts received comparatively little mention. Few respondents distinguished between watching and participating in sports.[50] Some respondents mentioned the value of swimming, which is a real luxury for most poor people who usually lack access to public pools.

- *Music and dance.* Music was rated almost as highly as sport and received special emphasis from township dwellers, women and the young. Singing and dancing were also described as valuable recreational activities.

Singing appeared to be a fairly important community activity in Murraysburg. (In the evening it is often possible to hear the voices of the village children united in song.)

- *Reading.* Reading was also nominated as an important activity. This item commanded the most support from rural dwellers, women and children. This finding tends to confirm that the most disadvantaged groups in the fieldwork areas place a high premium upon the value of literacy and education.

- *Church activities.* Church meetings and other activities were also rated highly. In Murraysburg the church is responsible for organising many of the village's social activities. In addition to attending church and going to prayer meetings and bible reading sessions, several respondents specifically mentioned the value of participating in 'church bazaars', 'church singing' and 'church picnics'. Some people also mentioned the importance of working for the church and 'serving Jesus' in their spare time.

- *Socialising.* Socialising and visiting friends were regarded as important recreational activities by all groups of respondents. A large number of people (especially rural dwellers and men) also mentioned the value of meeting new people and making new friends (see Table I.10). In some cases this seemed to reflect dissatisfaction with the quality of existing friendships and a desire 'to meet better people'. A few respondents also mentioned the value of using free time to be with their family or improve personal relationships (Table I.10, items 12, 17 and 18).

- *Television and cinema.* Watching television and going to the cinema were also regarded as important forms of recreation – especially among the young (Table I.11). In general, informants indicated that they valued watching a broad range of programmes including the news and current affairs programmes, films, serials and sport (Table I.14).

There are grounds for challenging the validity and general relevance of some of these findings. It may seem surprising that activities such as reading and watching the news scored so highly (Tables I.11 and I.14). In fact, watching the news appears to be rated more highly than viewing films, serials and other forms of light entertainment. To some extent this probably reflects the high premium placed upon acquiring an education, a keen and active interest in politics, and a certain amount of curiosity about the outside world (see Table I.14). However, it is also likely that some informants chose to nominate the things they thought we wanted to hear or may have tried to impress the interviewer.

There are also some notable omissions in Table I.11. For example, hardly anybody mentioned the importance of drinking alcohol or smoking tobacco.[51] When we asked about these activities the vast majority of respondents were reluctant to endorse these items (Table II.1). Most of the people we interviewed insisted that they did not drink alcohol or smoke tobacco on the grounds that these activities damage health (Table I.15). These statements are not very convincing. Alcoholism, in particular, is widespread among the poor and often constitutes 'the only available form of relaxation' (Ntoane and Mokoetle, 1984; Wilson and Ramphele, 1989, pp.159–60). In fact, it is not uncommon to find the poor spending all their money in beerhalls (see Morifi, 1984, p.26). The consumption of liquor is a contentious issue in most poor communities. Women, in particular, tended to insist that the consumption of alcohol wastes money, jeopardises family relations and leads to 'trouble' or 'crime' and 'bad', 'violent' or 'abusive' behaviour. Several women also denounced drinking as 'wrong', 'immoral' and against their religious beliefs.[52] The fact that drinking and smoking causes all sorts of social and domestic problems and is usually frowned upon may have encouraged respondents to provide more conservative responses than were warranted.

Nevertheless, several informants did admit to drinking and/or smoking in order to facilitate relaxation, pleasure, and social activities.[53] Some of the people we spoke to also mentioned the importance of using drink or tobacco to calm their nerves, relieve depression, and drown their problems (Table I.15). But none of this demonstrates that alcohol and tobacco is an important part of a good life for these people. It is possible to desire and even consume alcohol and tobacco without genuinely valuing these items. There is some evidence to support this argument. Six of the people we questioned who had admitted to drinking or smoking also stated that they did not value these activities.[54] However, it is not possible to conclude that drinking and smoking were not regarded as valuable recreational activities by a sizeable number of survey participants.

Most respondents appear to have confined their examples of valuable recreational pursuits to the activities that take place in their own community. This helps to explain the interest in sport, socialising, church activities, television and possibly even reading.[55] Several informants also nominated other activities such as taking walks, gardening, needlework, cooking, knitting, cleaning the house, fixing things and repairing the home (see Table I.11). These responses imply that there is very little to do in terms of worthwhile recreation (although Murraysburg does appear to be more fortunate in terms of recreational facilities than many other poor communities). In the light of these remarks it is fair to say that the responses recorded in Table I.11 lack imagination and ambition. Few respondents mentioned the importance of holidays, driving sports cars, enjoying cool drinks or dining out at night.[56] (Two possible exception are Table I.11's items 23 and 28.) However, once given the chance to reflect more fully, most respondents strongly agreed that holidays, parties and driving cars are valuable forms of recreation (see Tables II.9 and II.6).

The findings presented so far can be generalised. When asked, almost all respondents confirmed that free time and recreation is important in order to facilitate happiness, relaxation, sleep and rest, and various social activities (Table II.8). Television, cinema, music and dance, sports, reading, games, parties and holidays were all generally regarded as worthwhile recreational activities (Table II.9). Efforts to uncover the motives behind these activities tend to confirm the fundamental importance of happiness, relaxation, rest and health as the findings presented in Chapter 2 and Tables I.12–I.15 and II.10–II.11 show.

However, respondents also agreed that 'thinking, daydreaming and remembering', 'appreciating nature and forms of beauty', 'visiting libraries museums and art galleries' and 'appreciating classical music' could be added to their list of valuable recreational activities (Table II.9). These capabilities were not spontaneously mentioned. In consequence, it is difficult to repose confidence in these responses.

4.3 Factors Influencing the Responses to Open-Ended Questions

We have seen that jobs, housing, education, income, family and friends and recreation are thought to be among the most important aspects of a good life. In Section 4.2 an effort was made to identify some of the most important human functions associated with these aspects of life. These findings have implications for the assessment of development ethics. Before considering these implications some words of caution are in order. I have already indicated that there are grounds for questioning some of the survey findings. It is time to consider some of these problems in greater depth.

It is clear that there is a strong connection between respondents' personal circumstances and the capabilities they chose to emphasise in the interviews. In particular, the responses to open questions were influenced by the socio-economic condition of informants. However, people's wants, hopes and expectations were not crushed by the harsh realities of poverty and social deprivation. While a great deal of weight was attached to basic achievements, this did not signify a general lack of social consciousness. Respondents *were* aware of many of the better things in life, but chose to emphasise their most *urgent* basic needs.[57] This is why so many respondents were able to talk with passion and zeal about the value of reasonable jobs, adequate housing and access to education and good incomes. These are all things their lives generally lacked in quantity and quality (see Section 2.3). The same reasoning helps to explain why human capabilities such as being able to take part in recreational activities and having access to reasonable working conditions were sometimes overshadowed by more pressing needs (see for example Tables I.1 and I.2).

Both survey areas were highly political. In spite of educational deprivation, most respondents had clear ideas about the problems facing their community and strong views about the things the authorities should do to improve their quality of life. In some cases respondents simply used the interview as an opportunity to put forward a list of demands or to criticise the government. Several informants responded to our questions by insisting that the government should do more to improve housing, job prospects and education. The lack of progress with housing programmes was a particularly sore point in Wallacedene:

> Our people especially have struggled . . . It is about time [that] they get what is owed to them. Good housing is not a privilege it is a right. (A 29-year old Black African man interviewed in Wallacedene. Translated from Xhosa)

Some respondents also wanted to know if our survey was likely to yield any practical benefits or influence local development projects.

In fact, it was evident that some respondents were attempting to use the interview to promote their own interests. People were not only aware of the government's pledge to improve education, housing, health, water, electricity and the job situation but were also familiar with the aims and objectives of the RDP which had been launched during the 1994 election (see GNU, 1994). Table I.1 reveals a striking resemblance between the most frequently mentioned aspects of a good life and the objectives of the RDP. The emphasis upon jobs, housing and education in our survey appears to reflect the fact that people were impatiently waiting for the RDP to deliver tangible results in these areas of life.[58] In other words, respondents were inclined to ask for the things the government might provide in the foreseeable future. These insights help to account for the relatively poor performance of many important capabilities in the private (personal) sphere of life such as intimate personal relationships, family happiness, solid friendships and self-respect.[59]

The survey results indicate that different groups of people frequently chose to emphasise different capabilities (Sections 4.1 and 4.2). This does not represent the absence of a broad commitment to a common set of ends (see Section 4.4). Instead, it reflects the fact that different groups of people often face different problems and have different interests. The most urgent and pressing problems facing the poor typically vary with their objective circumstances and position in society. Some notable examples from the preceding discussion include the relatively high premium placed on (1) housing in the slums of Wallacedene; (2) access to employment by women; and (3) education and training among the youth.

It would be helpful to compare our survey findings with visions of development in societies that are *not* as highly politicised. For example consider Naqvi, Sharpe and Hecht's (1995) survey of the Parry Sound region in Ontario, Canada. While their survey sample includes business as well as residential respondents and asked questions about what kind of development is familiar as well as what sort of development is desirable, their findings are informative. The top development priorities of ordinary people in the Parry Sound region (more jobs, education, social development and participation) are not completely at odds with the objectives of the South African people we interviewed (ibid., p.297 and table 1A). This is encouraging because it suggests that the responses we received to open-ended questions in South Africa have not been greatly distorted by a relatively tense political climate. It also implies that people in countries like South Africa and Canada who come from different cultural backgrounds and often face divergent social and economic conditions still share common goals and objectives – although there are some notable differences.[60]

Another potential source of bias is the inherent tendency to focus on *means* (inputs) rather than ultimate objectives, because these things facilitate the simultaneous realisation of multiple ends. As we have seen, much of the significance attached to jobs, housing, education, income, food, clothing and other resources derive from the fact that these items promote a wide range of human capabilities. Several of these inputs may have some intrinsic value (see Section 6). But the fact that respondents often focused on items that are primarily of instrumental value tends to direct attention away from the things that ultimately matter, i.e. the intrinsically valuable ends of life. The tendency to focus on means rather than ends robs the capability approach of potential support.

To a small extent guiding the thoughts of respondents by asking a series of open questions about *specific* aspects of life helps to address these difficulties. For example, by asking questions about the importance of family and recreation attention is directed away from more immediate needs and towards intrinsically valuable ends in the personal sphere of life. However, a much more direct approach is also required to achieve a more balanced and comprehensive overview of people's impressions of a good life.

4.4 The Ends of Life

In the final part of the interview respondents were asked to evaluate a pre-defined set of potentially valuable capabilities. The results of this exercise confirm the importance of jobs, housing and shelter, education, good health, happiness, family and friends, sleep and rest, basic clothing, income and wealth, self-respect, and free time and recreation (among other things). Nearly all respondents considered these capabilities to be 'valuable' or 'essential' components of a good life style (Table II.1). The apparent scale of the consensus is remarkable. No respondents considered any of these capabilities to be undesirable; and hardly anyone thought they were 'unimportant' or failed to pass judgement.

Table II.1 indicates that this consensus can be extended to include other items such as access to clean water and sanitation, personal safety, (negative) freedom, political rights, electricity, and transportation, *inter alia*. These are important aspects of human development. The reason most informants failed to mention these capabilities when we asked them to describe a good life requires some explanation (see below). Before proceeding with this task it is worth pausing to reflect on the value of these items.

4.4.1 Clean water
Access to clean water is a major problem in many poor areas. Water is often contaminated by cattle or sewerage and can pose a serious threat to health and life (see Section 4.2.2). Obtaining water can also be costly in terms of time, effort and money. In rural areas people often have to walk for several miles to fetch water from the nearest well or stream. Buying water by the bucket or barrel can be expensive. Wilson and Ramphele (1989, p.49) estimate that the contents of a drum of water in Port Elizabeth costs the poor 28 times more than the water flowing out of the taps of middle-class houses in Cape Town.[61] Dry spells and periodic drought often exacerbate these problems. Piped water is therefore perceived as one of the most urgent basic needs in many poor areas (see Horner, 1995; Moller, 1996; PSLSD, 1994), and has the potential to make an enormous contribution to the quality of life.

4.4.2 Physical infrastructure and the surrounding environment
Respondents also confirmed the importance of electricity, tarred roads, adequate transportation, good sanitation and clean living conditions (Table II.1). Access to shops, health care and other services are also valuable commodities (Section 4.2.2). These utilities make a valuable contribution to the overall quality of life by promoting a wide range of important capabilities (see Section 4.2.2; Tables II.12 and II.13; and Chapter 2).

4.4.3 Negative freedom and political rights
Freedom from arbitrary interference with personal affairs and the possession of civil and political rights are also important aspects of human development. Throughout Africa's troubled history political power has frequently been

used to exploit the poor and exclude the weak from resources (Iliffe, 1987). Until recently one of the most striking and well-known examples was the practice of apartheid in South Africa. At one point land alienation alone left the Black majority with just 13% of the territory (ibid., p.123). Basic civil and political liberties are necessary (but not sufficient) to prevent the abuse of power and protect human rights. It is therefore not surprising that virtually all of the South Africans we interviewed appreciated the value of freedom and self-determination, the right not to be deprived of personal property, equal employment opportunities, and the right to vote and hold public office (Table II.1).

4.4.4 Physical security and personal safety
Theft, rape and assault are common hazards in poor areas. Many neighbourhoods are terrorised by groups of gangsters who prey on the poor and compete for power. Walking home from work with wages, leaving the house at night or living alone can be a risky business (especially for women). Fights frequently break out between rival mobs of gangsters leading to knife attacks, gun battles and serious loss of life (Wilson and Ramphele, 1989, pp.152–6; see also Ntoane and Mokoetle, 1984). Domestic violence and abuse is also a common problem and is often provoked by excessive drinking and stress. In places that lack proper civil and political rights the state itself or the prospect of civil war often threatens physical security.[62]

The reasons why most respondents did not spontaneously mention the value of these items are implicit in the proceeding discussion (Section 4.3). Most of the people living in the survey areas already had access to clean water, reasonable sanitation and electricity. In consequence, none of these goods were big concerns in Murraysburg or Wallacedene. This has not always been the case. I am reliably informed by Mr Faldie Esau (and others involved with the Public Works Programme at the University of Cape Town) that water was a major concern in Murraysburg just a few months before our survey was conducted. However, the issue of adequate access to water has been effectively removed from the village's agenda following the recent installation of piped water in most backyards.[63] According to our informant Isaac Dokter the same can be said about the struggle for electrification in Murraysburg. The majority of the village was forced to march in protest before demands for electricity were met (Dokter, 1996, p.7). Now three-quarters of the village has electricity (ibid.), most villagers are preoccupied with other (now more pressing) needs (see Table I.1.1). The same can be said about political reform in South Africa. Since the end of apartheid and the election of the democratic Government of National Unity, the right to vote and freedom of speech have ceased to be the chief concerns of Black South Africans (see Moller, 1995).

Some respondents did nominate personal safety and peace in the household and community as important aspects of a good life (Table I.1; see also Tables I.3 and I.9). These items however, received less emphasis than might be expected. Crime and violence (along with unemployment) are considered to be the most pressing problems in South Africa (Moller, 1996, pp.21–2). A likely explanation for this apparent difference in attitudes is that the incidence of crime and violence is low by national standards in both survey areas. While several cases of housebreaking and sheep slaughtering were recorded in Murraysburg during 1995, only three cases of rape and two incidents of murder were reported (Dokter, 1996, p.8).[64] These statistics compare favourably with Cape Town and many other parts of South Africa where violent crime is extensively reported in the media and confirmed in police statistics.

Similar links between the incidence of *different forms* of physical security and the level of public concern can be found at the local and national level. Security from violence was perceived as the most pressing issue in Murraysburg and Wallacedene, but was closely followed by law and order, protection of personal property and risk of accidental injury (Table II.14.A). This implies that survey participants were not predominately concerned with any single aspect of physical security. For South Africa as a whole, crime and violence remain serious problems. But concern has shifted from political violence to security from crime since the 1994 election (Moller, 1996, pp.52–3).

The apparent lack of support for transportation and quality roads in Table I.1 requires some further explanation. In Murraysburg the majority of roads are not tarred and have no paving which makes travel a difficult and hazardous task. Internal transport is mainly by foot, bicycle or donkey cart. There is no bus or rail service. Taking a taxi to other distant villages and towns is expensive (Dokter, 1996, pp.7–8). It follows that Murraysburg would benefit from a reliable transport system. Nevertheless, access to good transport was *not* perceived as a high priority need. The village itself is small (with a radius of no more than 1.5 km), which makes internal travel relatively easy. Few people appeared to travel to other villages or bigger towns on a regular basis. Wallacedene on the other hand is served by roads of good quality and is conveniently situated close to the city of Cape Town. The township also appeared to benefit from a regular and cheap mini-bus service. These observations tend to confirm that a range of practical and political considerations influenced the responses to open questions.

Returning to the analysis of the responses to tutored questions helps to throw some additional light on perceptions of development in our survey areas. For example, respondents confirmed the value of several important functionings in the personal sphere of life. In particular, most people agreed that the concept of a good life could be extended to include internal powers like practical reason (defined as the capacity to think, reason and make choices), 'natural assets' such as determination, motivation and self-reliance, and physical exercise (see Table II.1). Even the most perceptive and impartial observers can easily overlook these capabilities.

On the other hand, respondents did indicate that there are clear limits to the scope of a potential consensus. A significant number of informants refused to endorse some of the pre-defined capabilities in Table II.1. In particular several respondents disputed the importance of wearing fashionable clothing, drinking Coca-Cola, watching television, visiting the cinema and taking a keen interest in sport (Table II.1). These activities are important aspects of many good life styles. But none of these activities are essential components of *all* good forms of life.

Some of the responses recorded in Table II.1 are a little more puzzling. A substantial number of rural as well as urban respondents indicated that access to land and cattle are unimportant (Table II.1.1), although in many pastoral societies access to land and livestock sometimes provide the only practical means of survival. It is not difficult to find examples of groups of people and even whole societies that have been plunged into extreme poverty and famine by competition for resources, exclusion from the means of production (especially land alienation), natural disasters such as drought, excessive rain and locust or cattle plagues (see Iliffe, 1987). Land and cattle are also potentially valuable assets that can be used as collateral for loans or sold to make ends meet in a crisis (see Dasgupta, 1993, ch. 9.5). However, in South Africa, the urban and rural poor have increasingly relied upon wage labour, the old age pension and other social security payments (such as disability allowances) to survive. In particular, the extension of the pension system to cover all citizens of pensionable age and the growth of social security sets South Africa apart from most other developing countries. A significant number of rural households now live off grandma's pension instead of the land.[65]

Several respondents also refused to endorse the value of having children (Table II.1). Children are regarded as another potentially valuable asset in poor countries. Not only do they provide poor households with a cheap source of labour but they also guarantee insurance against old age and ill-health (see Dasgupta, 1993, chs 12–13). But with the expansion of schooling and the growth of public pensions in South Africa, the economic benefits of large families have been eroded. Much progress has also been made in terms of providing sex education and family planning. In contrast to many other impoverished areas, attitudes towards family planning among men and women are positive (see Table II.1.2).

The fact that more than one-fifth of survey participants questioned the value of 'living long' does provide some grounds for concern (Table II.1). This finding appears to run counter to intuition and human nature. The source of this peculiarity can probably be traced to the harsh living conditions and poor quality of life most respondents have to endure. For those at the bottom of the heap life can be especially tough. Sometimes the destitute simply lose faith. It is not uncommon to hear broken victims of extreme poverty claim: 'All I am waiting for is my dying day' (Morifi, 1984, pp.8 and 11). However, there is some evidence to suggest that ageing concentrates the mind. Everybody we interviewed over the age of 59 appreciated the value of being able to live a long life (Table II.1.3).

5. IMPLICATIONS FOR DEVELOPMENT ETHICS

The data I have collected is extensive and has taken a considerable amount of time to analyse and digest. It is now time to use the survey results presented above to evaluate some of the theoretical accounts of well-being and human development explored in the last chapter. How far do the items recorded in Table 3.2 reflect the values and attitudes of ordinary people? A crude effort to throw some light on this question was made in Section 4.1. Now that we have reviewed all the survey results it is possible to present a more balanced and detailed assessment of Nussbaum and Sen's development ethic. The conclusions that emerge from this exercise are mixed and provide neither an unequivocal vindication nor a resounding indictment of the TVTG.

5.1 The Specifics

For clarity, an effort has been made to summarise the main implications of the survey findings for the TVTG and the ATG in Table 4.2. In some ways Nussbaum and Sen's account of development performs well. Most of the items included on their list of intrinsically valuable capabilities were spontaneously mentioned by a significant number of people. Further probing revealed that the vast majority of respondents agreed that most of these capabilities are important aspects of a good life style. More than 98% of informants chose to endorse the value of good health, avoiding hunger, shelter, happiness, knowledge and friendship, *inter alia*. Hardly any of the human capabilities advanced by Nussbaum and Sen were not ratified by at least 94% of the people we questioned (see Table 4.2). The most notable exceptions include the capability to live long, opportunities for sexual satisfaction and being able to take part in literary and scientific pursuits, which were rejected by a significant proportion of people. In fairness to Nussbaum and Sen, however, there are grounds for questioning the reluctance to endorse the value of sexual fulfilment and living long (see Sections 4.2.6 and 4.4).

The crux of the problem with Nussbaum and Sen's theory of the good appears to emanate from other quarters. Table 4.2 reveals that the TVTG tends to overlook the value of access to income, basic necessities (such as clean water and food), adequate housing, education, training and skills, and reasonable job opportunities. The survey findings also confirm that Nussbaum and Sen's theory pays insufficient attention to the importance of free time, sleep and rest, relaxation and opportunities for recreation. Yet these items performed just as well as the capabilities featured in the original version of the TVTG. A little prompting revealed that respondents also appreciated the value of civil and political rights and personal safety. (A few people freely acknowledged the importance of physical security.)

These findings imply that Nussbaum and Sen's list of human capabilities should be *augmented* to include these items (as suggested in Chapter 3). But the ATG does start to take some liberties by overstating the potential for achieving a genuine consensus. Some of the people we spoke to objected to the idea of adding the 'capability for exercise' and 'being able to avoid noise pollution' to a broadly universal account of the good. Several respondents also expressed doubts about the value of 'being able to travel' and the 'capability for adventure'. Some reservations were also expressed about the value of watching television and visiting the cinema. These things do not appear to be universal components of a good life (see Table 4.2).[66]

Unfortunately, it is not possible to provide a complete assessment of the TVTG or the ATG. There are some gaps in column 5 of Table 4.2. This is because it was not feasible to inquire about the importance of every single capability described in the TVTG and the ATG. (It was not practical or reasonable to subject respondents to longer interviews.) A decision was therefore taken to omit questions about some of the items that are least likely to be contentious, such as the ability to move around, being able to use the five senses and the capability to avoid non-beneficial pain. We can infer that some of these capabilities were valued from the responses survey participants provided to related questions (For example, see the notes in Table 4.2 for items 2i, 2*c and 3b.) There is also strong anecdotal evidence (from both the responses to open questions and secondary sources) to suggest that opportunities for 'Affiliation' and 'Participation in Society' are likely to be broadly universal components of a good life (Table 4.2's items 5, 5* and 7b–7c).[67]

There also appears to be a case for revising the specification of some of the capabilities recorded in Table 4.2. For example, the evidence we have collected implies that Sen's capability to 'keep warm' should be supplemented with the 'ability to keep cool', which is equally important in hot climates (see Sections 4.2.2 and 4.2.5.2). There also seems to be grounds for supplementing the 'ability to love' (item 5b) with ample opportunities for being loved (see Section 4.2.6). The notes in Table 4.2 indicate how we might go about adjusting some of the other capabilities featured in the TVTG and the ATG (e.g. items 4e, 7a and 10a–10b). Few revisions of any consequence appear to be in order.

The survey results also imply that a wide range of potentially valuable capabilities is not accounted for in Table 4.2. An effort has been made to summarise some of the most notable examples of these capabilities in Table 4.3. In particular the theoretical accounts of development we have considered do not explicitly include important human functions such as being clean and hygienic, saving money, having confidence, achieving status, enjoying sport(s) and living a good Christian life. While none of these items are explicitly mentioned by Nussbaum or Sen, many of the capabilities recorded in Table 4.3 (such as confidence, peace of mind and helping others) fit naturally into the Aristotelian framework. Several respondents however, also mentioned capabilities like being respected, feeling proud and achieving status and prestige. These capabilities (vices?) go against the spirit if not the letter of the Aristotelian project, which is committed to the idea of 'virtuous' functioning.

In most cases a precise estimate of how much support each of the items in Table 4.3 commands is not available. In order to gather this information it would have been necessary to process and analyse the responses to open-ended questions before designing and implementing the final part of the survey. This was not a viable option. Returning to the fieldwork sites would have doubled the cost of the survey and created logistical problems in terms of re-locating our original informants. However, an attempt was made to assess the overall performance of some potentially valuable capabilities that are not commonly featured in theoretical accounts of the good.[68] From this exercise it is possible to conclude that certain items recorded in Table 4.3 were not regarded as valuable capabilities by the bulk of respondents. More than a third of respondents refused to endorse the value of achieving status and prestige (see Tables II.2–II.5). A substantial proportion of respondents also failed to endorse having children, wearing fashionable clothing and watching or playing sport (Table II.1). While it is incorrect to assume that these ends are without value, there are clear grounds for striking these things from a development ethic that aims to be as universal as possible. On the other hand, the vast majority of survey participants (96.2%) did confirm that having 'adequate living space' should be included in a practical conception of the good (Table II.3).[69]

5.2 General Conclusions

We can also draw some more general conclusions about the strengths and weaknesses of the TVTG and ATG from the survey findings and case studies reviewed above.

5.2.1 Relevance for the poor
One difficulty is that the reasoning behind the TVTG appears to overlook many of the harsh realities that face ordinary poor people. At times this tends to direct attention away from the capabilities that matter most. For example, consider the function of education. If the items included in Nussbaum and Sen's development ethic are interpreted literally, then the only obvious role for education is to promote the cognitive functions and the power of practical reason.[70] No explicit provisions are made for acquiring practical skills, improving job prospects or raising earnings. But as we have seen, achieving these objectives are the primary reasons for valuing education (Section 4.2.3) and have the potential to make a big difference to the quality of life (see Sections 4.2.1 and 4.2.4).

This defect is inherited from the Aristotelian tradition. In ancient times the Greeks looked down on farm hands and manual labourers whose life styles were thought to lack virtue. Aristotle notices

> . . . that some forms of labour are incompatible with good human functioning. Because they are monotonous and mindless, and demanding in their time requirements, they leave the worker less than fully human, able to perform other functionings only at a less than fully human level. (Nussbaum, 1990, p.230)

Some passages in Aristotle's writings use this kind of reasoning as a justification for excluding manual labourers and farm workers from civilised society. According to Martha Nussbaum, Aristotle's basic argument runs along the following lines:

> We want a good city. A city is good if and only if (all) its parts are good. Manual labourers and farm workers cannot achieve goodness, because their lives lack leisure, and leisure is necessary for virtue. So: don't let these people be parts (citizens) of the city . . . In other words, don't let them pollute the nice structure [virtuous society] we are creating. They may be necessary props or supports but don't let them be *parts*. (Nussbaum, 1988, p.156)

Of course Nussbaum and Sen (like most other contemporary thinkers) do not subscribe to such an extreme position. In fact, Nussbaum not only argues against the prejudicial application of development ethics but also takes the trouble to demonstrate that Aristotle's basic argument here is inconsistent with other elements in his writings. (For example, his criticism of regimes that fail to set aside some of the city's wealth to subsidise common meals for the poor.) In the end Nussbaum effectively concludes that we should design a system that permits 'each and every' manual labourer, farm worker and poor person to 'live well' (Nussbaum, 1988, pp.156–7).

However Nussbaum, like Aristotle before her, does not make any new or discernible provisions in (her version of) the TVTG for the likes of manual labourers and ordinary poor people who have to work for a living. Yet the harsh reality is that a sizeable proportion of the world's population must work and work hard (often in appalling conditions) to survive and make a living. If Nussbaum really wants to make 'each and every' manual labourer and poor person capable of 'living well' her account of the good ought to cater for the prevalence and ubiquity of such life styles.[71] Not everyone can enjoy a life of leisure and virtue.

In particular, Nussbaum's TVTG needs to say something solid about the nature and character of working life. In most poor countries employment in the informal sector of the economy accounts for a substantial part of many people's lives. Workers frequently have to put up with poor and hazardous working conditions and perform physically exhausting and monotonous tasks. Many labourers spend more than half the day at work, which leaves insufficient time for sleep and rest, to be with family and friends and for recreational activities (see Section 4.2.1). For Nussbaum such life styles do not qualify as fully human.[72]

Many kinds of employment however, are compatible not only with human forms of life but also with achieving good forms of life. Some of the theoretical accounts of the good reviewed in the last chapter have pointed towards the importance of 'job satisfaction' and creating valuable opportunities for 'control, skill use and variety in the work place' (see Table 3.2). Nussbaum and Sen's own list of functional capabilities also tends to favour certain occupations. For example, teachers and scientists (in marked contrast to manual labourers and farm workers) are particularly well disposed to take part in the pursuit of knowledge, understanding and wisdom, and cultivate the power of practical reason (Table 3.1's items 4, 6 and 12c).

Of course, the worthy forms of employment implicit in these theories are fundamentally different from the informal mode of employment encountered by the poor. For the vast majority of poor people employment is nothing more than a necessary evil. Wanting a job has very little to do with striving to achieve some 'higher' form of human functioning. Earning a *living* is the central overriding concern. If Nussbaum is serious about improving the quality of life for manual labourers and poor people her theory of the good must say something of substance about the importance of working in a good safe environment, reasonable working hours, job security and effective legal protection, *inter alia*. Most survey participants agreed that achieving these ends has the potential to make a big difference to the overall quality of life[73] (see Section 4.2.1). While these aspects of life have featured prominently in the applied development studies literature, they have often been neglected in purely theoretical accounts of human functioning and philosophical discussions of well-being (contrast Section 4.2.1 with Chapter 3, Section 6).

Other examples of the ways in which theories of the good can direct attention away from some of the most pressing aspects of development are not difficult to find. In Section 4.2.6 we saw that the most important role for family and kin in poor societies is to provide economic and emotional support. However, the specification of Nussbaum's 'Virtues of Affiliation' suggests a different role for family and friends, which seems to be restricted to providing companionship and opportunities to love others (see Table 3.1, items 5 and 7). Some theories of the good do acknowledge the importance of receiving care and support from family and friends (see Table 3.2), but these accounts rarely emphasise these aspects of development.

As far as opportunities for 'affiliation' are concerned, most of the development ethics we have considered focus on the importance of being able to behave and act in certain ways towards other individuals. Consider the emphasis placed upon the value of being friendly, loving others and the virtues of toleration, passion, generosity and sharing in Table 3.2. Most theories of well-being say relatively little about the other side of the equation. The emphasis is on *giving* rather than *receiving* of love, friendship and charity. Of course, the evidence presented above implies that this sentiment should be reversed: for those living on the edge what really matters is receiving aid and comfort. The crux of the problem is that some development ethics seem to be more concerned with recommending ways of interacting with other people that are consistent with 'virtuous' functioning, than with promoting the subject's *own* personal well-being.

These difficulties reflect the fact that most theories of the human good abstract from the practical side of survival and development in poor countries. The TVTG, in particular, is not sensitive to some important forms of poverty. No special provisions are made to improve working conditions or guarantee access to certain basic needs (see above). Theoretical accounts of the good life also tend to neglect the social consequence of extreme poverty. Yet we have seen that a high premium is often placed on achievements like escaping from stress and frustration and avoiding mischief and crime in poor societies. Most theories of human well-being also tend to neglect the fact that the family is not always a virtuous institution (see Section 4.2.6). For a stark contrast between theoretical and practical conceptions of development compare Table 4.2 with Table 4.3.

Nussbaum and Sen both intend the capability approach to be useful for understanding and evaluating different forms of poverty (see Nussbaum and Sen, 1993). In fact, Sen started to develop the 'Basic Capability' approach for this very purpose (Sen, 1980; 1984; 1993; 1999). In particular, Sen focuses on hunger and health in his extensive writings on famine, and has also made much of the importance of literacy and shelter, *inter alia*. The fact that these items appear in the TVTG means that Nussbaum and Sen's development ethic is not completely divorced from some of the most crucial aspects of poverty and deprivation.

Some accounts of development however, do seem to be a little more receptive to the dilemmas and concerns of poor people. In Chapter 3 we saw that some social scientists include items like income, basic goods, job opportunities and physical security in their account of the good. If the capability approach to poverty is to be used to its full potential it must not neglect these (and other) basic achievements. So far Sen has explored the moral and political implications of conceptualising poverty in terms of capability failure.[74] He has not yet developed a comprehensive list of basic capabilities on which to base his concept of poverty. The survey results presented in this book may be able to assist with this task.

In the main, Nussbaum and Sen are concerned with the full range of human capabilities that make up a *good* life style.[75] Human development is not confined to avoiding poverty (see Chapter 3, Section 2.2). In fact, the capability approach is designed to be just as applicable to rich countries. Nussbaum's theory of the good is deliberately 'vague' (abstract) in order to provide space for pluralism. This is a strength as well as a weakness.

On balance however, there does seem to be scope for including a (more) substantial list of 'basic capabilities' in a working conception of the good *without* compromising the methodological requirement for 'vagueness'. Different cultures and societies (irrespective of their achievements on the development frontier) can probably reach a sustainable agreement about the most basic human functionings and capabilities (see Chapter 2, Section 7). This implies that a broadly universal development ethic can take explicit account of most, if not all, forms of poverty encountered by the poor.

5.2.2 Physical and mental functioning

The evidence considered above confirms that the capability approach should concern itself with the *physical condition* of the person. Many important functions connected with quality housing and good living conditions are endorsed in Nussbaum and Sen's list of 'bodily capabilities', e.g. health, shelter and keeping warm. Adding the requirement for items like adequate living space and clean hygienic living conditions is a natural extension of this approach. Similar points can be made about the physical capabilities associated with the consumption of food and clothing.

However, respondents also valued the resources and activities we asked about in order to enhance their *state of mind* (as well as their physical condition). In particular, informants felt that things like money, good jobs, adequate housing, food and clothing, a solid family and recreation help to facilitate 'happiness', 'pleasure' and 'joy'. In fact, no other 'functioning' was associated with so many different activities (see Tables I.2–I.10 and I.12–I.15).[76] This is where the TVTG (like most other development ethics) is relatively weak. Respondents also mentioned the importance of relaxation, avoiding stress and frustration, self-confidence and status (see also Table 4.3). It follows that a comprehensive account of the psychology of human well-being must go beyond some basic notion of utility.

The basic needs approach appears to commit the same error by focusing on the person's physical condition at the expense of his or her state of mind. In contrast to Welfarism (which merely conflates different psychological functionings), the basic needs literature tends to overlook these aspects of human development altogether. On the other hand, some proponents of the capability approach (including Nussbaum and Sen) do point to the value of happiness, self-respect and relaxation. The capability approach can also be extended to incorporate a diverse range of psychological functionings without conflating or obscuring the different categories.

5.2.3 Recreation and 'good living'
For most people recreation makes the difference between achieving a minimally decent form of life and a good life. Indeed, for Aristotle and the Ancient Greeks a life of leisure is a prerequisite for human flourishing. Yet this is an area in which most contemporary development ethics have little to say. Some of these theories pay lip service to the importance of free time and recreation (see Table 3.2), but none of the schemes emphasise the contribution that recreation makes to personal well-being. Martha Nussbaum, for example, explicitly sets out to describe the central features of a good human life, and to argue that the state should ensure that each and every individual is able to function accordingly (e.g. Nussbaum, 1990).[77] The problem is that her development ethic says little of substance about the role of leisure (see Chapter 3, Section 6). The survey findings reviewed above, however, indicate that development ethics should say something solid about the value of a wide range of recreational pursuits such as sport, watching television, visiting the cinema, listening to music, singing and dancing and reading books (see Section 4.2.8). One of the reasons Nussbaum does not elaborate on the requirement for leisure is to avoid compromising the reach of

the TVTG.[78] Relativists would not have to go to much trouble to demonstrate that activities such as following sport, watching television and reading books are not valued by all cultures or by all groups of people living in communities that do value these ends (as the survey findings summarised in Section 4.2.8 confirm). One possibility is to develop a separate list of capabilities that includes some of the more popular recreational pursuits (and other 'higher' human functions) that are not generally valued by all individuals and societies. This list could be used to supplement the TVTG, and should be adapted for different cultures and societies in accordance with the methodology developed in the last chapter.

6. SOME CONCLUDING REMARKS

An effort has been made to confront some of the abstract concepts of development employed in the academic literature with the views of some ordinary poor people. In particular, I have attempted to examine the implications of this exercise for Nussbaum and Sen's development ethic. The conclusions are mixed. Much however, depends on how the survey findings are interpreted.

On one reading, development is about *economic security* and access to food, water, clothing and other basic necessities. (Many respondents expressed the desire for economic security in terms of acquiring money, reasonable jobs or the necessary education and skills to guarantee a regular wage. The need for security was also expressed in terms of the desire to save money in the bank, avoid debt and pay the rent on time.) Development is living in adequate housing that is properly furnished and has running water, proper drainage, reasonable toilet facilities and electricity. Development is also about personal liberty (negative freedom) and living in a safe environment. Belonging to a caring family and having loyal and reliable friends that can provide advice and support in times of trouble are also central features of development. For some people development also includes access to some of the 'better things in life' such as luxury goods and recreational and sports facilities.

An alternative interpretation of the survey findings views development in terms of the ends of life. What really matters is whether or not people can achieve their ultimate goals and objectives. On this reading of the survey findings development is about being able to achieve final ends such as good health, confidence, happiness, knowledge, friendship, love, rest, relaxation and independence. Nussbaum and Sen's capability approach helps to facilitate our understanding of human development by directing attention towards the ultimate ends of life. Their work has also accurately identified several examples of intrinsically valuable ends (see Table 4.2).

The distinction between means and ends adds clarity to the concept of development. Insofar as it is possible to draw a sharp distinction between these two categories we can separate the 'objects' of a good life from everything else. But the distinction between means (inputs) and ends (ultimate objectives) is much less robust than it appears. First, most if not all intrinsically valuable ends carry some instrumental significance. Health, confidence and happiness are all obvious examples of valuable ends that can promote good human functioning in other spheres of life. In a word, the ends recorded in Table 4.2 are also means. Second, many of the objects frequently construed as means may also qualify as valuable ends. A good job may carry intrinsic value insofar as it endows life with meaning and substance or represents a valuable accomplishment.[79] The acquisition of knowledge, understanding and skills and the cultivation of natural assets (such as conscientiousness) are more obvious examples of potentially valuable ends that have sometimes been portrayed as nothing more than means. Physical security, civil liberty and freedom, family and friends and recreation also seem to possess large elements of both intrinsic and instrumental value.

Economic resources such as food, clean water and electricity may also carry at least some intrinsic value. But as one of my critics has pointed out: 'Because poor people think that clean water is important does not necessarily mean that clean water has intrinsic rather than instrumental value'.[80] This is a valid observation. Notice however, that the argument works both ways. In fact, the realisation that poor people attach so much weight to the importance of clean water suggests that we should not automatically dismiss the possibility that clean water may have some *intrinsic* value. Furthermore, it is unlikely that many of the people we interviewed would be inclined to agree that key resources such as water lack intrinsic value. This supposition was confirmed on a recent trip to Murraysburg. Even after the distinction between intrinsic and instrumental value was explained to a local community leader, he continued to insist that 'water is valuable in its own right because nothing can or will happen without it' (Interview with Isaac Dokter, 26 May 1999).[81]

It follows that most objects of value have intrinsic and instrumental significance. In some cases it is difficult to decide what should count as means and what should count as ends. As far as I am aware, Nussbaum and Sen have not yet confronted this issue. In some essays, Sen cites 'the power to fulfil one's requirements for clothing' as an example of an intrinsically valuable capability (e.g. Sen, 1984, p.281; 1992, p.110). Clothing clearly is essential for the promotion of valuable functionings such as avoiding shame, keeping warm and being fashionable. But it is not clear why Sen thinks clothing is a valuable end in itself.[82] Nor is it clear why clothing is considered to have intrinsic value while food and jobs only appear to have extrinsic significance for Sen (see Sen, 1987a). If clothing can count as a valuable end in its own right so can resources such as food, water and jobs.

There also appears to be some disagreement in academic circles about how to categorise some of these items. Paul Streeten (1994) distinguishes between Humanitarians and Resource Developers. According to Streeten, the Humanitarians tend to value things like participation and education for their own sake. In contrast, the Resource Developers regard these things as pure means (ibid., pp.233–4).

The lack of an obvious boundary between means and ends raises difficulties for the capability approach, which aims to conceptualise development in terms of ultimate objectives only. One way of tackling this problem is to appeal to the values of local people and let them decide what counts as intrinsically valuable. The survey findings considered above imply that several items traditionally viewed as pure means (such as food, water, electricity, housing and jobs) may well qualify as worthwhile ends in their own right. (While respondents were not asked to distinguish between means and ends, we encouraged them to focus on the latter by repeatedly asking about the objects of a good life style.)

Insofar as we are concerned with the concept and meaning of development we can restrict attention to the identification and clarification of valuable ends. In terms of devising development strategy and policy however, a good understanding of the objectives we want to achieve is not sufficient. Attention must also be devoted to the means for achieving these ends. It follows that Nussbaum and Sen's development ethic needs to be supplemented with a list of economic primary goods, i.e. the material things necessary to facilitate good human functioning.[83] Notice that this argument does not depend on demonstrating that inputs such as food and water possess some intrinsic value and therefore warrant inclusion in a credible development ethic.

Policy makers however, must proceed with caution and take care not to lose sight of the ends that ultimately matter. Means have a nasty habit of acquiring the characteristics of undesirable ends (Streeten, 1994, p.233). Focusing on means can also lead to the neglect of those aspects of development least connected with raising economic production, such as housing and civil rights in contrast to inputs like education and employment. Concentrating exclusively on means can be counter-productive. Ultimately, some hard choices must be made.

7. POSTSCRIPT

The fieldwork findings presented in this book are supported by the results of a recent survey on the *Essentials of Life*, which I administered in Murraysburg, Kwanonqaba and Khubus in June and July 2001. The aim of this survey was to help define poverty by investigating how ordinary people view the essential things in life. Preliminary findings indicate that jobs, housing, education, health, nutrition, food and water, safety, freedom, self-respect, survival and religion are core components of a minimally decent life style (see Clark and Qizilbash, 2002). It should be emphasised that this survey asked about the 'bare essentials' of life 'without which a [typical] person cannot cope or manage at all' rather than some more ambitious notion of 'good living' or human development.

Table 4.2 A Normative Evaluation of Nussbaum and Sen's list of 'Functional Capabilities' and the ATG

(A) Physical Capabilities	TVTG	ATG	(4) Item Nominated?	(5) Level of Consensus	Notes
1. Capability to Live a Long Life	N&S	Yes		x	Like 'survival'. See Tables I.4, I.5 and I.7
2. Bodily Capabilities					
(a) Being able to have good health	N&S	Yes	✓	✓✓	See Tables I.1, I.3, I.7, I.8, I.10 and II.1
(b) Being able to be adequately nourished	N&S	Yes	✓	✓✓	See Tables I.7 and II.7
(c) Capability to be free from hunger	S	Yes	✓	✓✓	See Tables I.7 and II.7
(d) Being able to have adequate shelter	N&S	Yes	✓	✓✓	See Tables I.3, I.8 and II.1
(e) The power to fulfil one's requirements for clothing	S	Yes	✓	✓	See Tables I.1, I.2, I.5, I.6, I.8 and II.1
(f) Being able to keep warm	S	Yes	✓	na	Also 'Keep Cool'. See Table I.8
(g) Having opportunities for sexual satisfaction	N	Yes		x	See Table II.1
(h) Having opportunities for choice in matters of reproduction	N	Yes		x	'Family planning' in Table II.1
(i) Being able to move from place to place	N&S	Yes		na	But see item 2*(d) below
(j) Being able to sleep and rest	-	Yes	✓	✓	See Tables I.3, I.10 and I.11
(k) Being able to exercise	-	Yes	?	x	'Physical fitness'. See Tables I.10 and II.1
2* Essential Inputs					
(a) Access to basic necessities, including	-	Yes	✓	na	See Tables I.2 and I.5
(i) Nutritional food	-	Yes	✓	✓✓	'Enough Food'. Tables I.1, I.2, I.6 and II.5
(ii) clean water	-	Yes	✓	✓✓	See Tables I.3, II.1 and II.3
(iii) clothing	-	Yes	✓	✓✓	See item 2(e) above
(iv) sanitation and	-	Yes	✓	✓✓	See Tables I.3, II.1 and II.3
(v) fuel for cooking and heating	-	Yes		✓✓	See Table II.1
(b) Access to adequate housing	-	Yes	✓	✓✓	See Tables I.1, I.2, I.4–I.6 and II.1
(c) Access to medical and health care	-	Yes		na*	But see item 2(a) above
(d) Access to appropriate means of transportation	-	Yes		✓	See Table II.1

Table 4.2 (cont.)

(B) Mental Well-being and Intellectual Development	TVTG	ATG	(4) Item Nominated?	(5) Level of Consensus	Notes
3. Capacity for Pleasure and Pain					
(a) Being able to have pleasurable experiences	N&S	Yes	✓	✓ ✓	'Joy', 'Happiness'. See Tables I.1–I.10 and II.1
(b) Being able to avoid unnecessary and non beneficial pain, so far as is possible	N	Yes		na	But see item 3(a) above
4. Cognitive Capabilities (Understanding, Knowledge and Skills)					
(a) Being able to use the five senses	N	Yes		na	'Think, learn and gain experience'. See Tables I.10 and II.1
(b) Being able to imagine, think, and to reason	N	Yes	?	✓	Like 'Knowledge'. See Tables I.2, I.4 and II.4
(c) Being acceptably well informed	S	Yes	?	✓ ✓	See Tables I.4 and II.4
(d) Being able to read, write, count and communicate	S	Yes	✓	✓	'Skills', 'Qualifications'. See Tables I.1, I.4, I.10 and II.4
(e) Being able to use (other) basic skills and abilities	-	Yes	✓	✓ ✓	See Table II.4
(f) Being able to take part in literary and scientific pursuits	S	Yes		x	
4a Other Natural Capabilities (or 'Natural assets')					
(a) Capability to be creative	-	Yes		na	
(b) Capacity for receptiveness, curiosity and intuition	-	Yes		na	
(c) Capacity for discipline, determination and motivation	-	Yes		✓	See Table II.1
4* Essential Inputs					
(a) Access to education	-	Yes	✓	✓ ✓	See Tables I.1, I.4–I.6 and II.1

See the *notes* at the end of this table

Continued/....

Table 4.2 (cont.)

(C) **Relating and Interacting**	TVTG	ATG	(4) Item Nominated?	(5) Level of Consensus	Notes
5. Opportunities for Affiliation I (Compassion)					
(a) Being able to have attachments to things and persons outside ourselves	N	Yes	?	✔ ✔	Good Family/ Personal Relationships See Tables I.1, I.3, I.9 and II.1
(b) Being able to love, to grieve, to experience longing and gratitude; and	N	Yes	?	na	'Love Each Other', 'Being Loved'. See Tables I.1 and I.9
Capacity for toleration, passion, generosity, appreciation and sharing		Yes	?	na	Support family, help others. See Tables I.1, I.2, I.5, I.6, I.9 and II.5
5* Essential Inputs					
(a) Access to the care and support of family and friends	-	Yes	✔	na	Also 'Good Family'. See Tables I.1 and I.9
7. Opportunities for Affiliation II (Friendship and Participation in Society)					
(a) Being capable of friendship; and	N	Yes	✔	✔ ✔	'Good friends', 'New Friends'. See Tables I.1, I.8–I.10, I.15 and II.1
Being able to visit and entertain friends	S	No	✔	✔	See Tables I.5, I.9, I.10 and II.8
(b) Being able to participate in the life of the community; and	S	No	?	na	Overlaps with items 7(a), 9 and 9*
(c) Being able to participate in certain meaningful social activities	-	Yes	?	na	Overlaps with items 7(a), 9 and 9*
7* Essential Inputs					
(a) Being able to obtain and participate in employment	-	Yes	✔	✔ ✔	See Tables I.1, I.2, I.4 and II.1
(b) Access to good working conditions	-	Yes		✔ ✔	See Table II.2 and Section 4.2.1 above
(c) Opportunities for control, skill use and variety in the work place	-	Yes		na	

8. Interaction with the Environment

(a) Being able to live with concern for and in relation to animals, plants and the world of nature	N	Yes	✓	✓✓	See Table II.12
(b) Being able to live in a clean environment; and	-	Yes	✓	✓	Being 'clean and hygienic'. See Tables I.3, I.8 and II.1
Being able to breathe unpolluted air	S	Yes	✓✓	✓✓	See Table II.12
(c) Capability to avoid noise pollution	-	Yes		x	See Table II.12

9. Opportunities for Recreational Activities

(a) Having opportunities for free time	-	Yes	?	✓	'Time to do important things', etc. See Tables I.10, I.11 and II.1
(b) Being able to laugh, to play, to enjoy recreational activities	N	Yes	✓	✓	See Tables I.1 and II.1. Also 'social activities' in Tables II.5 and II.8
(c) Being able to relax, daydream and remember	-	Yes	✓	✓✓	'Relaxation'. See Tables I.1, I.3, I.10 and II.8
(d) Being able to absorb, appreciate and enjoy nature	-	Yes	?	na*	'Taking walks', 'gardening', 'nature reserves'. See Table I.11
(e) Being able to respond to forms of beauty	-	Yes	✓	na*	
(f) Capability for adventure	-	Yes	✓	x	See Tables I.10 and II.8

9* Activities Worthy of Investigation

(a) Being able to travel and go on vacation	S	Yes	✓	x	See Tables I.5, I.6, I.10, I.11 and II.8
(b) Being able to play games	-	Yes	✓	na*	See Table I.11
(c) Being able to watch television and go to the cinema	-	Yes	✓	x	See Tables I.10, I.11 and II.1
(d) Being able to go to pubs, clubs and parties	-	Yes		na*	

Continued/....

Table 4.2 (cont.)

(D) Personal Autonomy and Freedom	TVTG	ATG	(4) Item Nominated?	(5) Level of Consensus	Notes
6. Capacity for Practical Reason					
(a) Being able to form a conception of the good	N&S	Yes		na	But see items 6(b) and 6(c) below
(b) Capability to choose; ability to form goals, commitments, values	S	Yes		✓	Like 'capacity to think, reason and make choices' in Table II.4
(c) Being able to engage in critical reflection about the planning of one's own life	N&S	Yes		✓✓	'Improving ability to plan life and make choices' in Table II.1
10. Separateness (Negative Freedom and Civil and Political Rights)					
(a) Being able to live one's own life and nobody else's; freedom to 'rule one's own life'	N	Yes	?	✓✓	'Independence', in Tables I.1–I.5. 'Self-determination' in Table II.1
(b) Being able to live in one's very own surroundings and context; freedom from external interference with one's own affairs, including	N	Yes	?	✓✓	As above
(i) Physical security (personal safety): being able to avoid violence, physical harm and injury	-	Yes	✓	✓✓	See Tables I.1, I.3 and II.1
(ii) Political rights (right to vote, hold public office, freedom of speech and assembly)	-	Yes		✓✓	See Table II.1
(iii) Equality of opportunity and social mobility	-	Yes	✓	✓	'Opportunities for advancement'. See Tables I.2, I.4 and II.1
(iv) Right to hold private property	-	Yes		✓✓	See Table II.1
11. Self-respect					
(a) Capability to have self-respect	S	Yes	✓	na	See Tables I.2–I.5, I.9 and II.1
(b) Capability 'to appear in public without shame'	S	Yes		na	But see Section 4.2.5.2 above

12. Capability to Function (Positive Freedom)

(a) Ability to achieve valuable functionings	S	Yes	✓	na	Ability to 'Do the things you want'. See Tables I.4, I.5 and I.10

12* Essential Inputs

(a) Access to economic resources including				
(i) income and wealth	-	Yes	✓	'Good/more Income'. See Tables I.1–I.3, I.6 and II.1
(ii) goods and services	-	Yes	✓	See Tables I.2, I.5 and II.5
(b) Access to discretionary income, and luxury and consumer durable goods, such as	-	Yes	x	'Luxury goods'. See Tables I.2, I.5, II.1 and II.5
(i) Cars	-	Yes	✓ na*	See Tables I.1 and I.6
(ii) bicycles	-	Yes	✓ na*	See Table I.6
(iii) radios	-	Yes	✓ na*	See Tables I.6 and I.11
(iv) televisions	-	Yes	✓ na*	See Tables I.6 and I.11
(v) refrigerators, washing machines, irons, kettles, cookers, vacuum cleaners	-	Yes	? na*	'Electrical Appliances' in Table I.6
(vi) telephones	-	Yes	na*	

Notes

N = Nussbaum
S = Sen
TVTG = Thick Vague Theory of the Good
ATG = Augmented Theory of the Good

Source: Table 3.2 and Annex

Key for Column 4

✓ = Item spontaneously mentioned in interviews (and featured in Tables I.1–I.11)
? = Similar to item(s) spontaneously mentioned in interviews (and featured in Tables I.1–I.11)

Key for Column 5

✓✓ = Endorsed by at least 98% of all respondents
✓ = Endorsed by at least 94% of all respondents
x = Not endorsed by at least 94% of all respondents.
na = Question not asked.
na* = Question not asked but see Tables II.6 and II.9

Table 4.3 A Selection of Other Items Nominated as Valuable 'Functional Capabilities'

(A) Physical Capabilities	(B) Mental States and Intellectual Development
Being clean and hygienic	Confidence
Adequate living space	Peace of mind/ less worries
	Avoiding stress and frustration
Inputs:	Feel safe and secure
To save money	
Investment/ insurance	Status and prestige
Acquiring assets	Feel proud (pride)
Pay-off debts, bonds, loans/ settle bills	Feel good
Pay rent	To be somebody/ to be successful
	To be reliable/ responsible
Having a business	
	Privacy
Good/ fashionable clothes	
	To broaden view of life
Furniture	
	Satisfying appetite
Motor car	

Continued/....

Table 4.3 (cont.)

(C) Interacting/ Relating	(D) Personal Autonomy and Freedom
Living a religious/ Christian life	Independence
Strong family relations	1) Self sufficiency/ earn own money
Emotional security, moral support and comfort	2) 'Do own thing'
Avoiding loneliness	Convenience
Family provide advice and help	
Solve problems	Good/ secure future prospects
Having children	To comply with social protocol
Provide/ care for children	To be like others/ fit in
	Being fashionable/ having a good image
Support/ care for family and friends	
Assist/ help others	Being neat and tidy/ smart and presentable
Gain respect	Looking attractive/ beautiful
Mutual respect	
Respect others	Facing a challenge
Be successful/ achieve something	
Living in a good area ('live elsewhere')	
Keep occupied/ avoid boredom	
Keep away from crime, mischief and trouble	
Inputs:	
Sport(s)	
Music, singing and dancing	

Source: Tables I.1–I.11

NOTES

1. The surveys I have managed to locate that deal with perceptions of development in specific locations are usually confined to questions about the perceived quality of life and/or existing development projects. How satisfied are people with various different aspects of their lives and the overall standard of living? Is the quality of life expected to improve? Are people aware of current development initiatives? Have they benefited from or participated in local development projects? See for example Beukes and Van Der Colff (1997), Moller (1996; 1997), Naqvi et al. (1995) and PSLSD (1994, ch. 12), *inter alia*. This is rather like putting the cart before the horse if the objective is to promote community-based development. (In fairness, some of these surveys have included one or two open questions about the most pressing problems facing the community and the things the government could do to improve living conditions.)

    Similarly, most participatory poverty studies do no provide detailed information on perceptions of human well-being and development. Instead these studies are usually concerned with other issues such as identifying the cause of poverty or investigating possible strategies for sustainable human development. See for example MEPD (1997), Moore et al. (1998), Narayan et al. (2000) and SA-PPA (1998).
2. The design of the questionnaire benefited from the advice of experienced fieldworkers. I am particularly grateful to Dudley Horner, Peter Nolan, Valerie Moller and John Sender for helpful comments. Useful lessons were also learned from some of the difficulties encountered during the administration of the 1993 Living Standards and Development Survey in South Africa by SALDRU and the World Bank (PSLSD, 1994). Wilson and Horner (1996) have discussed some of these difficulties.
3. The two teams consisted of the following personnel: Mr S. Adams, Mr S. Broderick, Mr S. Kuhn, Mr W. Levendal (the Murraysburg interviewers), and Ms M. Grove, Ms S. Jacobs, Ms J. Mdlankomo, Ms L. Zondi (the Wallacedene interviewers). The fieldwork supervisors were Mr D. Clark (in Murraysburg), and Mr D. Clark and Ms J. Goldin (in Wallacedene).
4. Statistics derived from the 1996 Census (released after our survey) put the population of the village of Murraysburg at 4,335. The population of the village has increased since the 1991 Census, and is heavily skewed in favour of Coloured people who make up more than two-thirds of the population. There is a modest gender skew in favour of women, and a significant age bias in favour of young people and children (see CSS, 1992; SSA, 1999).
5. The sampling interval was obtained by dividing a rough estimate of the number of households in the village (2,800) by the sample size (80 people). Unfortunately, we significantly overestimated the number of houses in the village and were forced to revisit the terrain in order to complete the survey. (1,336 dwellings were enumerated in the 1996 Census (SSA, 1999).) A more realistic sampling interval would have been something like every 17th house. An effort was made to compensate for this error by visiting houses that fell roughly in-between the households we had already visited. By the end of the survey we had visited approximately every 15th to 18th household in the village.
6. The 1996 Census puts the total population of Wallacedene at 19,513, which is composed largely of Black African (13,866) and Coloured (5,287) people, and roughly equal numbers of men and women. The majority of these people were of working age (between 18 and 59 years old), and only a small minority had passed retirement age (see SSA, 1999).
7. The aim was to give every household in the township an equal chance of being selected.
8. These figures do not include those in full time education who were mostly children, and consistently denied receiving money or resources from any source whatsoever. It was evident however, that these individuals were in fact, supported by their family or friends.
9. The average monthly per capita income for South Africa as a whole in 1993 was R468 (PSLSD, 1994, table 13.1.2). More than half the people interviewed in both survey areas still received considerably less than this sum in terms of money and food in March 1998 (despite living in one of the richer provinces). The poorest 40% of the survey respondents (which included many Coloured people) reported receipt of a monthly income in 1998 broadly equivalent to the per capita income of the poorest racial group (the Black South

Africans) in 1993.

10. These figures are echoed at the national level. For South Africa as a whole, 54.5% of individuals aged over 14 completed at least Standard 6 (eight years of schooling) in 1993 and 37.5% of people aged over 16 had achieved Standard 8 (ten years of schooling) (PSLSD, 1994, table 3.6).

11. On this occasion I shall refrain from dividing the sample by race. Table 4.1 shows that the two main racial groups included in the survey sample are not evenly split between the two fieldwork sites. The Coloured people we interviewed were concentrated in Murraysburg while the Black Africans included in the sample resided mostly in Wallacedene. This implies that the results derived from analysing the fieldwork findings in terms of these two racial categories would probably correspond closely to the results derived from dividing the survey sample by location. No effort has been made to divide the survey sample according to income group. The vast majority of respondents were extremely poor and, as previously stated, it is the attitudes of poor people with which we are primarily concerned.

12. The idea of false consciousness – as we have seen – also provides a possible justification for abandoning utility based concepts of development in favour of a more objective account of the human good (such as the capability approach).

13. As we have seen the excerpt cited below contrasts sharply with other passages in Nussbaum's writings. See also Clark (1998).

14. These remarks do not necessarily imply that the preferences expressed by individuals in the survey areas were fully informed. There are many different levels of social consciousness. (I am grateful to Dudley Horner for drawing my attention to the example of a disadvantaged person who could imagine and expressed a preference to be a surgeon until he discovered that achieving this end would entail a lot of hard work and spending several years at medical school. Once fully informed, he promptly decided that endeavouring to become a surgeon was not such a good idea after all, and would not constitute a good kind of life for him.) Individual preferences in the fieldwork areas appear to be sufficiently well informed to provide a meaningful set of conclusions about the nature and form of a genuinely good life style for most of the people we interviewed. I shall have more to say about social consciousness in the two fieldwork areas when the survey results are discussed (see Section 4).

15. See also Beukes and Van Der Colff (1997), Hill (1984), Horner (1995), Manganyi (1984), Moller (1997), Morifi (1984), Ntoane and Mokoetle (1984), PSLSD (1994, table 12.2), Sender and Johnston (1996) and Standing et al. (1996).

16. Several other respondents mentioned the value of an education for others (usually their children). If these responses are included in the 'education' category the proportion of respondents mentioning this item rises to just over one half.

17. When we specifically asked about the value of jobs in the tutored part of interviews the result was reversed: jobs were rated more highly by men than by women (see Table II.1.2).

18. Slightly more emphasis was placed upon the importance of this item in Murraysburg. This is probably because personal incomes are particularly low in rural areas.

19. Both survey areas were predominately Christian and the Church was powerful. In some other parts of South Africa people would probably have mentioned the value of living Muslim, Hindu and Jewish life styles.

20. More than 60 other distinct items received a small number of mentions (from five people or fewer).

21. The relative importance of jobs, housing and schools for the South African poor was also picked up in the SALDRU survey (PSLSD, 1994, table 12.2). See also Beukes and Van Der Colff (1997) and Horner (1995).

22. The respondents' answers were eventually fitted into a total of 90 distinct categories although there is some overlap between different categories. For further details see the Annex.

23. This is a bold statement that I shall support in my discussion of Table II.1 and Tables II.1.1-II.1.3 (see Section 4.4). Valerie Moller's (1996, pp.33–4) survey of Kwa-Zulu Natal asked a question designed to test whether all of the RDP's development goals were considered to be equally pressing. Respondents were asked to decide which of the RDP's

five objectives (improving the education, housing, water, electricity or job situation) could be delayed if the government could not afford to attend to all these problems immediately. More than two-thirds of respondents thought that none of these objectives could be deferred. (Strictly speaking respondents were required to choose one of the five options. While the response category 'none' was recorded, it was not read out to respondents as a valid option.)

24. The financial aspect of independence was emphasised by respondents residing in Murraysburg where paid employment is relatively scarce.

25. Only 'opportunities for advancement' received enough mentions during our survey to earn a place in Table I.2. Job security (ranked in 53rd place) and good/safe working conditions (in 56th place) were also spontaneously mentioned by a small minority of respondents.

26. This includes a large number of people traditionally classified as self-employed or as working in agricultural activities.

27. Sometimes workers are forced to involve their entire family (including extremely young children) in the production process.

28. Breman points to the appearance of wrist-watches among the Indian poor.

29. Only a small number of respondents mentioned these items. The findings and conclusions in this paragraph must therefore be treated with care.

30. In some cases interviewers only recorded the word 'security' or 'protection' on the questionnaire form. I am fairly certain that respondents were referring to security from 'crime' and 'physical harm' and protection from 'danger'. I have therefore included these responses in a single category (Table I.3, item 2). However, it is possible that some respondents may have been referring to economic security or protection from the elements. I have made an effort to distinguish between these items in Table I.3.

31. In Murraysburg even the brick houses of the relatively affluent Coloureds only had thin wooden front doors.

32. For a good overview of the issues and some of the surveys conducted in South Africa see Wilson and Ramphele (1989, ch. 6). Breman (1996) discusses several aspects of poor housing and living conditions in India.

33. The translation of the Afrikaans text in this quotation is provided by Wilson and Ramphele (1989, p.125) and has been corrected to read '. . . because there is not enough space' instead of '. . . because there is not enough place'. I have confirmed that this is a more accurate translation in correspondence with Professor Wilson.

34. Some respondents also valued a good education on the grounds that it can improve the standard of living. Most of these respondents resided in the township of Wallacedene where living conditions are comparatively poor.

35. One reason for valuing the capability to read and write is to improve employment prospects and earn a living. In developing countries the criterion of literacy is often used by employers to help allocate scarce jobs. But the fact that literacy was rated highly by respondents who had reached (or were approaching) retirement age implies that this is not the only reason for valuing literacy. Several respondents (mostly in the youngest two age groups) simply stated that they valued an education in order to learn (Table I.4).

36. In South Africa pensions and social security transfers are also regarded as valuable sources of income by the poor (see Moller, 1996, pp.26, 28; Standing et al., 1996).

37. A commitment to a humanistic way of life that involves sharing, trust and treating all people with respect in an effort to promote the common good (see Sindane, 1995).

38. The ordinal rankings expressed in Tables I.5 and II.5.A does not simply reflect the fact that respondents who had not previously commented on the importance of supporting family and friends were required to evaluate this item in the tutored part of the interview. A closer inspection of the survey results shows that the attitudes of most individuals did change. In the untutored part of the interview fifteen people stated that the most important reason for valuing income was to support family and friends. But in the tutored part of the interview only seven people ranked this item in first place. More importantly, only two of the original fifteen respondents continued to maintain that supporting family and friends was the most important reason for wanting income.

39. Almost three-quarters of respondents mentioned this item. Nearly all these people stated

that spending on housing was their top priority.

40. SALDRU estimates that the poorest South Africans typically spend less that 10% of their budget on housing (PSLSD, 1994, table 8.5).

41. The number of cars encountered during my visit to Murraysburg could be counted on the fingers of one hand. As I pulled into the gas station for some petrol in a 1996 Honda the pump attendant asked if I was 'with the movies'.

42. I am reliably informed that some poor South Africans have expressed a desire to assist their local community by creating jobs. I owe this insight to Jaqui Goldin.

43. This approach has limitations. It is conceivable that a person may consciously choose to consume foods like chocolate cake, ice-cream and beef-burgers without actually valuing the ability to eat these products. Some men and children also objected to this question (and even refused to answer) on the grounds that it is not their responsibility to select the foods their household consumes.

44. This is reflected in the overall ranking of these two items in Table I.7.

45. Respondents also mentioned other practical issues such as the need for durable clothes, and a desire for clean clothes to promote personal hygiene and cleanliness. Some people even valued good clothes in order to facilitate personal autonomy ('being myself') or enhance their social life.

46. Even young adults (people in the 20–34 age bracket) were often reluctant to endorse the value of sexual fulfilment (Table II.1.3).

47. Unfortunately I failed to fully appreciate the importance of religion and the church prior to the administration of my surveys.

48. The importance of sleep and rest takes fifth place in Table I.10 and was mentioned by 12.1% of all respondents. This item can carry connotations of laziness and idleness, which are scorned in African culture. In consequence some respondents may have been reluctant to mention the value of this item. I owe this insight to Valerie Moller.

49. Wilson and Ramphele (1989) and Breman (1996) both touch on this point.

50. We can infer from Table II.1 that watching and playing sports were equally valued.

51. Only one person spontaneously mentioned the consumption of alcohol. Nobody mentioned smoking.

52. Some men appeared to share these views. The remarks in this paragraph also apply to smoking tobacco as well as the use of other stronger substances.

53. In Murraysburg, 23 people admitted to either drinking and/or smoking. A further 21 people admitted to participating in at least one of these activities in Wallacedene. Together these individuals account for approximately 28% of the survey sample. Isaac Dokter (1996, p.10) reports that alcohol and drug abuse is a major social problem in Murraysburg.

54. Unfortunately, I inadvertently included a skip instruction in the questionnaire (part II, question 10.1) that directed interviewers not to ask respondents if they valued drinking or smoking if they had confessed to taking part in these activities. Some interviewers had the sense to ignore this instruction.

55. Although Murraysburg lacks a park and theatre, the village does have some sports facilities (including two rugby fields, two tennis courts and one football pitch), a library, a social club for the elderly, and some youth clubs organised by the church (see Dokter, 1996, p.10). Respondents in both survey areas had access to radio and television.

56. These items were mentioned but did not receive enough support to earn a place in Table I.11. One or two respondents also mentioned the value of hiking and mountaineering, scuba-diving, horse riding, camping out and parties.

57. The idea of false consciousness implies that a disadvantaged person is unable to imagine a better life style and is satisfied with his or her lot in life.

58. I will account for the lack of support for water and electricity in Table I.1 later (see Section 4.4).

59. The intense form of political consciousness described here is common in South African society. A recent survey of Kwa-Zulu Natal found that three-quarters of people could describe the goals of the RDP by 1995 (even though only a few lead projects had been established at the time of that survey) (see Moller, 1996, p.23). The same study also points to the RDP's poor public image. While most people approved of the RDP's work, many

felt that local development committees do not represent ordinary people or care about the communities they were set up to serve (ibid., p.46). Several studies have also found that people are more likely to be dissatisfied with things in the public domain of life (such as education, adequate housing, job opportunities and public services) than with things in the private or personal sphere of life (e.g. Beukes and Van Der Colff, 1997; Moller, 1995, table 4). It is likely that rising expectations and rapid adaptation to new living standards in South Africa has resulted in a more critical assessment of the dimensions of development that fall within the public sphere of life.

60. Housing, for example, was ranked in seventeenth place in the Parry Sound survey and is not regarded as an important development priority by many Canadians.

61. For an informative discussion of these points see Wilson and Ramphele (1989, pp.48–51). See also Dasgupta (1993), Horner (1995) and Ntoane and Mokoetle, (1984).

62. Timerman (1987) provides a horrifying description of political repression in Chile under General Pinochet, which includes some disturbing eyewitness accounts of torture and bloody murder at the hands of the state. The World Bank estimates that there were 63 civil wars in developing countries that cost something like eight million lives during the 1970s and 1980s (Dasgupta, 1993, p.122).

63. Our survey appears to confirm that water no longer has a place on the agenda of people living in Murraysburg.

64. No firm statistics regarding the incidence of crime or violence in Wallacedene are readily available. However, the township is known to be relatively safe by South African standards. In some informal settlements on the Cape Flats it is not safe for outsiders to walk around the streets or visit shacks (even with a Black escort).

65. However, access to firewood was valued highly by most respondents. This is probably because the people we interviewed lacked access to alternative forms of cooking and heating. (Nobody seemed to have access to gas or own an electric cooker or heater). The CSS (1996, p.30) estimates that 60% of Africans cannot always obtain all the firewood they need.

66. It is worth bearing in mind that the majority of respondents did declare their support for these items (see Tables II.1, II.8 and II.12).

67. In retrospect it would probably have been worth asking about 'opportunities for control, skill use and variety in the work place' and the value of natural talents such as 'creativity' and 'intuition'. These are not serious omissions.

68. Some of the categories in Tables II.1–II.13 were derived from a series of informed guesses inspired by intuition, the findings of past poverty surveys and the advice of experienced field operatives.

69. Respondents also passed judgement on a small number of items not featured in Tables 4.2 or 4.3 (see Tables II.1–II.13). These results indicate that access to electricity and job security deserve a place in any realistic approximation of the good, *inter alia* (see Section 4.4). I shall refrain from examining the implications of these findings for the TVTG and the ATG.

70. Nussbaum (1990, p.233) contends that 'Education is required for each of the major functionings . . .' featured in the TVTG.

71. For Nussbaum the role of the state is to ensure that citizens are capable of functioning in the ways specified by the TVTG (see Chapter 3, Section 2.2).

72. These life styles violate some of the conditions for crossing Nussbaum's level 1 threshold for 'human' functioning. Nussbaum's criteria for human functioning is described in Chapter 3.

73. Most respondents also agreed that 'job satisfaction' is important. Of course achieving job satisfaction is inextricably bound up with good working conditions (among other things). Several respondents however, were sceptical about the value of seeking employment to add 'meaning and substance' to life.

74. Hence Sen's call for equality in the space of capability.

75. In most of his major publications Sen does not distinguish between basic and non-basic capabilities (e.g. Sen, 1985, 1985a). He also cites several examples of non-basic capabilities, such as taking part in literary and scientific pursuits and being able to

entertain friends.

76. Health and self-respect are also good examples of functionings thought to be connected with many different activities (see the *Notes* in Table 4.2 for other examples).

77. This is an ambitious project. Most development economists have been content to focus on basic needs.

78. Another reason is that Nussbaum and Sen are concerned with improving the standard of living for all people (especially the poor), whereas Aristotle tends to focus on the well-being of an elite (all qualified citizens). This helps explain why Nussbaum and Sen, unlike Aristotle, pay insufficient attention to leisure and often focus on the physical condition of people.

79. See Griffin (1986, ch. IV) on the value of accomplishment.

80. Anonymous referee commenting on a paper submitted to the *Cambridge Journal of Economics*.

81. Dokter maintained that water is of intrinsic value for poor people throughout the interview. Yet many of the justifications he put forward for valuing water (e.g. to grow crops) pointed to the instrumental importance of an adequate water supply.

82. Griffin (1993, p.135) contends that Sen's list of functionings 'is so wide that it includes both means to substantive goods [the objects of a good life] and the substantive goods themselves'.

83. One important contrast which might have been explored in a longer book is between Sen's focus on 'people as the ultimate concern', abstracting from the production process, and Marx's insistence that the appropriate conceptual framework for a discussion of human welfare is the social relations of production.

5. Conclusion

This inquiry has grappled with one of the most fundamental and difficult questions in moral philosophy and social science. It is a question that economists and social scientists have tried to avoid but must answer – especially for policy purposes. The concept of 'development' lies at the heart of economics and development studies. While the study of development ethics is viewed as a potential minefield, its neglect serves only to impoverish the subject and jeopardise the design of appropriate policies.

This book constitutes a unique combination of philosophical reflection and practical fieldwork that attempts to breathe new life into potentially sterile debates concerning the nature of human well-being and development. The main findings of this book are summarised below (see also Chapter 2, Section 6 and Chapter 4, Sections 4–5). Our inquiry began with an attempt to identify and clarify some of the abstract concepts of development employed in social science (Chapter 1). These concepts offer some useful but incomplete insights into different aspects of economic, social, political and cultural development. Behind all these concepts is some deeper notion of human development.

In Chapter 2 we argued that the capability approach (as developed by Amartya Sen) is the best available framework for conceptualising human development. This approach, in contrast to accounts that reduce human well-being to some notion of opulence or commodity command, concerns itself with the development of people rather than the development of things. Furthermore, unlike approaches based on narrow concepts of utility (or basic needs), the capability framework readily accommodates the entire range of 'beings' and 'doings' that contribute to a good life.

While the capability approach provides the most accurate and comprehensive framework for thinking about development, efforts to inject some empirical content into this framework suggest greater overlap with welfare and resource based concepts of well-being than we might expect. More room needs to be made for utility and mental functioning within the general approach of capabilities. There is also a case for supplementing the capability approach with a list of economic primary goods. Resources such as water, food and clothing may have some intrinsic value as well as considerable instrumental importance. The fact that some activities carry instrumental significance reflects the other side of the coin. Some 'beings' and 'doings' (e.g. the act of riding a bicycle to get to work or to promote physical fitness) may only be of extrinsic importance for good living.

The foundations of the capability approach also appear to require further elaboration and clarification. In particular, we need to be clear about what we mean by the term 'capability'. A capability is more than just a bare opportunity. It reflects a person's actual ability to function (or effective freedom to pursue that opportunity) in accordance with rational deliberation (see Chapter 2, Addendum). The capability approach must also be adapted to accommodate some potentially antagonistic aspects of development. The pursuit of some ends (such as the 'satisfaction' derived from the consumption of junk food or tobacco) inevitably generates *negative* functionings as a by-product. More generally, the capability to achieve pure functioning in just about any area of human life seems to be beyond mere mortals. Efforts to achieve pure functioning may also entail high opportunity costs (Chapter 2, Section 6). The human good is not necessarily a quest for perfection. Somehow, the capability approach must weigh the costs and benefits of engaging in different activities.

Ultimately, Sen's framework needs to be supplemented with a list of intrinsically valuable capabilities. Several accounts of good living can be found in the literature. Some of these schemes seem to be objectionably paternalistic (e.g. Baran and Sweezy's account of 'genuine human needs'). Much however, depends on how a list of human capabilities or needs is developed and applied. While there is scope for the misuse and abuse of these frameworks, it is possible to avoid the problem of paternalism by developing an account of the good based on the values of ordinary people. Chapter 3 proposed a methodology that is particularly well suited for this task. Ultimately, sufficient steps must be taken to respect the rational desires of all people (including potential dissenters).

In Chapter 4 the results of fieldwork derived from a questionnaire designed to collect information about perceptions of development (a good life) were presented and used to evaluate some academic concepts of human well-being and development. The fieldwork results are compelling. They suggest that most people do in fact share a common set of human values; and that these values are not fundamentally at odds with most, but not all, of the human capabilities and needs proposed by social scientists and philosophers like Nussbaum and Sen (see Table 4.2). These findings fly in the face of traditional wisdom, but cannot be dismissed out of hand. The views of most respondents appear to be reasonably well informed and there is anecdotal evidence (from poverty studies) that suggests many of our survey findings can be generalised.

Our survey findings, however, do not provide a complete vindication of the TVTG or the ATG. The crux of the problem is not that these theories go too far in terms of advancing a thick conception of the common good. In fact, it is quite the reverse. None of these theories seem to go far enough (see Table 4.3). It is worth emphasising the following points:

(1) Many of the people we interviewed possessed fairly ambitious desires and could imagine a substantially better life style than Nussbaum's account of the good seems to imply. In particular, the TVTG and ATG need to give more prominence to recreational pursuit. Many respondents were keen to emphasise the value of sport, television, socialising and music and dance. Not all of these activities are universal aspects of a good life. Ultimately, different people and societies may have to develop their own distinct accounts of good recreation.

(2) The 'good life' is not necessarily incompatible with virtue (as Aristotle maintained). Several respondents stressed the value of being able to live a spiritual ('religious') life style. Some people also mentioned the importance of being able to avoid mischief and crime. Acts of altruism such as supporting family and friends or helping the community were also highly prized. Most people however, placed the emphasis on benefiting from benevolent acts rather than on rendering aid to others. This may reflect the fact that most poor people cannot afford to be altruistic. Several respondents also mentioned the value of achieving status, prestige, success and pride. These capabilities (vices?) go against the spirit of the Aristotelian approach. In addition, some respondents were sceptical about the value of virtues such as physical exercise, travel and adventure, and literary and scientific pursuits (see Table 4.2).

(3) Most development ethics focus on the person's physical condition at the expense of his or her state of mind. This is a mistake. The survey findings indicate that happiness, pleasure and joy are key aspects of a good life. In fact, the concept of utility needs to be stretched to include a diverse range of mental functionings such as feeling relaxed, avoiding stress, achieving self-confidence and experiencing pride. In short, a more substantial and sophisticated account of the psychology of well-being is required. Our survey findings may be able to assist with this task.

(4) Many accounts of human well-being are divorced from some of the practical aspects of survival and development in poor countries. Some of the ways in which the TVTG abstracts from the harsh realities of life in developing countries were illustrated by examining the function of

education, employment and the family in the last chapter. In particular, development ethics needs to say something solid about the value of good working conditions, which have the potential to make an enormous difference to the overall quality of life. It may also be possible to expand on Sen's concept of poverty (as basic capability failure) by drawing on our survey findings.

(5) Respondents indicated that many of the things traditionally viewed as 'means' (inputs) may well possess some intrinsic value. This is particularly true of basic necessities such as clean water, food, housing and clothing. The distinction between 'means' and 'ends' also seems to lack a clear boundary, which makes it particularly difficult to categorise items such as health, education and skills, civil liberties and family. Some of the items that have been categorised as 'means' may actually deserve a place in the TVTG after all. A theory of 'means' is also required to guide public policy – though care must be taken not to lose sight of the ends that ultimately matter.

These conclusions rest on the study of perceptions of development in two poor South African communities located in the Province of the Western Cape. Apart from their poverty, these two locations have little in common. One is an isolated rural village situated deep in the Karoo desert. The other is a semi-urban squatter camp located on the outskirts of Cape Town. Yet both communities appear to share a common vision of a good life. Our survey findings can therefore be used to forge a first approximation of a working theory of the good, which should be developed and applied in line with the methodology described in Chapter 3. However, further study is required to test the strength of our findings. In particular, it would be useful to investigate human values in poor communities that are not Christian or Westernised.

Annex: Statistics and Questionnaire

1. INTRODUCTION

This annex contains a selection of tables derived from fieldwork in Murraysburg and Wallacedene and a copy of the questionnaire employed. It is divided into three main parts:

Part One: Responses to Open Questions
Part Two: Responses to Pre-Defined Questions
Part Three: The Questionnaire

Not all of the tables that were compiled are reproduced here. A complete set of tables (which break down the results to all the questions we asked by location, gender and age) will be deposited in the archives at SALDRU (see Clark, forthcoming). The questionnaire is reproduced in the same format as it was used in the field.

2. COMPILATION OF TABLES

2.1 Open Responses

Informants were asked to provide up to five responses to each of the core questions. Each response has been fitted into a distinct category for the purpose of aggregation. An effort was made to preserve the essence and substance of individual answers and to capture, rather than to conceal, possible ambiguities. In particular, we refrained from aggregating similar sets of responses whenever: (1) useful insights could be gained by *not* conflating similar items (e.g. Table I.1's items 3 and 12; Table I.5's items 3, 22 and 23; Table I.10's items 4, 12 and 27, etc.); or (2) certain responses could be merged with two or more *distinct* categories.

Most of the items in these tables appear as they were recorded on the questionnaires. (In most cases, interviewers translated responses into English first.) Some responses are not as precise as I would have liked. In some cases, it is difficult to be certain about what respondents meant (e.g. Table I.14's item 24). My interpretation of the findings should not be regarded as definitive (see Chapters 2 and 4). The construction and presentation of the tables is designed to leave the reader with the maximum freedom to interpret the results for his-or-herself.

Individual responses to each question were eventually fitted into between 50 and 90 different categories. Respondents were asked to rank their answers in order of priority. This information was used to calculate a total weight for each category. For example, in the case of the first question (question 1 in Part II of the questionnaire), each time a person ranked an item as the most important aspect of a good life it received five points. Four points were awarded each time an item was ranked as the second most important aspect of a good life, three points for the third most important aspect, and so forth. In the case of item 2 in the table below, the total number of points awarded is calculated as follows:

$$Total\ Weight\ (of\ 'Housing') = (5x24)+(4x28)+(3x20)+(2x7)+(1x8) = 314$$

An ordinal rank of the top 30 responses to each question is recorded in Tables I.1–I.16. (The top 25 items are recorded in the tables that provide a break down of the results by location, gender and age.) The first columns of these tables (especially the top five or six items) are the most significant. Note that the ordinal ranks expressed in the tables often conceal large gaps in relative values. (I have highlighted the most striking contrasts in Chapters 2 and 4.) The gap between subsequent categories narrows as we move down the tables (as Table A.1 shows). In general, the top four or five items in each table were nominated by at least half of all survey participants. The last two or three items were rarely mentioned by more than three or four respondents.

Some items towards the end of the tables scored the same number of points. In these cases, the item(s) with the most nominations in first place was ranked highest. If two or more items were still equivalent, the category with the most nominations in second place was ranked highest, and so forth. As a last resort items were ranked alphabetically.

A complete ranking of all items was constructed for each of the tables compiled (including those not reproduced here) using a computer program written specifically for this task. The results of this exercise are available on a collection of Microsoft Excel worksheets. (Note that some of the findings mentioned in Chapters 2 and 4 are not featured in Tables I.1–I.16, which only summarise the top 25 or 30 responses to our questions.)

Finally, with the exception of Table I.15, I have refrained from including negative responses to the questions we asked (though these responses are reported and discussed in the text). In most cases, few respondents disputed the value of the objects we asked them to evaluate (see Table II.1).

Table A.1 Cardinal Ranking of the Top 10 Aspects of a 'Good Life' in Murraysburg and Wallacedene

Rank Item	Total number of respondents					
	Total Weight	Ranked First	Ranked Second	Ranked Third	Ranked Fourth	Ranked Fifth
1 Jobs	355	38	31	11	4	0
2 Housing	314	24	28	20	7	8
3 An Education	266	30	13	18	4	2
4 Adequate/ Regular Income	212	8	19	24	9	6
5 A Good Family	127	7	9	11	9	5
6 Living a Religious /Christian Life	103	16	3	3	1	0
7 Good Health	84	3	11	3	8	0
8 Enough Food	68	4	3	7	7	1
9 Happiness/ Joy	67	4	4	4	7	5
10 Love (each other)	49	2	5	3	5	0

Source: Fieldwork database

2.2 Closed (Tutored) Responses

Most of these questions were designed to supplement the responses to open questions. In cases where a new question was introduced, respondents were given the opportunity of adding their own suggestions to the pre-defined ends we asked them to evaluate (e.g. questions 3.3, 3.4, 7.3.1, 7.6.1 and 12.3 in Part III of the questionnaire). In some cases, respondents were also given the chance to explain their reason(s) for not valuing certain activities (e.g. questions 4.5 and 7.7). Few informants chose to take advantage of these opportunities. I have not tried to include the results of these exercises in the tables below.

The percentages and rankings expressed in these tables were calculated using a computer program designed to interface with the fieldwork database. The rankings were constructed in line with the procedure described above.

3. ACKNOWLEDGEMENT

The construction of the fieldwork database and the compilation of tables were long and painful tasks. I am extremely grateful to Mr Stephen Morris for designing the necessary software to perform many of the long and tedious calculations required. Without this software a full set of tables would have taken years instead of months to compile.

ANNEX: PART ONE

RESPONSES TO OPEN QUESTIONS

1. THE PRIORITIES OF LIFE

Table I.1 Normative Ranking of the Top 30 Aspects of a 'Good Life' in Murraysburg and Wallacedene

1 Jobs	16 Support of family
2 Housing	17 Relaxation
3 An education	18 Good area to live/ live elsewhere
4 Adequate/ regular income	19 Nice/ good clothes
5 A good family	20 Security/ safety
6 Living a religious/ Christian life	21 Having/ caring for children
7 Good health	22 Respect (especially for others)
8 Enough food	23 Sport(s)
9 Happiness/ joy	24 To get married
10 Love (each other)	25 Independence (especially financial)
11 Good friends	26 Peace in the household/ community
12 Education for children	27 Recreation
13 Motor car	28 Communication (between people)
14 Owning a business	29 Acquiring skills/ qualifications
15 Understanding (between people)	30 Furniture

Source: based on question II.1

Table I.1.1 Normative Ranking of the Top 25 Aspects of a 'Good Life' in Murraysburg and Wallacedene by Location

Village of Murraysburg	Township of Wallacedene
1 An education	1 Jobs
2 Jobs	2 Housing
3 Adequate/ regular income	3 An education
4 Housing	4 Adequate/ regular income
5 Living a religious/ Christian life	5 A good family
6 A good family	6 Happiness/ joy
7 Good health	7 Education for children
8 Love (each other)	8 Owning a business
9 Enough food	9 Good health
10 Understanding (between people)	10 Enough food
11 Good friends	11 Good friends
12 Relaxation	12 Motor car
13 Happiness/ joy	13 Living a religious/ Christian life
14 Respect (especially for others)	14 Support of family
15 Motor car	15 Good area to live/ live elsewhere

Continued/.....

Table I.1.1 (cont.)

Village of Murraysburg	Township of Wallacedene
16 Sport(s)	16 To get married
17 Support of family	17 Nice/ good clothes
18 Peace in the household/ community	18 Security/ safety
19 Recreation	19 Independence (especially financial)
20 Communication (between people)	20 Having/ caring for children
21 Acquiring skills/ qualifications	21 Healthy environment
22 Being punctual/ industrious	22 Love (each other)
23 Security/ safety	23 Better home for children
24 To help each other	24 Clothe/ feed children
25 Having/ caring for children	25 Good future/ better life for children

Source: based on question II.1

Table I.1.2 Normative Ranking of the Top 25 Aspects of a 'Good Life' in Murraysburg and Wallacedene by Gender

Men	Women
1 An education	1 Jobs
2 Jobs	2 Housing
3 Housing	3 An education
4 Adequate/ regular income	4 Adequate/ regular income
5 A good family	5 Living a religious/ Christian life
6 Good health	6 A good family
7 Living a religious/ Christian life	7 Good health
8 Happiness/ joy	8 Enough food
9 Enough food	9 Love (each other)
10 Motor car	10 Happiness/ joy
11 Support of family	11 Education for children
12 Good area to live/ live elsewhere	12 Good friends
13 Good friends	13 Owning a business
14 Owning a business	14 Understanding (between people)
15 Understanding (between people)	15 Relaxation

Continued/.....

Table I.1.2 (cont.)

Men	Women
16 Sport(s)	16 Nice/ good clothes
17 Love (each other)	17 Communication (between people)
18 Security/ safety	18 Respect (especially for others)
19 Nice/ good clothes	19 Security/ safety
20 Education for children	20 Having/ caring for children
21 Acquiring skills/ qualifications	21 Furniture
22 Having/ caring for children	22 Support of family
23 Respect (especially for others)	23 Peace in the household/ community
24 To get married	24 Independence (especially financial)
25 Relaxation	25 To get married

Source: based on question II.1

Table I.1.3 Normative Ranking of the Top 25 Aspects of a 'Good Life' in Murraysburg and Wallacedene by Age

Individuals aged 12–19	Individuals aged 20–34
1 An education	1 Jobs
2 Adequate/ regular income	2 Housing
3 Jobs	3 An education
4 Housing	4 Adequate/ regular income
5 A good family	5 A good family
6 Living a religious/ Christian life	6 Owning a business
7 Good health	7 Happiness/ joy
8 Good friends	8 Education for children
9 Motor car	9 Enough food
10 Happiness/ joy	10 Living a religious/ Christian life
11 Love (each other)	11 Good health
12 Respect (especially for others)	12 Good friends
13 Enough food	13 Support of family
14 Relaxation	14 Motor car
15 Sport(s)	15 Love (each other)

Continued/....

Table I.1.3 (cont.)

Individuals aged 12–19	Individuals aged 20–34
16 Good area to live/ live Elsewhere	16 Having/ caring for children
17 Understanding (between people)	17 Independence (especially financial)
18 Acquiring skills/ qualifications	18 Understanding (between people)
19 Support of family	19 Nice/ good clothes
20 Nice/ good clothes	20 Relaxation
21 To get married	21 Better home for children
22 Buy parents a home	22 Communication (between people)
23 Money for children	23 Security/ safety
24 Recreation	24 Clothe/ feed children
25 To be famous	25 Good future/ better life for children

Continued/.....

Table I.1.3 (cont.)

Individuals aged 35–59	Individuals aged 60 plus
1 Housing	1 Living a religious/ Christian life
2 Jobs	2 Housing
3 Adequate/ regular income	3 Good health
4 An education	4 Adequate/ regular income
5 Good health	5 Enough food
6 Enough food	6 Jobs
7 Happiness/ joy	7 A good family
8 Love (each other)	8 Love (each other)
9 A good family	9 Being punctual/ industrious
10 Education for children	10 Remaining economically active as long as possible
11 Living a religious/ Christian life	11 An education
12 Understanding (between people)	12 Loyalty to employer
13 Good area to live/ live elsewhere	13 Security/ safety
14 Nice/ good clothes	14 Happiness/ joy
15 To get married	15 Healthy environment

Continued/.....

Table 1.1.3 (cont.)

Individuals aged 35–59	Individuals aged 60 plus
16 Peace in the household/ community	(Insufficient sample to construct further rankings)
17 Furniture	
18 Job satisfaction	
19 Having/ caring for children	
20 Motor car	
21 Security/ safety	
22 To help each other	
23 Independence (especially financial)	
24 Ability to choose/ do the things you want	
25 Adequate means of supply	

Source: based on question II.1

2. JOBS

Table I.2 Normative Ranking of the Top 30 Reasons for Valuing 'A Good Job' in Murraysburg and Wallacedene

1 Good income/ earn money	16 Peace of mind/ less worries
2 To buy house/ improve housing	17 Self sufficiency/ support yourself
3 To support/ care for family and friends	18 Opportunities for advancement
4 Happiness/ satisfaction	19 Provides a challenge
5 Send children to school/ educate children	20 Learn things/ improve knowledge
6 Buy food/ clothes	21 To help others
7 To improve life/ live a good life	22 Buy regular things/ necessities
8 To get job benefits	23 Independence
9 To be secure	24 To plan for the future
10 To buy goods/ facilitate expenditure	25 To buy furniture
11 To provide for children	26 Financial independence/ earn own money
12 Acquiring good things in life/ luxury goods	27 To pay rent
13 To be confident	28 A good job is important
14 Enhances status and prestige	29 Gives assurance in life
15 Enhances self-respect	30 Need to work/ can't be without work

Source: based on question II.3

3. HOUSING

Table I.3 Normative Ranking of the Top 30 Reasons for Valuing 'Good Housing' in Murraysburg and Wallacedene

1 Shelter from the elements
2 Security, safety and protection
3 Happiness/ joy
4 Adequate living space (per person)
5 Improve family relations ('togetherness'/ 'oneness')
6 Facilitates good health
7 Live in good/ reliable house
8 Enhance quality of life/ standard of living
9 Live in your own house
10 Need better/ reliable housing
11 Place where you feel safe/ secure
12 Place to sleep and rest/ accommodation
13 Housing is a good investment
14 Give you pride/ feel proud
15 Stay with family

16 Enhances self-respect/ self-image
17 Home for family/ children
18 Move away/ live in a better place
19 Privacy
20 Relaxation/ puts mind at rest
21 To have a family/ children
22 For status and prestige
23 Feel good
24 It's neat, clean and hygienic
25 Access to water and sanitation
26 Responsibility
27 Facilitates independence
28 Comfortable in own house
29 Place family can 'meet', 'gather', 'share'
30 Can't always live in shack/ squatter camp

Source: based on question II.12

4. EDUCATION

Table 1.4 Normative Ranking of the Top 30 Reasons for Valuing Education in Murraysburg and Wallacedene

1 To get a good/ better job
2 Raise income/ earn good money
3 Acquiring knowledge/ understanding
4 Facilitates a better/ good life
5 Learning to read, write and count
6 Happiness/ joy
7 Acquiring skills/ qualifications
8 To improve future prospects
9 Enhances security
10 To be somebody, get somewhere, achieve something
11 It's good/ important to get an education
12 Promotes general opportunities
13 Improve communication with other people
14 To be better equipped
15 To educate children/ education important for children

16 Can do nothing without an education
17 Survival
18 Improves standard of living/ living conditions
19 To learn
20 Can't be stolen from you/ taken away
21 Facilitates independence
22 To be successful
23 Enhances self-respect/ self-image
24 Education is the basis of life
25 Education makes you a better person
26 To start a business
27 To learn more about/ broaden view of life
28 Improves social life
29 Helps you through life
30 To buy a house

Source: based on question II.2

5. INCOME AND WEALTH

Table I.5 Normative Ranking of the Top 30 Reasons for Valuing Income and Wealth in Murraysburg and Wallacedene

1 Supporting family and friends	16 To care for/ support children
2 Acquiring enough food	17 To gain respect/ enhance self-image
3 To buy things (in general)	18 Makes you reliable
4 Buy house/ improve home/ have adequate housing	19 Facilitates independence (do your own thing)
5 Avoid/ pay-off debt/ settle bills	20 Acquiring status and prestige
6 Enhances well-being/ quality of life	21 Provide food/ clothes for children or family
7 Facilitates happiness	22 To purchase necessities
8 Pay for education/ to study further	23 Acquiring luxury goods/ consumer durables
9 To have money	24 Secures future
10 To provide education for children and family	25 Independence (self-sufficiency)
11 Can't survive/ live without money	26 Provide children with livelihood
12 Enables you to do the things you want to	27 Buy clothes/ shoes
13 To save money	28 To travel, go overseas/ on holiday and visit friends
14 Can do nothing without money	29 Shapes your thinking
15 Provides security	30 For social security

Source: based on questions II.6.2 and II.6.3

6. GOODS AND SERVICES

Table I.6 Normative Ranking of the Top 30 Spending Priorities in Murraysburg and Wallacedene

1 Housing/ home improvements	16 Television
2 Cars/ new car	17 Bicycle
3 Saving (in bank)/ investment or insurance	18 Holiday
4 Furniture/ quality furniture	19 Clothes/ shoes for children/ family
5 Food	20 Buy farm
6 Clothing/ shoes	21 Entertainment
7 Start or expand own business	22 Hi-fi/ music centre (radio excluded)
8 Support family and friends	23 Build swimming bath
9 Assist others/ help the community	24 Gambling
10 Education (for self)	25 'Treat'/ 'spoil' family
11 Education for children/ family	26 Computer
12 Fashionable/ smart clothing	27 Pleasure
13 Pay-off debts, bond, loans/ pay account	28 Radios
14 Acquiring assets	29 Electrical appliances
15 Travel/ go overseas	30 Money in house/ enough money

Source: based on questions II.6.4 and II.6.5

7. FOOD

Table I.7 Normative Ranking of the Top 30 Reasons for Choosing Between Different Foods in Murraysburg and Wallacedene

1 Promotes good health
2 Enjoyment/ like taste
3 Cheap(er) food/ food you can afford
4 Good quality foods
5 Food that's easily accessible/ readily available
6 Avoiding hunger
7 Facilitating social events
8 (Must be) fresh vegetables/ food
9 Avoiding malnutrition
10 To diet/ maintain a healthy diet
11 Food must be wholesome
12 Religious reasons
13 Brand loyalty/ good trade mark
14 Buy popular foods
15 Cater for family's choice/ tastes

16 Availability of money
17 Purchasing as much food as possible
18 Convenience in preparation
19 Maintain body
20 Another person in household buys food
21 Good prices
22 Buy luxury foods (when affordable)
23 (Satisfying) appetite
24 Necessary for survival
25 For consumption
26 Buy what you need/ staple foods
27 Deriving energy
28 Food in house
29 Foods with special/ good ingredients
30 When I return home (from far away)

Source: based on question II.7

8. CLOTHING

Table I.8 Normative Ranking of the Top 30 Reasons for Valuing Clothing in Murraysburg and Wallacedene

1 Body must be covered
2 Protection from the elements
3 Keep warm (or cool)
4 Look smart/ presentable
5 Look good/ beautiful
6 Fashionable clothing/ good image
7 Self-respect
8 Happiness/ like nice clothes
9 Attracting spouse/ look attractive
10 Must be of good quality
11 Look neat and tidy
12 Durability
13 To be hygienic/ cleanliness
14 Reflect inner-most self/ says a lot about a person
15 Achieving status

16 Draw attention
17 To comply with social protocol (e.g. dress for church)
18 Perfect way of mixing colours
19 Health
20 To be/ feel myself
21 Enhances friendship/ social life
22 To be like others/ fit in
23 Enhances feeling of well-being
24 People judge you by the state of your clothes
25 Social pressure
26 Reveals/ reflects tastes
27 Helps identify people
28 'Basic clothes for everyone'
29 Clothes are necessary, indispensable, essential
30 Decorates

Source: based on question II.13

9. FAMILY AND FRIENDS

Table I.9 Normative Ranking of the Top 30 Reasons for Valuing Family and Friends in Murraysburg and Wallacedene

1 Access to the care and support of family and friends
2 Help/ support each other
3 Help to solve problems/ give advice
4 Improves communication
5 Strengthen relationships with family and friends
6 Strengthens understanding (of each other)
7 Happiness, pleasure and joy
8 To share food
9 Provides emotional security, moral support and comfort
10 Being loved
11 Mutual respect (among family and friends)
12 Culture
13 Visiting family and friends
14 For socialising
15 Not to be alone/ spend life with someone

16 Can learn/ exchange ideas with friends
17 Share joys and sorrows of life with family/ friends
18 Companionship/ friendship
19 Security
20 To love each other
21 Need family and friends
22 Can always rely on family
23 To talk to someone
24 To share with family and friends
25 Family always there for you
26 Facilitates a better/ good life
27 Enhances self-image/ feeling of self-worth
28 Family is important
29 Family and friends care for you
30 Providing for family and friends

Source: based on question II.4

10. RECREATION

Table I.10 Normative Ranking of the Top 30 Reasons for Valuing Recreation in Murraysburg and Wallacedene

1 Relaxation
2 Promotes health/ physical fitness
3 Happiness/ enjoyment
4 Make new friends/ meet new friends
5 Sleep and rest
6 Time to think, learn and gain experience
7 To keep occupied/ avoid boredom
8 Relieving stress/ frustration
9 To socialise
10 Refreshes mind/ helps you think better
11 To preserve nature
12 Spend time with family/ friends
13 Keep away from trouble and crime/ avoid mischief
14 Provides a change of scene
15 Time alone/ for myself

16 To exchange ideas/ learn from each other
17 Understanding
18 Facilitates good communication
19 Enhances quality of life/ facilitates a good life
20 To learn about new cultures
21 Can do what you want/ like best
22 Travel and adventure
23 Television/ movies
24 Improves abilities
25 Time to do important things
26 To solve/ discuss problems
27 Visiting friends
28 To help family and friends
29 Togetherness/ brings you closer together
30 For entertainment

Source: based on questions II.5.2 and II.5.3

11. RECREATIONAL ACTIVITIES

Table I.11 Normative Ranking of 30 most Valuable Recreational Activities in Murraysburg and Wallacedene

1 Sports	16 Athletics
2 Music	17 Gardening
3 Reading	18 Cricket
4 Church meetings and activities	19 Needlework
5 TV/ cinema	20 Listening to the radio
6 Football	21 Chess
7 Rugby	22 Playing games
8 Socialise/ visit friends	23 Travel/ see other places
9 Netball	24 Volleyball
10 Singing	25 Cooking
11 Swimming	26 Knitting
12 Tennis	27 Rest/ sleep
13 Drama/ plays	28 Hiking/ mountaineering
14 Dancing	29 Cycling long distances
15 Taking walks	30 Spending time with family

Source: based on questions II.5.4 and II.5.5

12. COCA-COLA

Table I.12 Normative Ranking of the Top 30 Reasons for Valuing Coca-Cola and Soft Drinks in Murraysburg and Wallacedene

1 Enjoyment/ like taste	16 Feels good
2 Quenches thirst	17 Fulfil liquid needs
3 Cool drink ('cools you down')	18 Not too sweet
4 Like fizziness/ gas	19 Provides energy
5 Popular drink/ everyone drinks it	20 Linked to competitions and prizes
6 Good for stomach ache, wind and diarrhoea	21 Feels well/ better
7 Promotes health	22 Can be a medicine
8 Easily available	23 Relives migraine attacks
9 Refreshing	24 Drink I know the best
10 'Coke is best'/ Coke is 'top', 'no.1'	25 It's marketing promotes social development
11 It's cheap/ not too expensive	26 Not too much gas
12 To relax	27 Used to it
13 It's a healthy, clean drink	28 Like the colour/ design on the can
14 Enhances social life/ friendships	29 Tastes sweet
15 Brand loyalty	30 Makes you feel strong

Source: based on question II.8

13. WATCHING SPORT

Table I.13 Normative Ranking of the Top 30 Reasons for Watching Sport(s) in Murraysburg and Wallacedene

1 Yields happiness, enjoyment and excitement
2 Facilitates relaxation ('cooling nerves')
3 Learn from sports (rules, tactics and new techniques)
4 Contributes to social life/ spend time with friends
5 Interest/ fascination
6 Love of competition and contest
7 Sportsman/ player myself
8 Think creatively/ critical analysis
9 To play better/ improve sports skills
10 Entertaining
11 Get experience
12 Passes time/ keep occupied
13 Keeps you out of trouble
14 See favourite players/ know sports stars
15 Healthy body and mind/ keep fit and exercise

16 For records
17 Watch game/ observe sports skills
18 Know what goes on
19 Enhance discipline
20 Grew up participating in sports
21 Keep up to date with sports events
22 Helps enhance communication
23 Support local team/ watch South Africa
24 To talk about sports/ provides topic of conversation
25 Watch players put in their best
26 Sports is good/ important
27 Good activity
28 To give advice/ helps to be a coacher
29 Can become your future
30 Check opponents' tactics

Source: based on question II.9

14. TELEVISION AND CINEMA

Table I.14 Normative Ranking of the Top 30 Reasons for Valuing Television and Cinema in Murraysburg and Wallacedene

1 Education/ information and knowledge
2 Relaxation
3 Pleasure/ enjoyment
4 Watch news/ current affairs
5 Watch films and serials/ good stories
6 See other places/ what's going on in world
7 Watch sports
8 Passes the time/ keep busy
9 Entertaining
10 See or learn new things
11 Understand different cultures
12 Takes mind off worries
13 Find interesting
14 Broadens way of thinking
15 Good pastime

16 Helps understand better
17 Share programmes with family and friends
18 To be cool and fashionable
19 Enhances communication
20 Takes you away from reality/ imagine and daydream
21 Enlightening
22 Social activities/ topic of conversation
23 To do something different
24 Be groomed
25 Because own a TV/ it's there
26 Watch certain programmes
27 Watch documentaries
28 Helps learn language
29 Learn a lot about how to love
30 Keeps you out of trouble/ mischief

Source: based on question II.11

15. ALCOHOL AND CIGARETTES

Table 1.15 Normative Ranking of the Top 30 reasons for Valuing/ Not Valuing Alcohol and Tobacco in Murraysburg and Wallacedene

Valuing Alcohol/ Tobacco	Not Valuing Alcohol/ Tobacco
1 Facilitates relaxation	1 Unhealthy/ causes disease
2 Pleasure/ satisfies desires	2 Waste of money
3 Facilitates social interaction with friends	3 Jeopardises family relations/ breaks unity
4 Calms nerves, relieves depression, drowns sorrows	4 Not good for body
5 Cultural purposes	5 Can kill/ risk of death
6 To forget problems	6 Leads to trouble/ crime
7 Addiction/ won't stop	7 Against religious/ Christian beliefs
8 Facilitates being cool and fashionable	8 Wrong, immoral, against principles
9 Refreshing to drink beer	9 Not good for children
10 Way I was brought up	10 It's dangerous/ not good for you
11 Feel like it	11 Risk of addiction/ can't stop
12 Medication	12 Makes you sick
13 Alcohol is stimulating	13 Destroys life
14 Don't know/ no reason	14 Too young/ old

Continued/.....

Table I.15 (cont.)

Valuing Alcohol/ Tobacco	Not Valuing Alcohol/ Tobacco
15 Feel better	15 Causes problems
16 Helps me think	16 Encourages bad, abusive, violent behaviour
17 Quenches thirst	17 Family disapprove/ won't tolerate it
18 Started as a prank when young	18 Not good for brain
19 Starts day	19 Serves no useful purpose/ no need for it
20 It's a habit	20 Makes you do the wrong thing
21 If don't think	21 Bad habit
22 Has no future	22 It's not good at all
23 Like colour	23 Provide example to others
24 Pastime	24 Dislike taste/ don't enjoy
25 Help me dance a lot	25 Not ladylike
26 Been doing it some time	26 Gives you bad image
27 Like smell	27 'Breaks down'/ 'does not build'
28 Feel part of world	28 Loses friends
29 Wine alters personality	29 There is no life
30 Helps control appetite	30 Can't afford/ can cost a lot of money

Source: based on question II.10

16. ADVERTISING

Table I.16 Normative Ranking of the Top 30 Reasons for Valuing Advertising in Murraysburg and Wallacedene

1 View products/ make products known	16 Information regarding product use
2 Provides useful information/ knowledge	17 Make money/ profit for companies
3 See new products	18 Provides information about latest fashions/ styles
4 Promotes choice between products	19 See where things are on sale
5 To see/ compare prices	20 Builds understanding
6 So people can buy/ sell products	21 Advertise product
7 Expand product market/ promote product	22 Advertising means business
8 Educates/ learn from advertising	23 Important for consumer
9 Helps to compare products	24 It's pretty
10 Get value for money/ save money	25 Teaches values
11 Generates interest in article	26 Communication to public
12 Encourages competition	27 Advertising is likeable/ nice to see
13 Creative marketing	28 Allow me to dream of future
14 Can be entertaining/ amusing	29 Business needs advertising
15 Information about obtaining product	30 Connection with people

Source: based on question II.14

ANNEX: PART TWO

RESPONSES TO PRE-DEFINED QUESTIONS

1. NORMATIVE EVALUATION OF 38 PRE-DEFINED 'FUNCTIONAL CAPABILITIES'

Table II.1 Normative Evaluation of 38 different 'Functional Capabilities' in Murraysburg and Wallacedene

	PERCENTAGE OF SAMPLE				
	Essential	Valuable	Unimportant	Undesirable	No Response
1 Jobs	89.81	10.19	0	0	0
2 Access to clean water and sanitation	81.53	17.2	0.64	0	0.64
3 Housing and shelter	93.63	6.37	0	0	0
4 Family and friends	70.06	29.3	0.64	0	0
5 Personal safety and physical security	78.34	20.38	0	0	1.27
6 An education	93.63	6.37	0	0	0
7 Happiness	70.06	28.03	1.27	0	0.64
8 Good health	82.8	16.56	0	0	0.64
9 Sleep and rest	63.69	33.76	0.64	0	1.91
10 Fuel for cooking and heating	52.23	43.31	3.18	0	1.27
11 Access to family planning	38.22	44.59	7.01	0	8.92
12 Exercise	42.68	49.04	7.64	0	0.64
13 Capacity to think, reason and make choices	56.05	40.76	1.91	0	1.27
14 Sexual satisfaction	14.65	35.67	25.48	3.18	21.02
15 Basic clothing	63.69	30.57	4.46	0	1.27
16 Fashionable clothing	27.39	42.68	28.66	0	1.27
17 Freedom/ self-determination	63.06	35.03	1.91	0	0
18 Income and wealth	64.33	29.94	3.82	0	1.91

Continued/.....

Table II.1 (cont.)

	PERCENTAGE OF SAMPLE				
	Essential	Valuable	Unimportant	Undesirable	No Response
19 Consumer durable and luxury goods	29.94	43.95	21.66	1.27	3.18
20 Self-respect	76.43	20.38	1.27	0	1.91
21 Land and cattle	27.39	42.04	26.11	2.55	1.91
22 Living in a clean natural environment	67.52	28.03	1.91	0	2.55
23 Coca-Cola (or other fizzy drink)	19.75	35.03	38.85	4.46	1.91
24 Transportation	54.78	40.13	3.18	0	1.91
25 (All weather) roads	52.23	41.4	2.55	0	3.82
26 Watching sport(s)	40.76	40.13	14.65	2.55	1.91
27 Playing sport(s)	43.31	34.39	19.11	1.27	1.91
28 Electricity	78.34	20.38	0	0	1.27
29 Free time/ recreation	41.4	53.5	3.82	0	1.27
30 Having children	40.76	33.12	15.29	1.27	9.55
31 Watching TV/ going to the cinema	29.94	47.13	17.83	1.91	3.18
32 Drinking alcohol	3.82	7.01	33.76	54.78	0.64
33 Living long	36.31	40.13	15.92	5.73	1.91
34 Smoking cigarettes	5.1	8.28	31.21	54.14	1.27
35 Property rights (right to own personal property)	61.78	36.31	1.27	0	0.64
36 Equal opportunities for personal advancement	58.6	38.85	2.55	0	0
37 Determination, motivation, self-reliance	58.6	38.22	1.91	0	1.27
38 Political rights (right to vote, hold public office and freedom of speech and association)	65.61	29.3	3.82	1.27	0

Source: based on question III.1

Table II.1.1 Normative Evaluation of 38 'Functional Capabilities' in Murraysburg and Wallacedene by Location

	MURRAYSBURG (Percentage)					WALLACEDENE (Percentage)				
	Essential	Valuable	Unimportant	Undesirable	No Response	Essential	Valuable	Unimportant	Undesirable	No Response
1 Jobs	87.5	12.5	0	0	0	92.21	7.79	0	0	0
2 Access to clean water and sanitation	76.25	23.75	0	0	0	87.01	10.39	1.3	0	1.3
3 Housing and shelter	88.75	11.25	0	0	0	98.7	1.3	0	0	0
4 Family and friends	66.25	33.75	0	0	0	74.03	24.68	1.3	0	0
5 Personal safety and physical security	75	23.75	0	0	1.25	81.82	16.88	0	0	1.3
6 An education	96.25	3.75	0	0	0	90.91	9.09	0	0	0
7 Happiness	66.25	31.25	2.5	0	0	74.03	24.68	0	0	1.3
8 Good health	86.25	13.75	0	0	0	79.22	19.48	0	0	1.3
9 Sleep and rest	73.75	25	1.25	0	0	53.25	42.86	0	0	3.9
10 Fuel for cooking and heating	51.25	43.75	3.75	0	1.25	53.25	42.86	2.6	0	1.3
11 Access to family planning	41.25	37.5	5	0	13.75	35.06	51.95	9.09	0	3.9
12 Exercise	51.25	45	3.75	0	0	33.77	53.25	11.69	0	1.3
13 Capacity to think, reason and make choices	62.5	33.75	2.5	0	1.25	49.35	48.05	1.3	0	1.3
14 Sexual satisfaction	16.25	31.25	13.75	0	38.75	12.99	40.26	37.66	6.49	2.6
15 Basic clothing	75	25	0	0	0	51.95	36.36	9.09	0	2.6
16 Fashionable clothing	30	45	23.75	0	1.25	24.68	40.26	33.77	0	1.3
17 Freedom/ self-determination	65	32.5	2.5	0	0	61.04	37.66	1.3	0	0
18 Income and wealth	62.5	35	1.25	0	1.25	66.23	24.68	6.49	0	2.6
19 Consumer durable and luxury goods	23.75	52.5	22.5	0	1.25	36.36	35.06	20.78	2.6	5.19
20 Self-respect	81.25	15	2.5	0	1.25	71.43	25.97	0	0	2.6
21 Land and cattle	31.25	46.25	17.5	1.25	3.75	23.38	37.66	35.06	3.9	0

22 Living in a clean natural environment	71.25	26.25	1.25	0	1.25	63.64	29.87	2.6	0	3.9
23 Coca-Cola (or other fizzy drink)	22.5	38.75	32.5	3.75	2.5	16.88	31.17	45.45	5.19	1.3
24 Transportation	56.25	41.25	1.25	0	1.25	53.25	38.96	5.19	0	2.6
25 (All weather) roads	62.5	33.75	1.25	0	2.5	41.56	49.35	3.9	0	5.19
26 Watching sport(s)	48.75	42.5	8.75	0	0	32.47	37.66	20.78	5.19	3.9
27 Playing sport(s)	48.75	37.5	12.5	0	1.25	37.66	31.17	25.97	2.6	2.6
28 Electricity	77.5	22.5	0	0	0	79.22	18.18	0	0	2.6
29 Free time/ recreation	47.5	52.5	0	0	0	35.06	54.55	7.79	0	2.6
30 Having children	42.5	27.5	15	0	15	38.96	38.96	15.58	2.6	3.9
31 Watching TV/ going to the cinema	37.5	46.25	15	0	1.25	22.08	48.05	20.78	3.9	5.19
32 Drinking alcohol	0	2.5	48.75	48.75	0	7.79	11.69	18.18	61.04	1.3
33 Living long	47.5	41.25	10	0	1.25	24.68	38.96	22.08	11.69	2.6
34 Smoking cigarettes	1.25	2.5	46.25	48.75	1.25	9.09	14.29	15.58	59.74	1.3
35 Property rights (right to own personal property)	58.75	41.25	0	0	0	64.94	31.17	2.6	0	1.3
36 Equal opportunities for personal advancement	61.25	37.5	1.25	0	0	55.84	40.26	3.9	0	0
37 Determination, motivation, self-reliance	55	41.25	2.5	0	1.25	62.34	35.06	1.3	0	1.3
38 Political rights (i.e. right to vote, hold public office and freedom of speech and association)	55	40	5	0	0	76.62	18.18	2.6	2.6	0

Source: based on question III.1

Table II.1.2 Normative Evaluation of 38 'Functional Capabilities' in Murraysburg and Wallacedene by Gender

	MEN (Percentage)					WOMEN (Percentage)				
	Essential	Valuable	Unimportant	Undesirable	No Response	Essential	Valuable	Unimportant	Undesirable	No Response
1 Jobs	92.86	7.14	0	0	0	87.36	12.64	0	0	0
2 Access to clean water and sanitation	80	18.57	1.43	0	0	82.76	16.09	0	0	1.15
3 Housing and shelter	92.86	7.14	0	0	0	94.25	5.75	0	0	0
4 Family and friends	64.29	35.71	0	0	0	74.71	24.14	1.15	0	0
5 Personal safety and physical security	81.43	18.57	0	0	0	75.86	21.84	0	0	2.3
6 An education	91.43	8.57	0	0	0	95.4	4.6	0	0	0
7 Happiness	67.14	31.43	1.43	0	0	72.41	25.29	1.15	0	1.15
8 Good health	82.86	17.14	0	0	0	82.76	16.09	0	0	1.15
9 Sleep and rest	62.86	35.71	0	0	1.43	64.37	32.18	1.15	0	2.3
10 Fuel for cooking and heating	54.29	41.43	4.29	0	0	50.57	44.83	2.3	0	2.3
11 Access to family planning	37.14	48.57	7.14	0	5.71	39.08	41.38	6.9	0	11.49
12 Exercise	48.57	44.29	7.14	0	0	37.93	52.87	8.05	0	1.15
13 Capacity to think, reason and make choices	54.29	40	4.29	0	1.43	57.47	41.38	0	0	1.15
14 Sexual satisfaction	11.43	45.71	21.43	0	21.43	17.24	27.59	28.74	5.75	20.69
15 Basic clothing	65.71	30	4.29	0	0	62.07	31.03	4.6	0	2.3
16 Fashionable clothing	31.43	42.86	25.71	0	0	24.14	42.53	31.03	0	2.3
17 Freedom/ self-determination	71.43	28.57	0	0	0	56.32	40.23	3.45	0	0
18 Income and wealth	62.86	31.43	2.86	0	2.86	65.52	28.74	4.6	0	1.15
19 Consumer durable and luxury goods	35.71	44.29	18.57	0	1.43	25.29	43.68	24.14	2.3	4.6
20 Self-respect	77.14	20	1.43	0	1.43	75.86	20.69	1.15	0	2.3
21 Land and cattle	27.14	47.14	22.86	1.43	1.43	27.59	37.93	28.74	3.45	2.3

22 Living in a clean natural environment	68.57	25.71	2.86	0	2.86	66.67	29.89	1.15	0	2.3
23 Coca-Cola (or other fizzy drink)	27.14	40	27.14	5.71	0	13.79	31.03	48.28	3.45	3.45
24 Transportation	58.57	40	1.43	0	0	51.72	40.23	4.6	0	3.45
25 (All weather) roads	54.29	44.29	0	0	1.43	50.57	39.08	4.6	0	5.75
26 Watching sport(s)	47.14	47.14	4.29	1.43	0	35.63	34.48	22.99	3.45	3.45
27 Playing sport(s)	50	38.57	10	1.43	0	37.93	31.03	26.44	1.15	3.45
28 Electricity	77.14	22.86	0	0	0	79.31	18.39	0	0	2.3
29 Free time/ recreation	44.29	50	5.71	0	0	39.08	56.32	2.3	0	2.3
30 Having children	48.57	31.43	12.86	0	7.14	34.48	34.48	17.24	2.3	11.49
31 Watching TV/ going to the cinema	31.43	51.43	15.71	0	1.43	28.74	43.68	19.54	3.45	4.6
32 Drinking alcohol	4.29	7.14	44.29	44.29	0	3.45	6.9	25.29	63.22	1.15
33 Living long	41.43	41.43	11.43	4.29	1.43	32.18	39.08	19.54	6.9	2.3
34 Smoking cigarettes	5.71	7.14	38.57	48.57	0	4.6	9.2	25.29	58.62	2.3
35 Property rights (right to own personal property)	62.86	35.71	1.43	0	0	60.92	36.78	1.15	0	1.15
36 Equal opportunities for personal advancement	57.14	42.86	0	0	0	59.77	35.63	4.6	0	0
37 Determination, motivation, self-reliance	51.43	45.71	2.86	0	0	64.37	32.18	1.15	0	2.3
38 Political rights (i.e. right to vote, hold public office and freedom of speech and association)	62.86	34.29	2.86	0	0	67.82	25.29	4.6	2.3	0

Source: based on question III.1

Table II.1.3 Normative Evaluation of 38 'Functional Capabilities' in Murraysburg and Wallacedene by Age

	INDIVIDUALS AGED 12–19 (Percentage)					INDIVIDUALS AGED 20–34 (Percentage)				
	Essential	Valuable	Unimportant	Undesirable	No Response	Essential	Valuable	Unimportant	Undesirable	No Response
1 Jobs	88	12	0	0	0	93.85	6.15	0	0	0
2 Access to clean water and sanitation	80	20	0	0	0	81.54	16.92	0	0	1.54
3 Housing and shelter	94	6	0	0	0	93.85	6.15	0	0	0
4 Family and friends	70	30	0	0	0	73.85	24.62	1.54	0	0
5 Personal safety and physical security	78	20	0	0	2	87.69	12.31	0	0	0
6 An education	94	6	0	0	0	96.92	3.08	0	0	0
7 Happiness	62	38	0	0	0	72.31	23.08	3.08	0	1.54
8 Good health	82	18	0	0	0	83.08	15.38	0	0	1.54
9 Sleep and rest	80	16	2	0	2	58.46	38.46	0	0	3.08
10 Fuel for cooking and heating	52	44	2	0	2	49.23	46.15	3.08	0	1.54
11 Access to family planning	40	38	4	0	16	44.62	49.23	1.54	0	4.62
12 Exercise	52	42	6	0	0	43.08	49.23	6.15	0	1.54
13 Capacity to think, reason and make choices	62	30	6	0	2	56.92	41.54	0	0	1.54
14 Sexual satisfaction	6	24	18	0	52	20	47.69	26.15	6.15	0
15 Basic clothing	78	16	6	0	0	53.85	38.46	6.15	0	1.54
16 Fashionable clothing	34	46	18	0	2	29.23	41.54	29.23	0	0
17 Freedom/ self-determination	76	24	0	0	0	63.08	35.38	1.54	0	0
18 Income and wealth	68	30	2	0	0	66.15	26.15	4.62	0	3.08
19 Consumer durable and luxury goods	30	52	16	0	2	40	33.85	18.46	3.08	4.62
20 Self-respect	88	8	0	0	4	72.31	26.15	1.54	0	0
21 Land and cattle	34	42	20	2	2	26.15	40	29.23	3.08	1.54

22	Living in a clean natural environment	78	18	2	0	2	61.54	32.31	3.08	0	3.08
23	Coca-Cola (or other fizzy drink)	34	30	32	2	2	16.92	38.46	35.38	7.69	1.54
24	Transportation	66	30	4	0	0	53.85	38.46	4.62	0	3.08
25	(All weather) roads	66	30	4	0	0	53.85	40	0	0	6.15
26	Watching sport(s)	58	26	12	4	0	36.92	47.69	10.77	1.54	3.08
27	Playing sport(s)	60	30	8	2	0	41.54	35.38	18.46	1.54	3.08
28	Electricity	84	16	0	0	0	75.38	21.54	0	0	3.08
29	Free time/ recreation	66	32	2	0	0	33.85	60	4.62	0	1.54
30	Having children	40	18	22	0	20	47.69	41.54	7.69	1.54	1.54
31	Watching TV/ going to the cinema	40	42	14	2	2	26.15	52.31	13.85	3.08	4.62
32	Drinking alcohol	0	6	36	58	0	9.23	7.69	29.23	52.31	1.54
33	Living long	52	38	8	2	0	30.77	36.92	20	10.77	1.54
34	Smoking cigarettes	2	4	32	60	2	10.77	9.23	26.15	52.31	1.54
35	Property rights (right to own personal property)	68	30	2	0	0	61.54	36.92	1.54	0	0
36	Equal opportunities for personal advancement	68	32	0	0	0	56.92	40	3.08	0	0
37	Determination, motivation, self-reliance	60	36	2	0	2	63.08	36.92	0	0	0
38	Political rights (i.e. right to vote, hold public office and freedom of speech and association)	62	34	4	0	0	75.38	21.54	0	3.08	0

Continued/....

Table II.1.3 (cont.)

	INDIVIDUALS AGED 35–59 (Percentage)					INDIVIDUALS AGED 60 PLUS (Percentage)				
	Essential	Valuable	Unimportant	Undesirable	No Response	Essential	Valuable	Unimportant	Undesirable	No Response
1 Jobs	87.1	12.9	0	0	0	81.82	18.18	0	0	0
2 Access to clean water and sanitation	83.87	12.9	3.23	0	0	81.82	18.18	0	0	0
3 Housing and shelter	96.77	3.23	0	0	0	81.82	18.18	0	0	0
4 Family and friends	74.19	25.81	0	0	0	36.36	63.64	0	0	0
5 Personal safety and physical security	70.97	25.81	0	0	3.23	45.45	54.55	0	0	0
6 An education	87.1	12.9	0	0	0	90.91	9.09	0	0	0
7 Happiness	77.42	22.58	0	0	0	72.73	27.27	0	0	0
8 Good health	80.65	19.35	0	0	0	90.91	9.09	0	0	0
9 Sleep and rest	51.61	48.39	0	0	0	54.55	45.45	0	0	0
10 Fuel for cooking and heating	58.06	35.48	6.45	0	0	54.55	45.45	0	0	0
11 Access to family planning	29.03	41.94	22.58	0	6.45	18.18	54.55	9.09	0	9.09
12 Exercise	32.26	51.61	16.13	0	0	27.27	72.73	0	0	0
13 Capacity to think, reason and make choices	54.84	45.16	0	0	0	27.27	72.73	0	0	0
14 Sexual satisfaction	12.9	29.03	35.48	3.23	19.35	27.27	36.36	27.27	0	9.09
15 Basic clothing	58.06	38.71	0	0	3.23	72.73	27.27	0	0	0
16 Fashionable clothing	22.58	38.71	35.48	0	3.23	0	45.45	54.55	0	0
17 Freedom/ self-determination	54.84	38.71	6.45	0	0	27.27	72.73	0	0	0
18 Income and wealth	58.06	32.26	6.45	0	3.23	54.55	45.45	0	0	0
19 Consumer durable and luxury goods	12.9	51.61	32.26	0	3.23	18.18	45.45	36.36	0	0
20 Self-respect	77.42	16.13	3.23	0	3.23	45.45	54.55	0	0	0
21 Land and cattle	22.58	38.71	32.26	3.23	3.23	18.18	63.64	18.18	0	0

22 Living in a clean natural environment	67.74	29.03	0	0	3.23	54.55	45.45	0	0	0
23 Coca-Cola (or other fizzy drink)	9.68	35.48	51.61	3.23	0	0	36.36	54.55	0	9.09
24 Transportation	51.61	48.39	0	0	0	18.18	72.73	0	0	9.09
25 (All weather) roads	35.48	58.06	3.23	0	3.23	27.27	54.55	9.09	0	9.09
26 Watching sport(s)	29.03	41.94	22.58	3.23	3.23	18.18	54.55	27.27	0	0
27 Playing sport(s)	29.03	35.48	32.26	0	3.23	18.18	45.45	36.36	0	0
28 Electricity	80.65	19.35	0	0	0	63.64	36.36	0	0	0
29 Free time/recreation	25.81	64.52	6.45	0	3.23	18.18	81.82	0	0	0
30 Having children	25.81	41.94	22.58	3.23	6.45	45.45	27.27	9.09	0	18.18
31 Watching TV/ going to the cinema	19.35	48.39	29.03	0	3.23	36.36	36.36	27.27	0	0
32 Drinking alcohol	0	9.68	35.48	54.84	0	0	0	45.45	54.55	0
33 Living long	22.58	41.94	25.81	3.23	6.45	36.36	63.64	0	0	0
34 Smoking cigarettes	0	16.13	32.26	51.61	0	0	0	54.55	45.45	0
35 Property rights (right to own personal property)	61.29	35.48	0	0	3.23	36.36	63.64	0	0	0
36 Equal opportunities for personal advancement	51.61	41.94	6.45	0	0	45.45	54.55	0	0	0
37 Determination, motivation, self-reliance	58.06	32.26	6.45	0	3.23	27.27	72.73	0	0	0
38 Political rights (i.e. right to vote, hold public office and freedom of speech and association)	61.29	35.48	3.23	0	0	36.36	36.36	27.27	0	0

Source: based on question III.1

2. JOBS

Table II.2 Normative Evaluation of 12 Possible Reasons for Valuing 'A Good Job' in Murraysburg and Wallacedene (Percentages)

	Essential	Valuable	Unimportant	Undesirable	No Response
Good income/ standard of living	87.9	12.1	0	0	0
Job security/ regular work	82.17	17.2	0.64	0	0
Good/ safe working conditions	68.79	30.57	0	0	0
Enhancing self-respect	58.6	40.13	0.64	0	0.64
Enhancing status and prestige	19.11	46.5	33.76	0	0.64
Enhancing influence and power	17.2	47.77	31.85	0.64	1.91
Reasonable working hours	47.77	48.41	2.55	0	0.64
Opportunities for advancement	52.87	39.49	6.37	0	1.27
Good relationship with employer	77.71	21.02	0.64	0	0.64
Opportunity to live at home (with family)	56.69	32.48	8.92	0.64	1.27
Job satisfaction	77.07	22.29	0.64	0	0
Giving life meaning and substance	56.05	29.94	13.38	0	0.64

Source: based on question III.11

Table II.2.A Normative Ranking of 12 Possible Reasons for Valuing 'A Good Job' in Murraysburg and Wallacedene

1 Good income/ standard of living	7 Reasonable working hours
2 Job security/ regular work	8 Opportunities for advancement
3 Good/ safe working conditions	9 Opportunity to live at home (with family)
4 Enhancing self-respect	10 Giving life meaning and substance
5 Job satisfaction	11 Enhancing status and prestige
6 Good relationship with employer	12 Enhancing influence and power

Source: based on question III.11

3. HOUSING

Table II.3 Normative Evaluation of 5 Possible Reasons for Valuing 'Good Housing' in Murraysburg and Wallacedene (Percentages)

	Essential	Valuable	Unimportant	Undesirable	No Response
Shelter from elements	87.9	9.55	1.27	0.64	0.64
Adequate living space (per person)	68.79	27.39	3.82	0	0
Facilitating status and prestige	17.83	49.04	31.21	1.27	0.64
Facilitating happiness	64.33	33.12	1.27	0	0.64
Access to water and sanitation	75.16	24.2	0.64	0	0

Source: based on question III.8

Table II.3.A Normative Ranking of 5 Possible Reasons for Valuing 'Good Housing' in Murraysburg and Wallacedene

1 Shelter from elements
2 Adequate living space (per person)
3 Access to water and sanitation
4 Facilitating happiness
5 Facilitating status and prestige

Source: based on question III.8

4. EDUCATION

Table II.4 Normative Evaluation of 8 Possible Reasons for Valuing Education in Murraysburg and Wallacedene (Percentages)

	Essential	Valuable	Unimpor-tant	Undes-irable	No Response
Raising income	82.17	17.83	0	0	0
Acquiring knowledge, understanding and wisdom	67.52	32.48	0	0	0
Acquiring training and skills for jobs	72.61	27.39	0	0	0
Acquiring training/ skills to better serve the community	62.42	35.03	2.55	0	0
Learning to read, write and count	81.53	17.2	0.64	0	0.64
Taking part in literary and scientific pursuits	26.11	55.41	14.01	2.55	1.91
Improving your ability to plan life and make choices	64.33	31.85	2.55	0.64	0.64
Enhancing status, influence and power	16.56	48.41	30.57	3.82	0.64

Source: based on question III.2

Table II.4.A Normative Ranking of 8 Possible Reasons for Valuing Education in Murraysburg and Wallacedene

1 Raising income	5 Acquiring training and skills to better serve the community
2 Acquiring knowledge, understanding and wisdom	6 Improving your ability to plan life and make choices
3 Acquiring training and skills for jobs	7 Taking part in literary and scientific pursuits
4 Learning to read, write and count	8 Enhancing status, influence and power.

Source: based on question III.2

5. INCOME AND WEALTH

Table II.5 Normative Evaluation of 11 Possible Reasons for Valuing Income and Wealth in Murraysburg and Wallacedene (Percentages)

	Essential	Valuable	Unimpor-tant	Undes-irable	No Response
Improving standard of living/ command over commodities	76.43	22.29	0.64	0	0
Acquiring food	76.43	22.29	0.64	0	0
Acquiring luxury goods/ consumer durables	17.2	49.68	28.03	0	4.46
Enhancing social life/ pursuing recreational activities	25.48	49.04	20.38	0	4.46
Achieving happiness	59.24	36.31	3.82	0	0
Acquiring status and prestige	13.38	44.59	36.94	0.64	3.82
Acquiring influence and power	7.64	41.4	45.22	3.18	1.91
Supporting family and friends	67.52	28.66	3.18	0	0
Working less hours/ increasing rest and recreation	26.75	52.23	19.75	0.64	0
Accumulating/ saving money for its own sake	60.51	29.3	9.55	0	0
Employing others/ job creation	46.5	34.39	17.83	0	0.64

Source: based on question III.9.1

Table II.5.A Normative Ranking of 11 Possible Reasons for Valuing Income and Wealth in Murraysburg and Wallacedene

1 Improving standard of living/ command over commodities	7 Enhancing social life/ pursuing recreational activities
2 Acquiring food	8 Acquiring luxury goods/ consumer durables
3 Achieving happiness	9 Working less hours/ increasing rest and recreation
4 Supporting family and friends	10 Acquiring status and prestige
5 Accumulating/ saving money for its own sake	11 Acquiring influence and power
6 Employing others / job creation	

Source: based on question III.9.1

6. COMMODITIES

Table II.6 Normative Evaluation of 18 Goods and Services in Murraysburg and Wallacedene by Location, Gender and Age (Average Mark out of 10)

	ALL	LOCATION		GENDER		INDIVIDUALS AGED			
		Murraysburg	Wallacedene	Men	Women	12–19	20–34	35–59	60 plus
1 Food	8.7	9.7	7.7	8.8	8.7	9.4	7.9	9	9.8
2 Clean water and sanitation	9.1	9.8	8.3	9.2	9	9.6	8.4	9.4	9.9
3 Clothing	8.3	9.4	7.1	8.2	8.4	9	7.9	7.7	9.5
4 Fuel for cooking and heating	8.6	9.3	7.9	8.6	8.6	8.7	8.4	8.6	9.3
5 Home improvements/ housing	8.7	9.2	8.1	8.8	8.6	9.2	8.2	8.8	8.8
6 Medical and health care	9.1	9.7	8.4	9.1	9	9.6	8.4	9.5	9.4
7 Education	9.2	9.8	8.5	9.3	9	9.8	8.5	9.3	9.8
8 Beer or alcohol	1.1	1.1	1	1.5	0.8	1	1.2	0.7	1.5
9 Cigarettes	1	1	1	1.3	0.8	0.8	1.1	1	1.4
10 Radios	6.9	7.5	6	7.1	6.7	7.3	6.7	6.2	7.3
11 Hi-fi/ music centre (radio excluded)	6.6	7.2	5.9	6.8	6.4	7.6	6.2	5.9	5.5
12 Televisions	8.1	8.8	7.4	8.2	8.1	8.5	8.3	7.3	7.9
13 Electric irons and kettles	8.2	9.2	7	8.1	8.4	8.7	7.9	7.9	8.8
14 Bicycles	5.8	7.4	3.8	6.3	5.4	7.3	5	4.8	6.1
15 Cars	8.6	8.8	8.4	8.8	8.5	9	8.5	8.3	8.6
16 Refrigerators, washing machines, vacuum cleaners	8.4	9.3	7.3	8.5	8.4	9	7.9	8.3	8.6
17 Telephones	8.7	9.3	8	8.7	8.6	9.1	8.3	8.5	8.9
18 Saving, investment or insurance	9.1	9.6	8.5	9.2	8.9	9.5	8.7	8.9	9.8

Note: Respondents were asked to indicate how valuable the goods and services listed in the table are by providing a mark out of ten for each of the items. The average mark for each item is recorded in the table. While respondents were asked to provide a mark between '1' and '10', some gave items like cigarettes and alcohol a mark of '0', which is reflected in the table. Unfortunately, the table does not adequately reflect the fact that several respondents wanted to denounce the value of cigarettes and alcohol.

Source: based on question III.9.3

7. FOOD

Table II.7 *Normative Evaluation of 6 Possible Reasons for Choosing Between Different Foods in Murraysburg and Wallacedene (Percentages)*

	Essential	Valuable	Unimportant	Undesirable	No Response
Avoiding hunger	80.25	19.75	0	0	0
Avoiding malnutrition	73.89	25.48	0.64	0	0
Convenience (in preparation, etc.)	27.39	47.13	24.84	0	0.64
Enjoyment	38.22	57.32	3.18	0	0.64
Planning social events	24.2	47.13	26.11	1.27	1.27
Maintaining a healthy diet	75.8	24.2	0	0	0

Source: based on question III.5

Table II.7.A *Normative Ranking of 6 Possible Reasons for Choosing Between Different Foods in Murraysburg and Wallacedene*

1 Avoiding hunger	4 Enjoyment
2 Avoiding malnutrition	5 Convenience (in preparation, etc.)
3 Maintaining a healthy diet	6 Planning social events

Source: based on question III.5

8. FREE TIME AND RECREATION

Table II.8 Normative Evaluation of 6 Possible Reasons for Valuing Free Time and Recreation in Murraysburg and Wallacedene (Percentages)

	Essential	Valuable	Unimportant	Undesirable	No Response
Happiness	72.61	23.57	2.55	0	0.64
Sleep and rest	55.41	41.4	2.55	0	0
Relaxation	63.06	34.39	1.91	0	0
Enhancing social life	35.67	51.59	12.1	0	0
Visiting family and friends	53.5	40.13	5.1	0	0.64
Travel and adventure	35.03	50.96	12.74	0.64	0

Source: based on question III.10.1

Table II.8.A Normative Ranking of 6 Possible Reasons for Valuing Free Time and Recreation in Murraysburg and Wallacedene

1 Happiness	4 Visiting family and friends
2 Relaxation	5 Enhancing social life
3 Sleep and rest	6 Travel and adventure

Source: based on question III.10.1

9. LEISURE ACTIVITIES

Table II.9 Normative Evaluation of 16 Recreational Activities in Murraysburg and Wallacedene by Location, Gender and Age (Average Mark out of 10)

	ALL	LOCATION		GENDER		INDIVIDUALS AGED			
		Murraysburg	Wallacedene	Men	Women	12–19	20 –34	35–59	60 plus
1 Watching television/ going to the cinema	7.8	8.7	6.8	7.9	7.7	8.4	7.4	7.3	8.6
2 Pop music	5.2	5.5	4.8	5.3	5.1	6.6	4.9	4.1	3.6
3 Township jazz	5.1	5	5.3	5.1	5.2	5.9	5.4	4	3.5
4 Drinking beer/ alcohol	1.3	1.3	1.4	1.7	1.1	0.9	1.9	1	1.4
5 Smoking cigarettes	1.4	1.2	1.6	1.7	1.2	0.9	1.9	1.2	1.8
6 Dancing	5.5	6	4.8	5.6	5.4	7.4	5.1	3.7	4
7 Watching sport(s)	6.8	8.4	5.1	7.7	6	8.1	6.2	5.5	7.9
8 Playing sport(s)	6.5	8	4.8	7.4	5.7	8.1	5.9	5.2	6.5
9 Playing games	7	8.8	5	6.8	7.1	7.8	6.1	7.7	6.2
10 Parties and clubs	6.1	6.4	5.8	6.2	6.1	7.2	6.3	4.6	4.4
11 Holidays	7.9	9	6.9	7.9	8	9	7	7.8	8.6
12 Reading books and literature	8.1	8.8	7.4	7.9	8.2	9.3	7.6	7.7	6.6
13 Thinking, daydreaming and remembering	7.6	7.7	7.5	7.3	7.8	7.9	7.9	7	6.1
14 Appreciating nature and forms of beauty	8.1	9.3	6.9	8.2	8	8.8	7.9	7.4	8.4
15 Visiting libraries, museums or art galleries	7.3	8.2	6.4	7.3	7.3	8.5	7.1	6.3	5.4
16 Appreciating classical music	6.1	6.8	5.4	5.9	6.3	6.7	6.4	5.1	4.5

Note: Respondents were asked to indicate how valuable the recreational activities listed in the table are by providing a mark out of ten for each of the items. The average mark for each item is recorded in the table. While respondents were asked to provide a mark between '1' and '10', some items like cigarettes and alcohol a mark of '0' which is reflected in the table. Unfortunately, the table does not adequately reflect the fact that several respondents wanted to denounce the value of cigarettes and alcohol.

Source: based on question III.10.3

10. PLAYING SPORT

Table II.10 Normative Evaluation of 6 Possible Reasons for Playing Sport(s) in Murraysburg and Wallacedene (Percentages)

	Essential	Valuable	Unimpor- tant	Undes- irable	No Response
Exercise and keeping fit	56.69	24.2	1.91	0	11.46
Acquiring skills	47.13	32.48	2.55	0	12.1
Enhancing social life	29.3	45.86	7.64	0	11.46
Pleasure	39.49	38.22	4.46	0.64	11.46
Love of challenge (including desire to win, score goal, etc.)	26.75	46.5	8.92	0.64	11.46
Enhancing personal status and prestige	14.65	43.31	24.2	0.64	11.46

Source: based on question III.4

Table II.10.A Normative Ranking of 6 Possible Reasons for Playing Sport(s) in Murraysburg and Wallacedene

1 Exercise and keeping fit	4 Enhancing social life
2 Acquiring skills	5 Love of challenge (e.g. desire to win, score goal, etc.)
3 Pleasure	6 Enhancing personal status and prestige

Source: based on question III.4

11. COCA-COLA

Table II.11 Normative Evaluation of 7 Possible Reasons for Valuing Coca-Cola and Soft Drinks in Murraysburg and Wallacedene (Percentages)

	Essential	Valuable	Unimpor-tant	Undes-irable	No Response
Obtaining nutrition	19.75	36.94	31.21	10.83	1.27
Helping to fulfil liquid needs	26.75	52.23	18.47	1.27	1.27
Obtaining a healthy, safe and clean drink	36.94	39.49	15.29	7.01	1.27
Obtaining a simple moment of pleasure	33.12	53.5	10.19	1.27	1.91
Facilitating social activities (e.g. interacting with friends)	19.11	52.23	23.57	3.18	1.91
Enhancing your image (being 'cool' or fashionable)	6.37	35.67	51.59	5.1	1.27
Enhancing personal status	8.92	28.66	53.5	7.64	1.27

Source: based on question III.6

Table II.11.A Normative Ranking of 7 Possible Reasons for Valuing Coca-Cola and Soft Drinks in Murraysburg and Wallacedene

1 Helping to fulfil liquid needs	5 Facilitating social activities (such as interacting with friends)
2 Obtaining a healthy, safe and clean drink	6 Enhancing your image (being 'cool' or fashionable)
3 Obtaining a simple moment of pleasure	7 Enhancing personal status
4 Obtaining nutrition	

Source: based on question III.6

12. THE ENVIRONMENT

Table II.12 Normative Evaluation of 5 'environmental virtues' in Murraysburg and Wallacedene (Percentages)

	Essential	Valuable	Unimpor-tant	Undes-irable	No Response
Respect for animals, plants and the world of nature	77.71	22.29	0	0	0
Taking steps to preserve/ protect the environment	59.87	39.49	0	0	0.64
Access to natural resources such as fertile land, etc.	44.59	47.13	8.28	0	0
Cleaner air	82.8	16.56	0	0	0.64
Avoiding noise pollution	39.49	47.13	10.83	1.91	0.64

Source: based on question III.3

Table II.12.A Normative Ranking of 5 'environmental virtues' in Murraysburg and Wallacedene

1 Respect for animals, plants and the world of nature	4 Access to natural resources such as fertile land, etc.
2 Cleaner air	5 Avoiding noise pollution
3 Taking steps to preserve/ protect the environment	

Source: based on question III.3

13. TRANSPORT

Table II.13 Normative evaluation of 7 Possible Reasons for 'Riding A Bicycle' in Murraysburg and Wallacedene (Percentages)

	Essential	Valuable	Unimpor-tant	Undes-irable	No Response
Exercise or keeping fit	57.32	29.94	8.28	1.27	3.18
Avoiding the pollution caused by other modes of transport	20.38	53.5	22.93	0	3.18
Visiting family and friends	49.04	39.49	7.64	0.64	3.18
Travelling to work	34.39	44.59	17.2	0.64	3.18
Getting to social events (e.g. local dance)	14.01	39.49	38.85	3.18	3.82
Moving aimlessly around	7.64	29.3	44.59	14.01	4.46
Enjoyment	37.58	48.41	8.92	1.91	3.18

Source: based on question III.7.2

Table II.13.A Normative Ranking of 7 Possible Reasons for 'Riding A Bicycle' in Murraysburg and Wallacedene

1 Exercise or keeping fit	5 Travelling to work
2 Visiting family and friends	6 Getting to social events (e.g. local dance)
3 Enjoyment	7 Moving aimlessly around
4 Avoid the pollution caused by other modes of transport	

Source: based on question III.7.2

Table II.13.B Normative Ranking of 3 Possible Reasons for Preferring to 'Travel by Car' (rather than by Bicycle) in Murraysburg and Wallacedene

	TOTAL NUMBER OF PEOPLE		
	Rank 1	Rank 2	Rank 3
Moving from A to B (more efficiently)	132	14	9
Achieving happiness (or realising a desire)	17	109	28
Enhancing status and respect among peers	4	33	118

Source: based on question III.7.5

14. PHYSICAL SECURITY

Table II.14.A Normative Ranking of 6 Aspects of Physical Security and Personal Safety in Murraysburg and Wallacedene

1 Threat of violence	4 Accidental injury
2 Law and order	5 Fear of war
3 Protection of personal property	6 Interference from state

Source: based on question III.12

THE QUESTIONNAIRE

SALDRU
PERCEPTIONS OF DEVELOPMENT

Murraysburg and Wallacedene, March 1998.

Write in <u>English</u> and in block capitals only. Mark with an 'X' if the respondent is unable or refuses to answer a question. Indicate if the question is not applicable by writing 'n/a'.

Name of Interviewer:_____.

(Interviewer please mark)

Interview Number:_____.

Date:_____.

Location: Murraysburg/ Wallacedene **(delete one)**

Household selection: original/ replacement.

Reason for Substitution (if applicable):_____.

Address:_____.

PART I: Personal Details

Say: 'Hello I'm _____, and we are conducting a survey for a research project at the University of Cape Town. The purpose of the study is to find out how South Africans perceive a good life. The answers you provide will be kept confidential and you will not be identified in any of the reports we plan to write'.

1.1 Respondent's Name:_____.

1.2 Home Village (where respondent comes from)

_____.

1.3 Gender of Respondent **(circle one)**
   Male   -1
   Female   -2

1.4 Population Group of Respondent.
   African   -1
   Coloured   -2
   Other (specify) -3
   _____.

1.5 Age of Respondent (in years last birthday):_____.

1.6 Marital Status
   Single   -1   Widowed   -4
   Married   -2   Divorced   -5
   Cohabiting -3   Seperated   -6

1.7 Does _____ have any physical or mental disabilities? Yes/No **(circle one)**
Specify (if applicable):_____.

1.8 Language of Respondent (main language spoken at home):

Afrikaans	-1
English	-2
Xhosa	-3
Other (Specify)	-4

_____.

1.9 Language interview is conducted in:

Interviewer please mark

Afrikaans	-1
English	-2
Xhosa	-3

2. Household Structure and Demographics

Note: list the names of all other individuals living in _____'s household in the grid below. (Definition of Household: All individuals who contribute to the common good of the household and who share food from a common source when they are together).

Code No.	2.1 First name	2.2 Relationship to respondent (use code box below)	2.3 Age (years last birthday)	2.4 Gender (Circle one).	2.5 Months spent away from household in last year	2.6 Reason for absence (if applicable) (use code box below)
01				M F		
02				M F		
03				M F		
04				M F		
05				M F		
06				M F		
07				M F		
08				M F		
09				M F		
10				M F		
11				M F		
12				M F		
13				M F		
14				M F		
15				M F		

2.7 Who is the household head? _____.
(Write 'respondent' or insert relevant code number from grid above).

2.8 Who is the residential head (if applicable)? _____.
(Write 'respondent' or insert relevant code number from grid above).

Codes for question 2.2	Codes for question 2.6
01 Wife or husband or partner	01 Employment
02 Son or daughter	02 Looking for employment
03 Father or Mother	03 Schooling
04 Grandchild	04 Student
05 Grandparent	05 Personal reasons
06 Mother or Father-in-law	06 Escape violence or political problems
07 Son or daughter-in-law	07 Visiting spouse or family
08 Brother or sister-in-law	08 Visiting friends
09 Aunt or Uncle	09 Living with other partner
10 Sister or brother	10 Prison
11 Niece or nephew	11 Vacation
12 Cousin	12 In hospital or clinic
13 Great-grandparent	13 Away on business
14 Household help (or relative of)	14 National service
15 Lodger or relative of lodgers	15 Other (specify)
16 Other family	
17 Other non-family.	

3. Income and Occupation

3.1 Main occupation (which of the following best describes your current occupation)?

Regular employment (salary)	-1
Casual/temporary employment (receive wage/food)	-2
Self employment (farming)	-3
Self employment (other)	-4
Housewife/ Child rearing	-5 ---->Go to 3.4
Retired/ pensioner	-6 ---->Go to 3.4
Formal education	-7 ---->Go to 3.4
Unemployed	-8 ---->Go to 3.4
Other	-9

3.2 Main occupation (specify):_____.

3.3 Does your job require you to live away from home?
Yes
No ---> **Go to question 3.3.2**

3.3.1 How many months have you spent away from home in the last year?
_____ months. **Go to question 3.4**

3.3.2 How long does it take you to get to work each day? _____.

3.4 Secondary job (specify if applicable):_____.

3.5 How much do you earn?
R_____ per week/fortnight/month.

3.6 How much do you receive in terms of free or subsidised (cheap) food or goods as payment for work?
R_____ per week/fortnight/month.

3.7 Have you received any money, food or goods from other sources?
Yes
No ---> **Go to question 4**

3.7.1 Please specify the source and amount in rands:-

Remittances   R_____ per week/fortnight/month
Pension   R_____ per week/fortnight/month

Other (Specify):

(i)_____   R_____ per week/fortnight/month

(ii)_____   R_____ per week/fortnight/month

(iii)_____   R_____ per week/fortnight/month

4. Education

4.1 Are you attending school, college or university? Yes/No

4.2 How many years of formal education has ____ completed?
_____ Years.

4.3 What is the highest educational qualification ____ has attained?
_____.

Official use only (to be completed by the fieldwork supervisor after the interview)

Total Income: R _____ per week/fortnight/month

PART II: Untutored Responses

1. The Priorities of Life

Say: 'Think about the things that make a good life. These items could be things that you already have, or things that you need, want or desire'.

1.1 What are the FIVE most important aspects of a good life?

Probe but do not prompt. Keep on probing until <u>FIVE</u> items have been mentioned. Use the table below to record the items mentioned by the respondent.

Table for question 1:

In grid?	Items: -	Rank (1-5)
	1.	
	2.	
	3.	
	4.	
	5.	

1.2 Which of these five things is the most important? **(mark with a '1').**
   Which one comes second? **(mark with a '2')**
   Which comes third? **(mark with a '3')**
   And finally, which comes fourth? **(mark with a '4')**

Say: 'Now I am going to ask you some questions about some specific aspects of life'.

2. Education

2.1 Do you value an education? Yes/No

2.2 Why?

Probe but do not prompt until <u>FOUR</u> reasons have been mentioned. Use the table below to record the respondent's answers.

Table for question 2:

In grid?	Reasons: -	Rank (1-4)
	1.	
	2.	
	3.	
	4.	

2.3 Which of these reasons is the most important? **(mark with a '1')**
   Which reason comes second? **(mark with a '2')**
   And which comes third? **(mark with a '3')**

3. Employment

3.1 Do you think a good job is important? Yes/No

3.2 Why?

Probe but do not prompt until <u>FOUR</u> reasons have been mentioned and record the respondent's answers in the table below.

Table for question 3:

In grid?	Reasons: -	Rank (1-4)
	1.	
	2.	
	3.	
	4.	

3.3 Which of these reasons is the most important? **(mark with a '1')**
   Which reason comes second? **(mark with a '2')**
   And which comes third? **(mark with a '3')**

4. Family and Friends

4.1 Do you think strong attachments to family and friends and a good relationship with family and friends is important? Yes/No

4.2 Why?

Probe until <u>FOUR</u> reasons have been mentioned and record the respondent's answers in the table below.

Table for question 4:

In grid?	Reasons: -	Rank (1-4)
	1.	
	2.	
	3.	
	4.	

4.3 Which of these reasons is the most important? **(mark with a '1')**
   Which reason comes second? **(mark with a '2')**
   And which comes third? **(mark with a '3')**

5. Leisure and Recreation

5.1 Do you value recreational activities? Yes/No

5.2 Why?

Probe until <u>FOUR</u> reasons have been mentioned and record the respondent's answers in the table below.

Table for question 5.2 and 5.3:

In grid?	Reasons: -		Rank (1-4)
	1.		
	2.		
	3.		
	4.		

5.3 Which of these reasons is the most important? **(mark with a '1')**
   Which reason comes second? **(mark with a '2')**
   And which comes third? **(mark with a '3')**

Go to question 6 if the answer to 5.1 is <u>NO</u>.

5.4 Which FIVE recreational activities would you most like to take part in?

Probe until <u>FIVE</u> activities have been mentioned and record the respondent's answers in the table below.

Table for question 5.4 and 5.5:

In grid?	Recreational activity: -		Rank (1-5)
	1.		
	2.		
	3.		
	4.		
	5.		

5.5 Which of these activities would you like to take part in the most? **(mark with a '1')**
   Which activity comes second? **(mark with a '2')**
   Which comes third? **(mark with a '3')**
   And which comes fourth? **(mark with a '4')**

6. Economic Resources

6.1 Do you think income and wealth is important? Yes/No

6.2 Why?

Probe until <u>FOUR</u> reasons have been mentioned and record the respondent's answers in the table below.

Table for questions 6.2 and 6.3:

In grid?	Reasons: -	Rank (1-4)
	1.	
	2.	
	3.	
	4.	

6.3 Which of these reasons is the most important? **(mark with a '1')**
    Which reason comes second? **(mark with a '2')**
    And which comes third? **(mark with a '3')**

Go to question 7 if the answer to 6.1 is <u>NO</u>.

6.4 Imagine that your income increases substantially. Which FIVE items would be your top spending priorities?

Probe until <u>FIVE</u> items have been mentioned and record the respondent's answers in the table below.

Table for question 6.4 and 6.5:

In grid?	Items:-	Rank (1-5)
	1.	
	2.	
	3.	
	4.	
	5.	

6.5 Which of these items would be your first spending priority? **(mark with a '1')**
    Which would be your second spending priority? **(mark with a '2')**
    Which would be your third spending priority? **(mark with a '3')**
    And which would be your fourth spending priority? **(mark with a '4')**

7. Food

7.1 Which motives other than saving money determines the choice of foods you usually consume?

Probe until <u>FOUR</u> motives have been mentioned and record the respondent's answers in the table below.

Table for question 7:

In grid?	Motives: -	Rank (1-4)
	1.	
	2.	
	3.	
	4.	

7.2 Which of these motives is the most important? **(mark with a '1')**
   Which motive comes second? **(mark with a '2')**
   And which comes third? **(mark with a '3')**

8. Coca-Cola

8.1 Do you drink Coca-Cola?
   Yes ---> **Go to question 8.2**
   No

8.1.1 Do you drink Fanta or fizzy (soft) drinks?
   Yes ---> **Go to question 8.2**
   No

8.1.2 Would you value the opportunity to drink Coca-Cola or any other fizzy (soft) drink(s)?
   Yes
   No ---> **Go to question 9**

8.2 Why?

Probe until <u>FOUR</u> reasons have been mentioned and record the respondents answers in the table below.

Table for question 8:

In grid?	Reasons: -	Rank (1-4)
	1.	
	2.	
	3.	
	4.	

8.3 Which of these reasons is the most important? **(mark with a '1')**
   Which reason comes second? **(mark with a '2')**
   And which comes third? **(mark with a '3')**

9. Watching Sport(s)

9.1 Do you watch sport(s)?
      Yes ---> **Go to question 9.2**
      No

9.1.1 Would you value the opportunity to watch sport(s)?
      Yes
      No ---> **Go to question 10**

9.2 Why?

Probe until <u>FOUR</u> reasons have been mentioned and record the respondent's answers in the table below.

Table for question 9:

In grid?	Reasons: -	Rank (1-4)
	1.	
	2.	
	3.	
	4.	

9.3 Which of these reasons is the most important? **(mark with a '1')**
      Which reason comes second? **(mark with a '2')**
      And which comes third? **(mark with a '3')**

10. Alcohol, Beer and Cigarettes

10.1 Do you drink alcohol or smoke?
      Yes ---> **Go to question 10.2**
      No

10.1.1 Would you value the opportunity to drink alcohol or smoke? Yes/No

10.2 Why?

Probe until <u>FOUR</u> reasons have been mentioned and record the respondent's answers in the table below.

Table for question 10:

In grid?	Reasons: -	Rank (1-4)
	1.	
	2.	
	3.	
	4.	

10.3 Which of these reasons is the most important? **(mark with a '1')**
      Which reason comes second? **(mark with a '2')**
      And which comes third? **(mark with a '3')**

11. TV and Cinema

11.1 Do you watch television or visit the cinema?
    Yes ---> **Go to question 11.2**
    No

11.1.1 Would you value the opportunity to watch television or visit the cinema? Yes/No

11.2 Why?

Probe until <u>FOUR</u> reasons have been mentioned and record the respondent's answers in the table below.

Table for question 11:

In grid?	Reasons: -	Rank (1-4)
	1.	
	2.	
	3.	
	4.	

11.3 Which of these reasons is the most important? **(mark with a '1')**
    Which reason comes second? **(mark with a '2')**
    And which comes third? **(mark with a '3')**

12. Housing

12.1 Do you think good housing is important? Yes/No

12.2 Why?

Probe until <u>FOUR</u> reasons have been mentioned and record the respondent's answers in the table below.

Table for question 12:

In grid?	Reasons: -	Rank (1-4)
	1.	
	2.	
	3.	
	4.	

12.3 Which of these reasons is the most important? **(mark with a '1')**
    Which reason comes second? **(mark with a '2')**
    And which comes third? **(mark with a '3')**

13 Clothing

13.1 Do you value clothing? Yes/No

13.2 Why?

Probe until FOUR reasons have been mentioned and record the respondent's answers in the table below.

Table for question 13:

In grid?	Reasons: -	Rank (1-4)
	1.	
	2.	
	3.	
	4.	

13.3 Which of these reasons is the most important? **(mark with a '1')**
    Which reason comes second? **(mark with a '2')**
    And which comes third? **(mark with a '3')**

14 Advertising

14.1 Do you value advertising? Yes/No

14.2 Why?

Probe until THREE reasons have been mentioned and record the respondent's answers in the table below.

Table for question 14:

In grid?	Reasons: -	Rank (1-3)
	1.	
	2.	
	3.	

14.3 Which of these reasons is the most important? **(mark with a '1')**
    Which reason comes second? **(mark with a '2')**

PART III: Tutored Responses.

1. I will read you a list of things which may or may not improve life. Are they essential, valuable, unimportant or undesirable?

Read the items on the list below one at a time and use the grid to record the respondent's answers. (Tick relevant box.)

Grid for question 1:-

Item	Essential (4)	Valuable (3)	Unimportant (2)	Undesirable (1)
1 Jobs				
2 Access to clean water and sanitation				
3 Housing and shelter				
4 Family and friends				
5 Personal safety and physical security				
6 An education				
7 Happiness				
8 Good health				
9 Sleep and rest				
10 Fuel for cooking and heating				
11 Access to family planning				
12 Exercise				
13 Capacity to think, reason and make choices				
14 Sexual satisfaction				
15 Basic clothing				
16 Fashionable clothing				
17 Freedom/ self-determination				
18 Income and wealth				
19 Consumer durable and luxury goods				
20 Self-respect				
21 Land and cattle				
22 Living in a clean natural environment				
23 Coca-Cola (or other fizzy drink)				
24 Transportation				
25 (All weather) roads				
26 Watching sport(s)				
27 Playing sport(s)				
28 Electricity				
29 Free time/ recreation				
30 Having children				
31 Watching TV/ going to the cinema				
32 Drinking alcohol				
33 Living long				
34 Smoking cigarettes				
35 Property rights (right to own personal property)				
36 Equal opportunities for personal advancement				
37 Determination, motivation, self-reliance				
38 Political rights (i.e. right to vote, hold public office and freedom of speech and association)				

2. Education

2.1 How important are the following possible reasons for seeking an education? Are they essential, valuable, unimportant or undesirable? **(Tick box).**

Grid for question 2:-

	Esse-ntial	Valu-able	Unim-portant	Undes-irable	Rank (1-8)
1 Raising income					
2 Acquiring knowledge, understanding and wisdom					
3 Acquiring training and skills for jobs					
4 Acquiring training and skills to better serve the community					
5 Learning to read, write and count					
6 Taking part in literary and scientific pursuits					
7 Improving your ability to plan life and make choices					
8 Enhancing status, influence and power					

2.2 **Ask the respondent to** <u>rank</u> **(in order of priority) the reason(s) for seeking an education which s/he considered to be essential. Repeat the exercise for the reason(s) the respondent considered to be valuable, unimportant and undesirable. Mark the most important reason with a '1' and the least important reason with a '8' in the grid above.**

3. The Environment

3.1 How important are the following ecological virtues? Are they essential, valuable, unimportant or undesirable? **(Tick box).**

Grid for question 3:

	Esse-ntial	Valu-able	Unim-portant	Undes-irable	Rank (1-5)
1 Respect for animals, plants and the world of nature					
2 Taking steps to preserve/ protect the environment					
3 Access to natural resources such as fertile land, etc.					
4 Cleaner air					
5 Avoiding noise pollution					

3.2 **Ask the respondent to** <u>rank</u> **(in order of priority) the environmental virtue(s) s/he considered to be essential. Repeat the exercise for the virtue(s) the respondent considered to be valuable, unimportant and undesirable. Mark the most important virtue with a '1' and the least important virtue with a '5' in the grid above.**

3.3 Can you think of any other important ecological virtues? Yes/No
Specify (if applicable): _____.

4. Playing Sports

4.1 Do you value taking part in sport(s)?
    Yes
    No ---> **Go to question 4.5**

4.2 How important are the following possible reasons for playing sport(s)? Are they very important, important, unimportant or undesirable? **(Tick box).**

Grid for question 4:-

	Very Impt.	Valu-able	Unim-portant	Undes-irable	Rank (1-5)
1 Exercise and keeping fit					
2 Acquiring skills					
3 Enhancing social life					
4 Pleasure					
5 Love of challenge (including desire to win, score goal, etc.)					

4.3 Ask the respondent to <u>rank</u> (in order of priority) the reason(s) for playing sport(s) that s/he considered to be very important. Repeat the exercise for the reason(s) the respondent considered to be important, unimportant and undesirable. Mark the most important reason with a '1' and the least important reason with a '6' in the grid above.

4.4 Can you think of any other important reasons for playing sports? Yes/No
Specify (if applicable): _____.

Go to section 5

4.5 Why? _____.

5. Food

5.1 How important are the following possible determinants of the selection of foods you consume? Are they very important, important, unimportant or undesirable? **(Tick box).**

Grid for question 5:-

	Very Impt.	Valu-able	Unim-portant	Undes-irable	Rank (1-6)
1 Avoiding hunger					
2 Avoiding malnutrition					
3 Convenience (in preparation, etc.)					
4 Enjoyment					
5 Planning social events					
6 Maintaining a healthy diet					

5.2 Ask the respondent to <u>rank</u> (in order of priority) the possible determinant(s) for choosing between different foods that s/he considered to be very important. Repeat the exercise for the determinant(s) the respondent considered to be important, unimportant and undesirable. Mark the most important reason with a '1' and the least important reason with a '6' in the grid above.

5.3 Can you think of any other important motives behind your choice of foods? Yes/No
Specify (if applicable): _____.

6. Coca-Cola

6.1 How important are the following possible reasons for drinking fizzy (soft) drinks such as Coca-Cola? Are they very important, important, unimportant or undesirable? **(Tick box).**

Grid for question 6:

	Very Impt.	Valu-able	Unim-portant	Undes-irable	Rank (1-7)
1 Obtaining nutrition					
2 Helping to fulfil liquid needs					
3 Obtaining a healthy, safe and clean drink					
4 Obtaining a simple moment of pleasure					
5 Facilitating social activities (such as interacting with friends)					
6 Enhancing your image (being 'cool' or fashionable)					
7 Enhancing personal status					

6.2 **Ask the respondent to <u>rank</u> (in order of priority) the reason(s) for drinking Coca-Cola (or fizzy drinks) that s/he considered to be very important. Repeat the exercise for the reason(s) the respondent considered to be important, unimportant and undesirable. Mark the most important reason with a '1' and the least important reason with a '7' in the grid above.**

7. Transport

7.1 Do you own a bicycle?
    Yes ---> **Go to question 7.2**
    No

Say: 'Imagine that you own and can ride a bicycle'.

7.2 How important are the following possible reasons for riding a bicycle? Are they very important, important, unimportant or undesirable? **(Tick box).**

Grid for questions 7.2 and 7.3:

	Very Impt.	Valu-able	Unim-portant	Undes-irable	Rank (1-7)
1 Exercise or keeping fit					
2 Avoiding the pollution caused by other modes of transport					
3 Visiting family and friends					
4 Travelling to work					
5 Getting to social events (e.g. local dance)					
6 Moving aimlessly around					
7 Enjoyment					

7.3 **Ask the respondent to <u>rank</u> (in order of priority) the reason(s) for riding a bicycle that s/he considered to be very important. Repeat the exercise for the reason(s) the respondent considered to be important, unimportant and undesirable. Mark the most important reason with a '1' and the least important reason with a '7' in the grid above.**

7.3.1 Can you think of any other important reasons for riding a bicycle Yes/No.
Specify (if applicable): _____.

7.4 Would you prefer travel by car if you could afford to do so?
　　Yes ---> **Go to question 7.5**
　　No ---> **Go to question 7.7**

7.5 Which of the following would be the main reason for preferring a car? **(mark with a '1')**

Grid for question 7.5 and 7.6:-

	Rank (1-3)
1 Moving from A to B (more efficiently)	
2 Enhancing status and respect among peers	
3 Achieving happiness (or realising a desire)	

7.6 Which come second, is it ___ or ___? **(mark with a '2')**

7.6.1 Can you think of any other important reasons for preferring a car? Yes/No. Specify (if applicable): _____.

Go to Section 8

7.7 Why? _____.

8. Housing

8.1 How important are the following aspects of good housing? Are they very important, important, unimportant or undesirable? **(Tick box).**

Grid for question 8:-

	Very Impt.	Valu-able	Unim-portant	Undes-irable	Rank (1-5)
1 Shelter from elements					
2 Adequate living space (per person)					
3 Facilitating status and prestige					
4 Facilitating happiness					
5 Access to water and sanitation					

8.2 **Ask the respondent to** <u>rank</u> **(in order of priority) the aspects of good housing s/he considered to be very important. Repeat the exercise for the aspect(s) of housing the respondent considered to be important, unimportant and undesirable. Mark the most important aspect with a '1' and the least important aspect with a '5' in the grid above.**

9. Economic Resources

9.1 How important are the following possible reasons for having income and wealth? Are they very important, important, unimportant or undesirable? **(Tick box).**

Grid for questions 9.1 and 9.2:

	Very Impt.	Valu-able	Unim-portant	Undes-irable	Rank (1-11)
1 Improving standard of living/ command over commodities					
2 Acquiring food					
3 Acquiring luxury goods/ consumer durables					
4 Enhancing social life/ pursuing recreational activities					
5 Achieving happiness					
6 Acquiring status and prestige					
7 Acquiring influence and power					
8 Supporting family and friends					
9 Working less hours/ increasing rest and recreation					
10 Accumulating/ saving money for its own sake					
11 Employing others/ job creation					

9.2 **Ask the respondent to <u>rank</u> (in order of priority) the reason(s) for having income and wealth that s/he considered to be very important. Repeat the exercise for the reason(s) the respondent considered to be important, unimportant and undesirable. Mark the most important reason with a '1' and the least important reason with a '11' in the grid above.**

9.3 Please indicate how valuable the following goods and services are by providing a mark out of 10.

Grid for question 9.3:-

	Mark (1-10):
1 Food	
2 Clean water and sanitation	
3 Clothing	
4 Fuel for cooking and heating	
5 Home improvements/ housing	
6 Medical and health care	
7 Education	
8 Beer or alcohol	
9 Cigarettes	
10 Radios	
11 Hi-Fi/ music centre (radio excluded)	
12 Televisions	
13 Electric irons and kettles	
14 Bicycles	
15 Cars	
16 Refrigerators, washing machines, and vacuum cleaners	
17 Telephones	
18 Saving, investment or insurance	

10. Leisure and Recreational Activities

10.1 How important are the following possible reasons for valuing free time and recreational activities? Are they very important, important, unimportant or undesirable? **(Tick box)**.

Grid for questions 10.1 and 10.2:

	Very Impt.	Valu- able	Unim- portant	Undes- irable	Rank (1-6)
1 Happiness					
2 Sleep and rest					
3 Relaxation					
4 Enhancing social life					
5 Visiting family and friends					
6 Travel and adventure					

10.2 Ask the respondent to <u>rank</u> (in order of priority) the reason(s) for valuing free time/recreation that s/he considered to be very important. Repeat the exercise for the reason(s) the respondent considered to be important, unimportant and undesirable. Mark the most important reason with a '1' and the least important reason with a '6' in the grid above.

10.3 Please indicate how valuable the following recreational activities are by providing a mark out of 10.

Grid for question 10.3:-

	Mark (1-10):
1 Watching television/ going to the cinema	
2 Pop music	
3 Township jazz	
4 Drinking beer/ alcohol	
5 Smoking cigarettes	
6 Dancing	
7 Watching sport(s)	
8 Playing sport(s)	
9 Playing games	
10 Parties and clubs	
11 Holidays	
12 Reading books and literature	
13 Thinking, daydreaming and remembering	
14 Appreciating nature and forms of beauty	
15 Visiting libraries, museums or art galleries	
16 Appreciating classical music	

11. Employment

11.1 How important are the following possible aspects of a good job? Are they very important, important, unimportant or undesirable? **(Tick box).**

Grid for questions 11.1 and 11.2:

	Very Impt.	Valu-able	Unim-portant	Undes-irable	Rank (1-12)
1 Good income/ standard of living					
2 Job security/ regular work					
3 Good/ safe working conditions					
4 Enhancing self-respect					
5 Enhancing status and prestige					
6 Enhancing influence and power					
7 Reasonable working hours					
8 Opportunities for advancement					
9 Good relationship with employer					
10 Opportunity to live at home (with family)					
11 Job satisfaction					
12 Giving life meaning and substance					

11.2 **Ask the respondent to <u>rank</u> (in order of priority) the possible aspect(s) of a good job that s/he considered to be very important. Repeat the exercise for the possible aspect(s) of good a job the respondent considered to be important, unimportant and undesirable. Mark the most important aspect of a good job with a '1' and the least important aspect with a '12' in the grid above.**

12. Personal Safety and Physical Security

12.1 Which of the following aspects of personal safety and physical security concern you the most? **(mark with a '1')**

	Rank (1-6)
1 Threat of violence	
2 Law and order	
3 Interference from state	
4 Accidental injury	
5 Protection of personal property	
6 Fear of war	

12.2 Which comes second, is it ___, ___, ___ or ___? **(mark with a '2')**
Which comes third, is it ___, ___ or ___? **(mark with a '3')**
Which comes fourth, is it ___ or ___? **(mark with a '4')**
And finally, which comes fifth, is it ___ or ___? **(mark with a '5')**

12.3 Can you think of any other aspects of personal safety or physical security that concern you?
Yes/No
Specify (if applicable)? _____.

THANK YOU FOR YOUR TIME AND CO-OPERATION.

Bibliography

Adelman, I. (1975), 'Development Economics – A Reassessment of Goals', *American Economic Review*, 65(2), 302–9.

Alkire, S. (2002), 'Dimensions of Human Development', *World Development*, 30(2), 181–205.

Alkire, S. and Black, R. (1997), 'A Practical Reasoning Theory of Development Ethics: Furthering the Capabilities Approach', *Journal of International Development*, 9(2), 263–79.

Allardt, Erik (1993), 'Having, Loving, Being: An Alternative to the Swedish Model of Welfare Research', in Martha C. Nussbaum and Amartya K. Sen (eds), *The Quality of Life*, Oxford: Clarendon Press, pp. 87–94.

Annas, Julia (1993), 'Women and the Quality of Life: Two Norms or One?', in Martha C. Nussbaum, and Amartya K. Sen (eds), *The Quality of Life*, Oxford: Clarendon Press, pp. 279–96.

APU (1996), *Asia Pacific Update*, Fourth Quarter, Hong Kong: Coca-Cola Company.

Arndt, Heinz W. (1987), *Economic Development: the History of an Idea*, Chicago: University of Chicago Press.

Ayres, Ronald I. and Briguglio, Lino (eds) (forthcoming), *Cultural Tourism in Islands and Small States*, to be published by the Islands and Small State Institute, University of Malta in Autumn 2002.

Ayres, R. I. and Clark, D. A. (1998), 'Capitalism, Industrialisation and Development in Latin America: the Dependency Paradigm Revisited', *Capital and Class*, 64, 75–104.

Badsha, Omar (ed.) (1986), *South Africa: the Cordoned Heart*, Cape Town: The Gallery Press.

Bagchi, Amiya K. (1989), 'Industrialisation', reprinted in Ronald I. Ayres (ed.) (1995), *Development Studies*, Dartford: University of Greenwich Press, pp. 665–77.

Baran, Paul and Sweezy, Paul (1966), *Monopoly Capital*, London: Monthly Review Press.

Bastar, N. (1972), 'Development Indicators: An Introduction', *Journal of Development Studies*, 8(3), 1–20.

Basu, K. (1987), 'Achievements, Capabilities, and the Concept of Well-being', *Social Choice and Welfare*, 4, 69–76.

Bauer, Peter (1981), *Equality, the Third World and Economic Delusion*, London: Weidenfeld and Nicolson.

Berlin, Isaiah (1958), 'Two Concepts of Liberty', reprinted in Isaiah Berlin (1982), *Four Essays on Liberty*, Oxford: Oxford University Press.

Beukes, Elwil and Van Der Colff, Anna (1997), 'Aspects of the Quality of Life in Black Townships in a South African City: Implications for Human Development', in Valerie Moller (ed.), *Quality of Life in South Africa*, London: Kluwer Academic Press, pp. 229–50.

Birdsall, N. (1977), 'Analytical Approaches to the Relationship of Population Growth and Development', *Population and Development Review*, 1 and 3, 63–74 and 77–92.

Boserup, Esther (1970), *Women's Role in Economic Development*, London: Allen and Unwin.

Bottomore, Tom (ed.) (1983), 'Class Consciousness', 'Idealism' and 'Ideology', in *A Dictionary of Marxist Thought*, Oxford: Basil Blackwell.

Braybrooke, David (1987), *Meeting Needs*, New Jersey: Princeton University Press.

Breman, Jan (1996), *Footloose Labour: Working in India's Informal Economy*, Cambridge: Cambridge University Press.

Brewer, Anthony (1990), *Marxist Theories of Imperialism: A Critical Survey*, Second Edition, London: Routledge.

Brock, Dan (1993), 'Quality of Life Measures in Health Care and Medical Ethics', in Martha C. Nussbaum and Amartya K. Sen (eds), *The Quality of Life*, Oxford: Clarendon Press, pp. 95–132.

Broome, J. (1991), 'Utility', *Economics and Philosophy*, 7, 1–12.

Bruton, H. J. (1990), 'Review of H. W. Arndt: Economic Development: the History of an Idea', *Economic Development and Cultural Change*, 38(4), 869–872.

Cardoso, Fernando H. and Faletto, Enzo (1979), *Dependency and Development in Latin America*, Berkley: University of California Press.

Carr-Hill, Roy A. (1986) 'An Approach to Monitoring Social Welfare', in Peter Nolan and Suzy Paine (eds), *Rethinking Socialist Economics*, Cambridge: Polity Press, pp. 291–309.

Chambers, R. (1994), 'The Origins and Practice of Participatory Rural Appraisal', *World Development*, 22(7), 953–69.

Chen, Martha (1995), 'A Matter of Survival: Women's Right to Employment in India and Bangladesh', in Martha C. Nussbaum and Jonathan Glover (eds), *Women, Culture and Development*, Oxford: Clarendon Press, pp. 37–57.

Chenery, Hollis, Robinson, Sherman and Syrquin, Moshe (1986), *Industrialisation and Growth – A Comparative Study*, Oxford: Oxford University Press.

Chenery, Hollis and Srinivasan, Thirukodikaval N. (eds) (1988), *Handbook of Development Economics*, Vol.1, North Holland: Elsevier Science Publishers.

Chenery, Hollis and Syrquin, Moshe (1986), 'Typical Patterns of Transformation', in Hollis Chenery, Sherman Robinson and Moshe Syrquin, *Industrialisation and Growth – A Comparative Study*, Oxford: Oxford University Press, pp. 37–83.

Clark, David A. (1995), *Radical Theories of Development and Industrialisation: A Reassessment with Special Reference to Latin America*,

MPhil Thesis, Department of Development Studies, University of Cambridge.

Clark, D. A. (1996), 'Three Systems of Equality', *At the Margin*, Lent, 29–32.

Clark, D. A. (1998), 'Towards A Methodology for Conceptualising Development: Some Reflections on Martha Nussbaum's Thick Vague Theory of the Good', *Greenwich Working Papers in Political Economy 4*, University of Greenwich.

Clark, D. A. (2000a), 'Concepts and Perceptions of Development: Some Evidence from the Western Cape', *SALDRU Working Paper 88*, University of Cape Town.

Clark, D. A. (2000b), 'Capability and Human Development: An Essay In Honour of Amartya K. Sen', *Faculty of Business and Management Working Paper 39*, University of Lincolnshire and Humberside.

Clark, David A. (2000c), *Conceptualising Development*, Ph.D. Thesis, Faculty of Economics and Politics, University of Cambridge.

Clark, D. A. (2001), 'Development Ethics: A Research Agenda', forthcoming in the *International Journal of Social Economics*. (Earlier version appeared as *SOAS Working Paper 110*, Department of Economics, University of London, November 2000).

Clark, David A. (forthcoming), *Perceptions of Development in the Village of Murraysburg and Township of Wallacedene: Baseline Subjective Statistics*, Typescript, Southern Africa Labour and Development Research Unit, University of Cape Town.

Clark, David A. and Qizilbash, Mozaffar (2002), *Core Poverty and Extreme Vulnerability in South Africa*, Typescript, Department of Economics and Social Studies, University of East Anglia.

Cohen, G. A. (1993), 'Equality of What? On Welfare, Goods and Capabilities', in Martha C. Nussbaum and Amartya K. Sen (eds), *The Quality of Life*, Oxford: Clarendon Press, pp. 9–29.

Crocker, D. A. (1991), 'Toward Development Ethics', *World Development*, 19(5), 457–83.

Crocker, D. A. (1992), 'Functioning and Capabilities: The Foundation of Sen's and Nussbaum's Development Ethic', *Political Theory*, 20(4), 584–612.

Crocker, David A. (1995), 'Functioning and Capability: The Foundation of Sen's and Nussbaum's Development Ethic, part II', in Martha C. Nussbaum and Jonathan Glover (eds), *Women, Culture and Development*, Oxford: Clarendon Press, pp. 153–98.

CSS, (1992), *Population Census 1991*, Pretoria: Central Statistics Service.

CSS, (1996), *Living Standards in South Africa: Selected Findings from the 1995 October Household Survey*, Pretoria: Central Statistics Service.

Dasgupta, Partha (1993), *An Inquiry into Well-Being and Destitution*, Oxford: Clarendon Press.

Diener, Ed and Suh, Eunkook (2000), *Culture and Subjective Well-Being*, Cambridge MA: MIT Press.

Dokter, Isaac (1996), *Murraysburg: A Community Profile*, SADEP/HSRC Community Profile Series, University of the Western Cape.

Dorfman, R. (1991), 'Review Article: Economic Development from the Beginning to Rostow', *Journal of Economic Literature*, 29(2), 573–91.

Dower, N. (1988), 'What is Development? A philosopher's answer', *Occasional Paper 3*, Centre for Development Studies, University of Glasgow.

Doyal, Len and Gough, Ian (1991), *A Theory of Human Need*, London: Macmillan.

Dworkin, Ronald (1985), 'Liberalism' in *A Matter of Principle*, Cambridge MA: Harvard University Press, pp. 181–204.

Easterlin, Richard A. (1974), 'Does Economic Growth Improve the Human Lot? Some Empirical Evidence', in Paul A. David and Melvin W. Reder (eds), *The Nation and Household in Economic Growth*, London: Academic Press, pp. 89–125.

Ekins, Paul and Max-Neef, Manfred (eds) (1992), *Real Life Economics – Understanding Wealth Creation*, London: Routledge.

Elster, Jon (1982), 'Sour Grapes – Utilitarianism and the Genesis of Wants', in Amartya K. Sen and Bernard Williams (eds), *Utilitarianism and Beyond*, Cambridge: Cambridge University Press, pp. 219–38.

Erikson, Robert (1993), 'Descriptions of Inequality: The Swedish Approach to Welfare Research', in Martha C. Nussbaum and Amartya K. Sen (eds), *The Quality of Life*, Oxford: Clarendon Press, pp. 67–83.

Fields, Gary S. (1980), *Poverty, Inequality and Development*, Cambridge: Cambridge University Press.

Fowler, H. W. and Fowler, F. G. (1975), *The Concise Oxford Dictionary*, Fifth Edition, Oxford: Oxford University Press.

Frank, Andre G. (1967), *Capitalism and Underdevelopment in Latin America*, London: Monthly Review Press.

Friedman, Milton and Friedman, Rose (1980), *Free to Choose – A Personal Statement*, London: Secker and Warburg.

Galbraith, John Kenneth (1958), *The Affluent Society*, London: Hamish Hamilton.

Gasper, D. (1996), 'Needs and Basic Needs: A Clarification of Meanings Levels and Different Streams of Work', *ISS Working Paper 210*, Institute of Social Studies, The Hague.

Gasper, D. (1996a), 'Culture and Development Ethics: Needs, Women's Rights, and Western Theories', *Development and Change*, 27(4), 627–61.

Gasper, D. (1997), 'Sen's Capability Approach and Nussbaum's Capabilities Ethic', *Journal of International Development*, 9(2), 281–302.

GNU (1994), *White Paper on Reconstruction and Development*, Cape Town: Ministry in the Office of the Deputy President.

Gorman, W. M. (1956), 'The Demand for Related Goods', *Journal Paper J3129*, Ames IO: Iowa Experimental Station.

Goulet, Denis A. (1971), *The Cruel Choice – A New Concept in The Theory of Development*, New York: Atheneum.

Griffin, James (1986), *Well-Being: It's Meaning, Measurement and Moral Importance*, Oxford, Oxford University Press.

Griffin, James (1993), 'Dan Brock: Quality of Life Measures in Health Care and Medical Ethics', in Martha C. Nussbaum and Amartya K. Sen (eds), *The Quality of Life*, Oxford: Clarendon Press, pp. 133–9.

Haq, Mahbub ul (1995), *Reflections on Human Development*, Oxford: Oxford University Press.

Harcourt, Geoff C. (1996), *Two Views on Development: Austin and Joan Robinson*, Kingsley Martin Memorial Lecture, Jesus College, University of Cambridge.

Heilbroner, R. (1973), 'Economics as a Value Free Science', *Social Research*, 40, 129–43.

Herrick, Bruce and Kindleberger, Charles P. (1983), *Economic Development*, Fourth Edition, London: McGraw Hill.

Hicks, N. and Streeten, P. (1979), 'Indicators of Development: The Search for a Basic Needs Yardstick', *World Development*, 7(6), 567–80.

Hill, P. (1984), 'The Study of Individual Poverty', *Carnegie Conference Paper 296*, Southern Africa Labour and Development Research Unit, University of Cape Town.

Hirsch, Fred (1977) [1995], *Social Limits to Growth*, Revised Edition, London: Routledge.

Hirschman, Albert O. (1968), *The Strategy of Economic Development*, New Haven CT: Yale University Press.

Hirschman, Albert. O. (1981), *Essays in Trespassing: Economics to Politics and Beyond*, Cambridge: Cambridge University Press.

Hodgson, Geoffrey, Samuels, Warren J. and Tool, Marc R. (eds) (1993), *Elgar Companion to Evolutionary and Institutional Economics*, Vol. A-K and Vol. L-Z, Aldershot, UK and Brookfield US: Edward Elgar.

Honderich, Ted (ed.) (1995), *The Oxford Companion to Philosophy*, Oxford: Oxford University Press.

Horner, Dudley (1995), *Choices: the Household Survey as an Instrument for Policy Makers*, Paper presented to the Urbanisation and Health Programme, 24 January.

Iliffe, John (1987), *The African Poor: A History*, Cambridge: Cambridge University Press.

Ingham, Barbara (1995), *Economics and Development*, London: McGraw-Hill.

Jadeja, Smita (1999), *Sen: A Non-Sen(se),* Unpublished email circulated around academic institutions in the UK and India, circa January 1999.

Kanbur, Ravi (1987), 'The Standard of Living: Uncertainty, Inequality and Opportunity', in Geoffrey Hawthorn (ed.), *The Standard of Living*, Cambridge: Cambridge University Press, pp. 70–93.

Kelley, A. C. (1991), 'The Human Development Index: Handle with Care', *Population and Development Review*, 17(2), 315–24.

Kerr, P. (1993), 'Adam Smith's Theory of Growth and Technological Change Revisited', *Contributions to Political Economy*, 12, 1–27.

Kindleberger, Charles P. (1958), *Economic Development*, London: McGraw-Hill.

Klasen, Stephan (1997), *Measuring Poverty and Deprivation in South Africa*, Centre for History and Economics, Kings College, Cambridge. Revised version published in March 2000 in the *Review of Income and Wealth*, 46(1), 33–58. [References refer to the former].

Kuznets, S. (1973), 'Modern Economic Growth: Findings and Reflections', *American Economic Review*, 63(3), 246–58.

Lancaster, K. J. (1966), 'A New Approach to Consumer Theory', *Journal of Political Economy*, 74(2), 132–57.

Lange, Oscar (1963), *Political Economy*, Vol.1, Oxford: Pergamon Press.

Larrain, Jorge (1989), *Theories of Development*, Cambridge: Polity Press.

Lewis, W. Arthur (1954), 'Economic Development with Unlimited Supplies of Labour', reprinted in Amar N. Agarwala and Sampat P. Singh (eds) (1958), *The Economics of Underdevelopment*, London: Oxford University Press, pp. 400–449.

Lewis, W. Arthur (1955), *The Theory of Economic Growth*, London: George Allen and Unwin.

Lewis, W. A. (1980), 'The Slowing Down of the Engine of Growth', *American Economic Review*, 70(4), 555–64.

Lewis, W. Arthur (1988), 'The Roots of Development Theory', in Hollis Chenery and Thirukodikaval N. Srinivasan (eds), *Handbook of Development Economics*, Vol.1, North Holland: Elsevier Science Publishers, pp. 28–37.

Little, Ian M. D. (1982), *Economic Development – Theory, Policy and International Relations*, New York: Basic Books Inc.

Manganyi, N. C. (1984), 'The Worst of Times: A Migrant Worker's Autobiography', *Carnegie Conference Paper 1*, Southern Africa Labour and Development Research Unit, University of Cape Town.

Marx, Karl (1848), 'Manifesto of the Communist Party', reprinted in Lewis S. Feuer (ed.) (1969), *Marx and Engels: Basic Writings on Politics and Philosophy*, London: Fontana Library, pp. 43–82.

Marx, Karl (1853), 'The British Rule in India', reprinted in Lewis S. Feuer (ed.) (1969), *Marx and Engels: Basic Writings on Politics and Philosophy*, London: Fontana Library, pp. 511–8.

Marx, Karl (1877), 'Russia's Pattern of Development', reprinted in Lewis S. Feuer (ed.) (1969), *Marx and Engels: Basic Writings on Politics and Philosophy*, London: Fontana Library, pp. 476–9.

Marx, Karl (1959), 'Excerpts from A Contribution to the Critique of Political Economy', reprinted in Lewis S. Feuer (ed.) (1969), *Marx and Engels: Basic Writings on Politics and Philosophy*, London: Fontana Library, pp. 83–7.

Max-Neef, Manfred (1992), 'Development and Human Needs', in Paul Ekins and Manfred Max-Neef (eds), *Real Life Economics – Understanding Wealth Creation*, London: Routledge, pp. 197–213.

May, Julian (ed.) (2000), *Poverty and Inequality in South Africa: Meeting the Challege*, London: Zed Books.

Meier, Gerald M. and Baldwin, Robert E. (1962), *Economic Development: Theory, History, Policy*, London: John Wiley and Sons Inc.

MEPD (1997), *Swaziland: Poverty Assessment by the Poor*, Report on Participatory Poverty Assessment, Swaziland: Ministry of Economic Planning and Development.

Miles, Ian (1992), 'Social Indicators for Real Life Economics', in Paul Ekins and Manfred Max-Neef (eds), *Real Life Economics – Understanding Wealth Creation*, London: Routledge, pp. 283–97.

Mill, John Stuart (1859) [1974], *On Liberty*, Harmondsworth: Penguin.

Mitchell, Brian R. (1998), *International Historical Statistics: Africa, Asia and Oceania*, Third Edition, London: Macmillan Reference.

Moller, V. (1995), 'Waiting for Utopia: Quality of Life in the 1990s', *Indicator South Africa*, 13(1), 47–54.

Moller, Valerie (ed.) (1996), *Perceptions of Development in KwaZulu Natal: A Subjective Indicator Study*, Durban: Indicator Press.

Moller, V. (1997), 'A Better Life for All – Views of Development in KwaZulu-Natal', *Indicator South Africa*, 14(1), 54–9.

Moore, M., Choudhary, M. and Singh, N. (1998), 'How Can We Know What They Want? Understanding Local Perceptions of Poverty and Ill-Being in Asia', *IDS Working Paper 80*, Institute of Development Studies, University of Sussex.

Morawetz, D., Atia, E., Bin-Nun, G., Felous, L., Gariplerden, Y., Harris, E., Soustiel, S., Tombros, G. and Zarfaty, Y. (1977), 'Income Distribution and Self-Related Happiness: Some Empirical Evidence', *Economic Journal*, 87, 511–22.

Morifi, M-J. (1984), 'Life Among the Poor in Philipstown', *Carnegie Conference Paper 33*, Southern Africa Labour and Development Research Unit, University of Cape Town.

Muellbauer, John (1987), 'Professor Sen on the Standard of Living', in Geoffrey Hawthorn (ed.), *The Standard of Living*, Cambridge: Cambridge University Press, pp. 39–58.

Myers, D. G. and Diener, E. (1996), 'The Pursuit of Happiness', *Scientific American*, May Issue, 54–6.

Myrdal, Gunnar (1962), *Value in Social Theory*, London: Routledge and Kegan Paul.

Myrdal, Gunnar (1970), *The Challenge of World Poverty – A World Anti Poverty Plan in Outline*, London: Allen Lane at the Penguin Press.

Naqvi, K., Sharpe, B. and Hecht, A. (1995), 'Local Attitudes and Perceptions Regarding Development: Parry Sound Ontario', *Canadian Journal of Regional Sciences*, 18(3), 283–305.

Narayan, Deepa, Patel, Raj, Schafft, Kai, Rademacher, Anne and Koch-Schulte, Sarah (2000), *Voices of the Poor: Can anyone Hear Us?* Oxford: Oxford University Press for the World Bank.

Nolan, P. (1993), 'The Causation and Prevention of Famines: A Critique of A. K. Sen', *Journal of Peasant Studies*, 21(1), 1–28.

Nolan, P. (1995), 'Joint Ventures and Economic Reform in China: A case study of the Coca-Cola business system with particular reference to the Tianjin Coca-Cola plant', *ESRC Centre for Business Research Working Paper 24*, Department of Applied Economics, University of Cambridge.

Nolan, Peter (1999), *Coca-Cola and the Global Business Revolution,* Cambridge: Judge Institute of Management Studies.

North, D. C. (1989), 'Institutions and Economic Growth: an Historical Introduction', *World Development*, 17(9), 1319–32.

North, Douglas C. and Thomas, Robert P. (1973), *The Rise of the Western World: A New Economic History*, Cambridge: Cambridge University Press.

Nozick, Robert (1974), *Anarchy, State and Utopia*, Oxford: Blackwell.

Ntoane, C. N. and Mokoetle, K. E. (1984), 'Major Problems as Perceived by the Community', *Carnegie Conference Paper 2*, Southern Africa Labour and Development Research Unit, University of Cape Town.

Nussbaum, M. C. (1988), 'Nature, Function and Capability: Aristotle on Political Distribution', *Oxford Studies in Ancient Philosophy*, Supl. Vol., 145–84.

Nussbaum, Martha C. (1990), 'Aristotelian Social Democracy', in Bruce Douglas, Gerald Mara and Henry Richardson (eds), *Liberalism and the Good*, New York: Routledge, pp. 203–52.

Nussbaum, M. C. (1992), 'Human Functioning and Social Justice: In Defence of Aristotelian Essentialism', *Political Theory*, 20(2), 202–46.

Nussbaum, Martha C. (1993), 'Non Relative Virtues: An Aristotelian Approach', in Martha C. Nussbaum and Amartya K. Sen (eds), *The Quality of Life*, Oxford: Clarendon Press, pp. 242–69.

Nussbaum, Martha C. (1995), 'Human Capabilities, Female Human Beings', in Martha C. Nussbaum and Jonathan Glover (eds), *Women, Culture and Development*, Oxford: Clarendon Press, pp. 61–104.

Nussbaum, Martha C. (2000), *Women and Human Development: the Capabilities Approach*, Cambridge: Cambridge University Press.

Nussbaum, Martha C. and Glover, Jonathan (eds) (1995), *Women, Culture and Development*, Oxford: Clarendon Press.

Nussbaum, Martha C. and Sen, Amartya K. (1989), 'Internal Criticism and Indian Rationalist Traditions', in Michael Krausz (ed.) *Relativism, Interpretation and Confrontation*, South Bend: University of Notre Dame Press, pp. 299–325.

Nussbaum, Martha C. and Sen, Amartya K. (eds) (1993), *The Quality of Life*, Oxford: Clarendon Press.

OED (1933), *The Oxford English Dictionary*, Vol. III, Oxford: Clarendon Press.

Osmani, Siddiqur R. (ed.) (1992), *Nutrition and Poverty*, Oxford: Clarendon Press.

Packard, Vance (1961), *The Waste Makers*, London: Longmans, Green.

Palma, Gabriel (1978), 'Underdevelopment and Marxism: From Marx to the Theories of Imperialism and Dependency', reprinted in Ronald I. Ayres (ed.) (1995), *Development Studies*, Dartford: University of Greenwich Press, pp. 161–210.

PSLSD (1994), *South Africans Rich and Poor: Baseline Household Statistics*, Project for Statistics on Living Standards and Development, Southern Africa Labour and Development Research Unit, University of Cape Town.

Qizilbash, M. (1996), 'Capabilities, Well-being and Human Development: A Survey', *Journal of Development Studies*, 33(2), 143–62.

Qizilbash, M. (1996a), 'Ethical Development', *World Development*, 24(7), 1209–21.

Qizilbash, M. (1998), 'The Concept of Well-Being', *Economics and Philosophy*, 14, 51–73.

Qizilbash, M. (2001), 'Amartya Sen's Capability View: Insightful Sketch or Distorted Picture?', *Discussion Paper 2001–5*, School of Economics and Social Studies, University of East Anglia.

Rao, J. Mohan (1994), 'Underdevelopment', in Philip Arestis and Malcolm Sawyer (eds), *The Elgar Companion to Radical Political Economy*, Aldershot, UK and Brookfield, US: Edward Elgar, pp. 443–8.

Rawls, John (1971), *A Theory of Justice*, Oxford: Clarendon Press.

Rawls, John (1982), 'Social Unity and Primary Goods', in Amartya K. Sen and Bernard Williams (eds), *Utilitarianism and Beyond*, Cambridge: Cambridge University Press, pp. 159–85.

Rawls, J. (1988), 'The Priority of Right and Ideas of the Good', *Philosophy and Public Affairs*, 17(4), 251–76.

RDP (1995), *Key Indicators of Poverty in South Africa*, Pretoria: RDP Office.

Rosenstein-Rodan, P. N. (1943), 'Problems of Industrialisation of Eastern and South-Eastern Europe', *Economic Journal*, 53, 202–11.

Rosenstein-Rodan, P. N. (1969), 'Criteria for the Evaluation of National Development Effort', *Journal of Development Planning*, 1, 1–13.

Rostow, Walt W. (1956), 'The Take-off into Self Sustained Growth' in Amar N. Agarwala and Sampat P. Singh (eds) (1958), *The Economics of Underdevelopment*, London: Oxford University Press, pp. 154–86.

Saith, R. (2001), 'Capabilities: the Concept and its Operationalisation', *QEH Working Paper Series 66*, Queen Elizabeth House, University of Oxford.

Samuelson, Paul A. (1961), *Economics*, Fifth Edition, New York: McGraw-Hill.

Samuelson, P. A. (1977), 'A Modern Theorist's Vindication of Adam Smith', *American Economic Review*, 67(1), 42–49.

Samuelson, Paul A. and Nordhaus, William D. (1992), *Economics*, Fourteenth Edition, London: McGraw-Hill.

SA-PPA (1998), *The Experience and Perceptions of Poverty: the South African Participatory Poverty Assessment*, Durban: Data Research Africa Report.

Schwartz, Catherine (ed.) (1993), *The Chambers Dictionary*, Edinburgh: Chambers Harrap.

Seers, Dudley (1969), 'The Meaning of Development', reprinted in Norman T. Uphoff and Warren F. Ilchman, (eds) (1972), *The Political Economy of Development Theory*, Berkley: University of California Press, pp. 123–9.

Seers, D. (1972), 'What are we Trying to Measure', *Journal of Development Studies*, 8(3), 21–36.

Sen, Amartya K. (1980), 'Equality of What', in Sterling M. McMurrin (ed.), *The Tanner Lectures on Human Value*, Salt Lake City: University of Utah Press, pp. 195–220.

Sen, A. K. (1980a), 'Description as Choice', *Oxford Economic Papers*, 32, 353–69.

Sen, A. K. (1980–81), 'Plural Utility', *Proceedings of the Aristotelian Society*, 81, 193–215.

Sen, Amartya K. (1981), *Poverty and Famines: An Essay on Entitlements and Deprivation*, Oxford: Clarendon Press.

Sen, Amartya K. (1982), *Choice, Welfare and Measurement*, Oxford: Basil Blackwell.

Sen, A. K. (1982a), 'Rights and Agency', *Philosophy and Public Affairs*, 11(1), 3–39.

Sen, A. K. (1983), 'Development: Which Way Now?', *Economic Journal*, 93, 745–62.

Sen, Amartya K. (1984), *Resources, Values and Development*, Oxford: Basil Blackwell.

Sen, A. K. (1984a), 'The Living Standard', *Oxford Economic Papers*, 36, 74–90.

Sen, Amartya K. (1985), *Commodities and Capabilities*, Oxford: Elsevier Science Publishers.

Sen, A. K. (1985a), 'Well-being, Agency and Freedom: the Dewey Lectures', *Journal of Philosophy*, 82(4), 169–221.

Sen, Amartya K. (1987), *The Standard of Living: The Tanner Lectures*, Cambridge: Cambridge University Press.

Sen, Amartya K. (1987a), 'Hunger and Entitlements: Research for Action', reprinted in Ronald I. Ayres (ed.) (1995), *Development Studies*, Dartford: University of Greenwich Press, pp. 72–87.

Sen, Amartya K. (1988), 'The Concept of Development', in Hollis Chenery and Thirukodikaval N. Srinivasan (eds), *Handbook of Development Economics*, Vol.1, North Holland: Elsevier Science Publishers, pp. 10–26.

Sen, A. K. (1989), 'Food and Freedom', *World Development*, 17(6), 769–81.

Sen, Amartya K. (1990), 'Development as Capability Expansion', in Keith Griffin and John Knight (eds), *Human Development and the International Development Strategy for the 1990s*, London: Macmillan, pp. 41–58.

Sen, A. K. (1991), 'Utility: Ideas and Terminology', *Economics and Philosophy*, 7, 277–83.

Sen, Amartya K. (1992), *Inequality Re-examined*, Oxford: Clarendon Press.

Sen, Amartya K. (1993), 'Capability and Well-being' in Martha C. Nussbaum and Amartya K. Sen (eds), *The Quality of Life*, Oxford: Clarendon Press, pp. 30–53.

Sen, Amartya K. (1999), *Development As Freedom*, Oxford: Oxford University Press.

Sen, Amartya K. (1999a), *Reason Before Identity: the Romanes Lecture for 1998*, Oxford: Oxford University Press.

Sen, A. K. (2001), 'Other People', *Proceeding of the British Academy*, 111, 319–35.

Sen, Amartya K. and Williams, Bernard (eds) (1982), *Utilitarianism and Beyond*, Cambridge: Cambridge University Press.

Sender, J. and Johnston, D. (1996), 'Some Poor and Invisible Women: Farm Labourers in South Africa', *Development Southern Africa*, 13(1), 3–16.

Sindane, J. (1995), 'Democracy in African Societies and Ubuntu', *Human Science Research Council Discussion Paper*, Johannesburg: HSRC.

Smith, Adam (1776), *An Inquiry into the Nature and the Causes of the Wealth of Nations*, reprinted in Edwin Cannon (ed.) (1976), *The Wealth of Nations*, Chicago: University of Chicago Press.

Soper, K. (1993), 'A Theory of Human Need', *New Left Review*, 197, 113–28.

South Commission (1990), *The Challenge to the South*, New York: Oxford University Press.

Spengler, Joseph J. (1949), 'Theories of Socio-economic Growth', in National Bureau of Economic Research (NBER) (ed.) *Problems in the Study of Economic Growth*, New York: NBER, pp. 45–114.

Srinivasan, T. N. (1994), 'Human Development: A New Paradigm or Reinvention of the Wheel?', *American Economic Review*, 84(2), 238–43.

SSA (1999), *The People of South Africa: Population Census 1996*, Pretoria: Statistics South Africa.

Standing, Guy, Sender, John and Weeks, John (1996), 'The Rural Labour Market' in *Restructuring the Labour Market: the South African Challenge*, Geneva: International Labour Office, pp. 236–87.

Streeten, P. (1979), 'From Growth to Basic Needs', *Finance and Development*, 16(3), 28–31.

Streeten, Paul (1981), *Development Perspectives*, London: Macmillan.

Streeten, P. (1984), 'Basic Needs: Some Unsettled Questions', *World Development*, 12(9), 973–8.

Streeten, P. (1994), 'Human Development: Means and Ends', *American Economic Review*, 84(2), 232–7.

Streeten, Paul (1995), 'The Evolution of Development Thought', in *Thinking About Development*, Cambridge: Cambridge University Press, pp. 5–83.

Sugden, R. (1986), 'Commodities and Capabilities by Amartya Sen', *Economic Journal*, 96, 820–822.

Sugden, R (1993), 'Welfare, Resources, and Capabilities: A Review of Inequality Reexamined by Amartya Sen', *Journal of Economic Literature*, 31, 1947–62.

Syrquin, Moshe (1988), 'Patterns of Structural Change', in Hollis Chenery and Thirukodikaval N. Srinivasan (eds), *Handbook of Development Economics*, Vol.1, North Holland: Elsevier Science Publishers, pp. 203–73.

Tawney, Richard H. (1931), *Equality*, London: Allen and Unwin.

Taylor, Charles (1982), 'The Diversity of Goods' in Amartya K. Sen and Bernard Williams (eds), *Utilitarianism and Beyond*, Cambridge: Cambridge University Press, pp. 129–44.

Thurow, L. C. (1971), 'The Income Distribution as a Pure Public Good', *Quarterly Journal of Economics*, 85(2), 327–36.

Timerman, Jacob (1987), *Chile – Death in the South*, Suffolk: Picador.

Timmer, Peter C. (1988), 'The Agricultural Transformation', in Hollis Chenery and Thirukodikaval N. Srinivasan (eds), *Handbook of Development Economics*, Vol.1, North Holland: Elsevier Science Publishers, pp. 276–331.

Todaro, Michael P. (1994), *Economic Development*, Fifth Edition, London: Longman.

Tower, C. (1987), 'Mother Teresa: Love in Action', *Readers Digest*, December Issue, 156–84.

UNDP (1990), *Human Development Report 1990*, Oxford: Oxford University Press.

UNDP (1992), *Human Development Report 1992: Global Dimensions of Development*, Oxford: Oxford University Press.

UNDP (1996), *Human Development Report 1996: Economic Growth and Human Development*, Oxford: Oxford University Press.

UNDP (1997), *Human Development Report 1997: Poverty from a Human Development Perspective*, Oxford: Oxford University Press.

Walsh, Patricia (1995), 'Well-Being', in Ted Hoderich (ed.), *The Oxford Companion to Philosophy*, Oxford: Oxford University Press, pp. 908–9.

Warren, B. (1973), 'Capitalism and Industrialisation', *New Left Review*, 81, 3–44.

Warren, Bill (1980), *Imperialism: Pioneer of Capitalism*, London: New Left Books.

Webster, Andrew (1993), 'Modernisation Theory', reprinted in Ronald I. Ayres (ed.) (1995), *Development Studies*, Dartford: University of Greenwich Press, pp. 104–20.

Wells, J. R. (1977), 'The Diffusion of Consumer Durables in Brazil and its Implications for Recent Controversies Concerning Brazilian Development' *Cambridge Journal of Economics*, 1, 259–79.

Wiarda, H. J. (1983), 'Towards A Nonethnocentric Theory of Development: Alternative Conceptions from the Third World', *Journal of Developing Areas*, 17(4), 433–52.

Williams, Bernard (1987), 'The Standard of Living: Interests and Capabilities', in Geoffrey Hawthorn (ed.), *The Standard of Living*, Cambridge: Cambridge University Press, pp. 94–102.

Wilson, Francis and Horner, Dudley (1996), 'Report on the Project for Statistics on Living Standards and Development: The South African Story', *Research Project 679–61, Working Paper 5*, World Bank.

Wilson, Francis and Ramphele, Mamphela (1989), *Uprooting Poverty: The South African Challenge*, New York: W. W. Norton and Company.

Witke, Roxane (1977), *Comrade Chiang Ch'ing*, London: Weidenfeld and Nicolson.

Wolf, Susan (1995), 'Martha C. Nussbaum: Human Capabilities, Female Human Beings', in Martha C. Nussbaum and Jonathan Glover (eds), *Women, Culture and Development*, Oxford: Clarendon Press, pp. 105–15.

World Bank (1987), *World Development Report 1987: Industrialisation*, Oxford: Oxford University Press.

World Bank (1991), *World Development Report 1991: The Challenge of Development*, Oxford: Oxford University Press.

World Bank (1992), *World Development Report 1992: Development and the Environment*, Oxford: Oxford University Press.

World Bank (1995), *World Development Report 1995: Workers in an Integrated World*, Oxford: Oxford University Press.

Index